International Series on Public Policy

Series Editors
B. Guy Peters
Department of Political Science
University of Pittsburgh
Pittsburgh, PA, USA

Philippe Zittoun
Research Professor of Political Science
LET-ENTPE, University of Lyon
Lyon, France

The International Series on Public Policy - the official series of International Public Policy Association, which organizes the International Conference on Public Policy - identifies major contributions to the field of public policy, dealing with analytical and substantive policy and governance issues across a variety of academic disciplines.

A comparative and interdisciplinary venture, it examines questions of policy process and analysis, policymaking and implementation, policy instruments, policy change & reforms, politics and policy, encompassing a range of approaches, theoretical, methodological, and/or empirical.

Relevant across the various fields of political science, sociology, anthropology, geography, history, and economics, this cutting edge series welcomes contributions from academics from across disciplines and career stages, and constitutes a unique resource for public policy scholars and those teaching public policy worldwide.

All books in the series are subject to Palgrave's rigorous peer review process: https://www.palgrave.com/gb/demystifying-peer-review/792492.

Clara Egger • Raul Magni-Berton
Eugénie de Saint-Phalle
Editors

Covid-19 Containment Policies in Europe

Editors
Clara Egger
Public Administration and Sociology
Erasmus University Rotterdam
Rotterdam, The Netherlands

Eugénie de Saint-Phalle
International Relations International
Organization
University of Groningen
Groningen, The Netherlands

Raul Magni-Berton
European School of Political
and Social Sciences
ESPOL-LAB Université Catholique
de Lille
Lille, France

ISSN 2524-7301 ISSN 2524-731X (electronic)
International Series on Public Policy
ISBN 978-3-031-52095-2 ISBN 978-3-031-52096-9 (eBook)
https://doi.org/10.1007/978-3-031-52096-9

Cover illustration: Westend61 GmbH / Alamy Stock Photo

This Palgrave Macmillan imprint is published by the registered company Springer Nature Switzerland AG.
The registered company address is: Gewerbestrasse 11, 6330 Cham, Switzerland

Paper in this product is recyclable.

ACKNOWLEDGMENTS

This publication is part of the project EXCEPTIUS: Exceptional powers in times of SarS-Cov-2 (with project number 10430032010026 of the research programme COVID-19—Social Dynamics which is financed by the Dutch Agency for Public Health Research and Development (ZonMw).

EXCEPTIUS received co-funding from the University of Grenoble-Alpes, Sciences Po Grenoble, the Maison des Sciences de l'Homme Alpes and the Centre National de la Recherche Scientific (France).

The open access publication of this volume was made possible by the support of the Erasmus University Rotterdam, the University of Groningen and ESPOL, Catholic Institute of Lille.

CONTENTS

NOTES ON CONTRIBUTORS

Gorka Urrutia-Asua is director of the Human Rights Institute and lecturer at the Faculty of Human and Social Sciences (University of Deusto). His main areas of research are human rights, migrations, diversity and religions. The most recent articles have been published in *The Age of Human Rights Journal* (2023) and *Religions* (2023).

Wojciech Brzozowski is Associate Professor of Law and Religion at the Faculty of Law and Administration, University of Warsaw (Poland). His research interests include constitutional law, human rights law, and law and religion, with a special focus on conscientious objection. In recent years, Wojciech has held fellowships at the University of Milan-Bicocca (Italy) and the Centre for Advanced Study Sofia (Bulgaria). He is a member of the International Consortium for Law and Religion Studies (ICLARS) and the Observatory on Religious Freedom in the Jurisprudence of the ECHR (ORFECT). In 2023 he was appointed Deputy Commissioner for Human Rights of Poland.

Malcolm Campbell-Verduyn is Assistant Professor of International Political Economy at the Department of International Relations and International Organization, University of Groningen. His research is generally concerned with the roles of emergent technologies, non-state actors and expert knowledge in contemporary global governance. He co-edited a special issue of *Global Perspectives* (2021, University of California Press) on the "Global Political Economy of COVID-19" and is co-editor of *Global Digital Data Governance: Polycentric Perspectives* (2024, Routledge).

Laura Chazel is a postdoctoral researcher at the *École des hautes études hispaniques et ibériques* (Casa de Velázquez) and a research associate at Sciences Po Grenoble. She holds a PhD in Political Science from Sciences Po Grenoble (realized in co-direction with the University Complutense of Madrid). She works on contemporary European left-wing parties: on the flow of ideas between political parties, on the relationship between social movements and political parties, and on the environmental and democratic programmes of left-wing populist parties. Her more recent articles were published in *Political Studies* (2023), *Journal for the Study of Radicalism* (2022) and *Partecipazione e Conflitto* (2021).

Cristina Churruca-Muguruza Associate Professor at the Human Rights Institute of the University of Deusto, she is Coordinator of the Erasmus+ Joint Master's Programme in International Humanitarian Action (NOHA). Her main areas of research are human security, in particular the protection of forced displaced people in border contexts and current trends and challenges in humanitarian action and peacebuilding and the European Union policy in these fields. She has widely published on these areas.

José Enrique Conde Belmonte is a lawyer, teacher and researcher at the Berg Institute in Madrid. José Enrique Conde is a professor in the Faculties of Law and International Relations at Universidad Pontificia Comillas de Madrid as well as European Union Law at the Faculty of Law of the CES Cisneros (centre attached to the Complutense University of Madrid) and at the Instituto de Estudios Bursátiles, honorary professor at the Faculty of Law of Complutense University of Madrid, and co-director and founder of the GIN Geopolitics and International Relations Association and has Doctor (cum laude) in Law from Alfonso X el Sabio University, Master in International Relations from the Alfonso X el Sabio University and post-graduate in Public International Law from The Hague Academy of International Law.

Anca Cretu is a PhD student at the Hegoa Institute for International Cooperation and Development Studies (University of the Basque Country, UPV/EHU). She has previous research experience in migration and asylum from a human rights perspective, with a particular focus on European Union policies and its relations with third countries. Her current research focuses on the contribution of universities to peacebuilding processes in societies affected by armed conflict.

Eugénie de Saint-Phalle is a permanent lecturer at the Department of International Relations and International Organization at the University of Groningen. Previously, she worked as a research fellow at the same institution. She defended her PhD in Political Science at the University of Lausanne in 2023, which investigates the textual images of political parties in campaign communication. She teaches seminars in international relations, statistical analysis and international political economy (IPE) of monetary relations. Her research interests lie in the field of content analysis, automated text analysis and interdisciplinary approaches. Currently, she is interested in analysing debates in the media on public debt in European countries.

Clara Egger is a senior assistant professor at the Department of Public Administration and Sociology of the Erasmus School of Social and Behavioural Sciences, Erasmus University Rotterdam (EUR). Her research agenda concerns the analysis of crisis management policies as well as the institutional drivers of societal resilience to various types of crises (mass violence, pandemic and disaster induced by natural hazards). Before joining the EUR, she was an assistant professor at the University of Groningen and a research lead at the Geneva Centre for Humanitarian Studies.

Piret Ehin is Professor of Comparative Politics and Deputy Head for Research at the Johan Skytte Institute of Political Studies at the University of Tartu (Estonia). Her research interests include democracy, elections and voting behaviour, legitimacy and political support, European integration and Europeanization. Her work has appeared in leading journals including the *European Journal of Political Research, Journal of Common Market Studies, Cooperation and Conflict, Politics and Government Information Quarterly.*

Rui Forte is a researcher at the Department of Political Science of the University of Minho. In 2022–2023 he worked as a research assistant on the project of the arms race in the Middle East. His field of study is arms control and nuclear security.

Oskar J. Gstrein is Associate Professor at the Department of Governance and Innovation of the interdisciplinary Faculty Campus Fryslân, University of Groningen (The Netherlands). He is also Programme Director of the BSc Data Science & Society and Theme Coordinator 'Data Autonomy' at the Jantina Tammes School of Digital Society, Technology and Artificial Intelligence. Oskar joined the University of Groningen to work with the first United Nations Special Rapporteur on the right to privacy. His overall research theme is 'Human Dignity in the Digital Age'. His research explores the transitions from abstract principles (e.g. human rights/ethical principles) into concrete legal or governance frameworks. His teaching is inspired by a contemporary interpretation of the Humboldtian model of higher education.

Maksymilian Hau is a PhD candidate at the Doctoral School of Social Sciences at the University of Warsaw. His dissertation will be devoted to the theory of corporate religious freedom, namely, the exercise of religious freedom by for-profit incorporated entities. Maksymilian has held fellowships at the University of Oxford (UK) and the Max Planck Institute for Social Anthropology (Germany).

Ana María Huesca González has been a director of the Security and Criminal Policy Research Group, since 2018. Since 2001, she has been Professor of Sociology and Criminology at the Comillas Pontifical University of Madrid. She is a UNED tutor in Criminology and Political Science. Previously, she was also Professor of Sociology at the Public University of Navarra and of Political Sciences at the UNED. Her main current research activity is focused on the study of subjective insecurity, in addition to other analyses of social problems such as those derived from unemployment, immigration or crime.

Daniel Kübler is a professor at the Department of Political Science and co-directs the Centre for Democracy Studies at the University of Zurich. He holds a PhD from the University of Lausanne and a Habilitation from the University of Zurich, both in political science. He works on direct democracy, democratic innovations, metropolitan and urban governance, as well as public policies, particularly in the field of public health.

Olga Litvyak is a researcher at the Department for E-Governance and Administration at the University for Continuing Education Krems. Previously, she was a postdoctoral researcher at the Computational Communication Science Lab at the University of Vienna. She holds a PhD in Political Science from the University of Lausanne and has been a visiting researcher at the University of Amsterdam and the Freie Universität (FU) Berlin. Her research explores the influence of crises on political communication and election campaigns, in particular framing strategies of political actors. She also researches the impact of digitalization and sustainability on public policies. Her work has been published in *Digital Journalism* and *Communication Methods and Measures*.

Raul Magni-Berton is Full Professor of Political Science at the Catholic University of Lille. Before his actual position, he worked at the universities of Paris-Sorbonne, Montréal, Bordeaux and Grenoble. He also taught at the universities of Geneva, Turin and Stuttgart. He mainly works on the democratic systems, their quality, their performance and their ability to prevent political violence. He published ten books and a hundred articles in peer-reviewed journals.

Roberto Merrill is Assistant Professor of Philosophy and Head of Department of Philosophy, at the School of Arts and Humanities at the University of Minho, where he also coordinates the MA in Political Philosophy. He is also a researcher at the Centre for Ethics, Politics and Society (CEPS), where he co-coordinates (with Stuart White, Oxford University) the UBIEXP project on Universal Basic Income (UBI) experiments and the PREDPOD project (with Alan Thomas, University of York) on pre-distribution and property-owning democracy. He is an associate researcher at CEVIPOF (Centre de recherches politiques de Sciences Po Paris) and a member of the Executive Committee of the Research Committee on Political Philosophy of the International Political Science Association. His research interests within political philosophy include liberal neutrality, perfectionism and value pluralism, as well as contemporary theories of distributive justice.

Ricardo Miguel holds a PhD scholarship in Law and Government at Dublin City University. Ricardo served as a data coder for the project "EXCEPTIUS Exceptional Powers in Times of Sars-CoV-2 Crisis" between 2021 and 2022. From 2022 to 2023, Ricardo was enrolled in the project "The Arms Race in the Middle East" as a research assistant at the Research Center in Political Science (CICP) at the University of Minho (Portugal). Additionally, he has showcased his work by presenting at various universities, including the University of Lisbon, the State University of Rio de Janeiro, and Pompeu Fabra University. His recent article about Chinese private security companies and the limit of coercion was published in *Small Wars and Insurgencies.*

Catarina Neves is a PhD candidate in Political Philosophy with a thesis on the philosophical justification of Unconditional Basic Income entitled "Justifying an Unconditional Basic Income: Reciprocity, Productive Justice and the Impact of UBI in the Labor Market". Her project is funded by FCT, the Portuguese Foundation for Science and Technology. She is also an invited teaching assistant at Nova School of Business and Economics, currently lecturing the course on "ethics." Catarina has written on reciprocity, inheritance and basic income, and she is the co-author of a book on basic income experiments: *Basic Income Experiments. A Critical Examination of Their Goals, Contexts, and Methods* (2022), published by Palgrave Macmillan.

Corentin Poyet is Associate Professor of Political Science at the University of Bergen (Norway). His research interests include legislative studies, electoral studies and party politics. His work has been published in *Electoral Studies, Legislative Studies Quarterly* and *Political Studies Review* among others.

Oliwia Rybczyńska is a PhD candidate at the Doctoral School of Social Sciences at the University of Warsaw. Her dissertation will be devoted to the freedom of religion or belief of non-religious people.

Liisa Talving is Associate Professor of Comparative Politics at the Johan Skytte Institute of Political Studies at the University of Tartu (Estonia). Her research focuses on public opinion and political behaviour. She has published in leading European political science journals such as *Journal of European Public Policy, West European Politics, Electoral Studies* and *European Union Politics.*

Paloma Villacián Goncer is a former researcher in the Security and Criminal Policy Research Group at Universidad Pontificia Comillas de Madrid and a graduate in International Relations and Global Communication from the same university, with a major in Economics and International Business. Her interests lie in development and growth economics, sustainability, corporate communication and IPE. Her recent research focuses on sustainability and communication in energy companies and green economic growth through renewable energies.

Rossella Vulcano is a PhD candidate in Sociology at the Rijksuniversiteit Groningen and Political Science at the University of Grenoble Alpes.

   Her research interests focus on investigating the causes that lead to the development of protests, individual noncompliance against governmental regulations and crisis management strategies in Europe.

Abbreviations

ECHR   European Convention on Human Rights
ECtHR European Court of Human Rights
EU   European Union
ICCPR International Covenant on Civil and Political Rights
MP   Members of Parliament
OECD   Organisation for Economic Co-operation and Development
SVA   Special Voting Arrangement
TFEU   Treaty on the Functioning of the European Union
WHO   World Health Organisation

LIST OF FIGURES

LIST OF TABLES

CHAPTER 1

A Comparative Journey into COVID-19 Policies in Europe

Clara Egger and Raul Magni-Berton

INTRODUCTION

The events are now well known. In December 2019, the city of Wuhan (Eastern China) went under lockdown to contain the spread of a fast-growing epidemic caused by a coronavirus. Shortly after the images of the sealed-off city reached European television screens and newspapers, the first cases were reported in Italy. After Asia, Europe became the second continent to be affected, with the first cases recorded in Italy on 31 January 2020 (Ritchie, 2020). On 13 March, the number of cases in Europe exceeded those in Asia, leading the World Health Organisation (WHO) to

C. Egger (✉)
Public Administration and Sociology, Erasmus University Rotterdam, Rotterdam, The Netherlands
e-mail: egger@essb.eur.nl

R. Magni-Berton
European School of Political and Social Sciences, ESPOL-LAB Université Catholique de Lille, Lille, France
e-mail: raul.magniberton@univ-catholille.fr

© The Author(s) 2024
C. Egger et al. (eds.), *Covid-19 Containment Policies in Europe*, International Series on Public Policy,
https://doi.org/10.1007/978-3-031-52096-9_1

1

declare Europe the epicentre of the crisis, with 40% of the world's cases and 68% of the deaths (WHO, 2020). In less than two months, several European governments were overwhelmed by the spread of the pandemic. Unlike their Asian counterparts, European decision-makers had little recent experience with coronavirus-induced respiratory infections. The last severe influenza pandemic occurred in 1968 and affected European countries mostly unevenly (Viboud et al., 2005). In addition, at the end of January 2020 there was little scientific knowledge about the virus, while in March 2020 expert advice was highly conflicting. The spread of the virus among children, its airborne nature, the mechanisms of immunity and its duration were among the major unknowns.

The COVID-19 pandemic presented European policymakers with a dilemma. They had to balance the need to protect the health of the population while maintaining the normal functioning of institutions. Giving absolute priority to protecting health can lead to restrictions on individual freedoms, including freedom of movement, privacy, trade and religion. Such a priority can also negatively impact political rights through the cancellation or postponement of elections, referendums and the restriction of petitions or demonstrations. Finally, the balance of powers can be altered, as the need for quick and coordinated decisions increases the power of the executive to the detriment of parliament, the judiciary and regional authorities. More specifically, exceptional crisis-management policies can have a negative impact on the economy and on the level of trust in the institutions, as well as creating opportunities for democratic backsliding. In contrast, giving priority to the normal functioning of institutions can lead to an out-of-control pandemic with dramatic consequences in terms of human lives.

In deciding on the best course of action, policymakers had little certainty and evidence, at least during the first wave of the pandemic. Faced with the same constraints, European policymakers responded in very different ways. Some activated constitutional emergency provisions, while others relied on crisis-management legislation. Several countries took a very centralised approach to pandemic management, while in others, policies were adopted at the regional or local level. In some countries, restrictions were very strict (including a curfew, a ban on leaving one's home for more than one kilometre, and strict police controls), whereas in others, people were called upon to exercise their sense of civic duty and solidarity by restricting their travel and daily activities. Neighbouring countries that share the same history, political culture, legal systems and institutions reacted in contrasting ways. For example, while the Dutch cabinet implemented one of the softest approaches to crisis-management in the early stages of the pandemic (January–March 2020), Belgium introduced a very strict lockdown early on (Massart et al., 2021).

Such different policy responses were however associated with a high degree of semantic proximity, making the analysis of legal responses even more arduous and possibly confusing. Although nearly all European countries—to the notable exception of Sweden—based their crisis-management strategy on a "lockdown," the amount of the restrictions decided upon as well as the level of coercion used in their implementation considerably vary (Engler et al., 2021; Egger et al., 2021).

This diversity of policy responses is even more striking as European nations are closely connected with one other and that pathways of policy diffusion and learning abound. In particular, the European Union (EU) offers coordination mechanisms in public health that go beyond the general guidelines of the WHO and drive from the 2014 EU Agenda on Health Systems (European Commission, 2020b). In addition, joint crisis-management mechanisms—through the EU civil protection instrument—are long established among European countries (European Commission, 2020a). Nevertheless, governments reacted to the pandemic in multiple and sometimes contrasting ways—and continued to do so well into autumn 2021. As a result, the cross-national variation in COVID-19 policy responses in Europe is very high and, as such, has sparked scholarly interest (Egger et al., 2021; Engler et al., 2021; Rausis & Hoffmeyer-Zlotnik, 2021).

Our edited volume aims to contribute to such a literature by providing a comparative account of COVID-19 policies across Europe. While most existing handbooks and edited volumes compare national case studies, mostly focusing on containment policies (see, inter alia, Hale et al., 2021; Cheng et al., 2020; Grogan & Donald, 2022), this volume brings together scholars of crisis-management policy, comparative politics and law to analyse the variation in the design and implementation of a wide range of COVID-19 containment policies at the national and subnational levels. To achieve this goal, we make use of new comparative data—collected during the EXCEPTIUS project—mapping the diversity of COVID-19 policies in 32 European countries based on the computational analysis of legal archives.

Mapping COVID-19 Containment Policies in the European Economic Area: The EXCEPTIUS Project

Empirically, the contributions to this volume draw on data collected by the EXCEPTIUS project (Egger et al., 2022). During the course of the pandemic, a group of 17 scholars representing five disciplines from the social sciences and humanities, coordinated by the University of Groningen (the Netherlands) and the University of Grenoble (France), came together to collect data on the modalities of exceptional decision-making and policy-making during the COVID-19 pandemic. Simply defined, exceptional measures impose extraordinary constraints on democratic governance, fundamental rights and everyday freedoms compared to pre-crisis business as usual. To achieve this goal, we have taken a three-pronged approach. First, we trace the measures back to their origins, creating a corpus of COVID-19 legislation that uniquely allows researchers to analyse the diversity of legal instruments used to contain the COVID-19 pandemic. Press releases or expert surveys, which are commonly used in competing projects (Hale et al., 2021; Cheng et al., 2020), capture such dimensions only indirectly and imperfectly. In contrast, legal sources detail the types of containment measures adopted, its modalities of implementation and the changes they introduce to pre-crisis governance. Analysing legal data allows to go beyond the semantic proximity of COVID-19 measures to uncover how a single measure (e.g., a lockdown) was implemented in a more or less stringent manner over time and space.

Second, our project defines the most comprehensive taxonomy of exceptional measures in the area of democratic governance, the rule of law and fundamental rights and freedoms. Four meetings took place among consortium members between May and September 2020 to draw up the project taxonomy. Classes and subclasses were identified by applying both top-down and bottom-up approaches. They are presented in Table 1.1 below.

The scientific board first did an extensive literature search to identify modalities of exceptional crisis-management measures in their relevant field. A sizeable literature has especially focused on the modalities and typologies of emergency powers (Rooney, 2019; Ferejohn & Pasquino, 2004; Gross & Aoláin, 2006; Bjørnskov & Voigt, 2018) allowing us to identify two first classes of events respectively focusing on: (1) state of emergency provisions—based on constitutional or ordinary law; (2)

Table 1.1   EXCEPTIUS Taxonomy of COVID-19 containment measures

Class	Subclasses
State of emergency provisions	State of emergency declaration Executive decision-making Suspension of parliamentary activities Suspension of elections Suspension of initiatives and referendums Suspension of constitutional courts Suspension of legal advisory bodies Suspension of ordinary courts Suspension of subnational competence Limitations to political opposition parties Limitations to civil society organizations/intermediary associations
Restrictions of fundamental rights and civil liberties Note: The fundamental rights and civil liberties listed correspond to the Charter of Fundamental Rights of the European Union	Restrictions on freedom of movement Neighbourhood lockdown (checkpoints) Restrictions on freedom of speech Restrictions on freedom of press Restrictions on freedom of religion Restrictions on the right of privacy Restrictions on the right to justice

(*continued*)

Table 1.1 (continued)

Class	Subclasses
Restrictions of daily liberties/activities	Social distancing (beyond household)
	Mask requirements
	Use of CoronaApp
	Quarantine requirements
	Stay-at-home requirements
	Compulsory self-filled form before leaving home
	Restrictions on private gatherings
	Radius authorized outside home
	Restrictions to visit vulnerable groups
	Restrictions on funeral attendance
	Restrictions on sport activities
	Compulsory medical procedures (tests, hospitalizations, vaccines)
	Vaccination
Closures/lockdowns	Closure of venues of entertainment and culture (e.g., museums, cinemas)
	Restrictions on public gatherings
	Daycare/kindergarten closure
	Primary school closure
	Secondary school closure
	University/tertiary school closure
	Closure of non-essential shops
	Workplace closure
	Restrictions on international travels
	Restrictions on internal travels
	Restrictions on public transport
	Closure of air traffic
	Closure of railway network
	Restrictions on commercial Schengen/international flights
	Curfew implementation
	Restrictions in prisons

(*continued*)

Table 1.1 (continued)

Class	Subclasses
Suspension of international cooperation and commitments	Changes of asylum-seeking procedures evaluation Suspension of trade agreements Suspension of visa/permits delivery Closure of embassies/consulates Repatriation of national citizens abroad Recall of foreign troops abroad Suspension of migration related procedures Suspension of migrant deportation Border closure
Police mobilization	Police mobilization Size of federal forces/national force mobilized Local forces Size of local forces mobilized Transportation police force Size of transportation police forces deployed Other additional public agents Number of additional public agents mobilized Private forces deployed Size of private forces deployed Extension of power (types of agents; types of powers granted) Ad hoc extension
Army mobilization	Support to health authorities Maintaining public order (patrolling the streets, securing buildings) Enforcing lockdown or curfew, policing duty (e.g., checking IDs) Deployment of the military in private buildings Extension of military powers/duties Types of power extension Prison sentences for non-compliance with the law

(*continued*)

Table 1.1 (continued)

Class	Subclasses
Governance oversight and transparency	Press conferences of the executive
	Publicity of executive measures
	Creation of specific (ad hoc) accountability mechanism
	Parliamentary investigation committee
	Other investigation committee
	Creation of certification of information by the government
Public administration and compensatory measures	Extension of administrative competence
	Suspension of administrative deadlines
	Changes in legal procedures
	Suspension of legal time frames for sale and notary agreements
	Suspension of procedural time limits (visas, passports, police custody, etc.)
	Compensatory measures
Emergency decision-making	Emergency decision-making
	Executive decision-making
	Suspension of parliamentary activities
	Suspension of elections
	Suspension of initiatives and referendums
	Suspension of constitutional courts
	Suspension of legal advisory bodies
	Suspension of ordinary courts
	Suspension of subnational competence
	Limitations to political opposition parties
	Limitations to civil society organizations/intermediary associations

derogations to fundamental rights and freedom—as listed in the European Convention on Human Rights. To identify countries that introduced exceptional measures based on crisis-management legal frameworks, we introduced a last class (10—emergency decision-making).

We added to these two seminal classes, a third one, that derives from the ability of governments to derogate from international human right treaties in times of emergencies (Hafner-Burton et al., 2011) and covers broader suspension to international agreements and commitments. We then reviewed the literature on pandemic management approaches as well as similar text analysis initiatives focusing on COVID-19 (Cheng et al., 2020; Porcher, 2020; Hale et al., 2021) to define two other classes. The first covers restrictions of daily liberties targeted at preventing the spread of the COVID-19. This includes restrictions placed to daily activities such as sport, different forms of private and public gathering but also obligation to maintain social distances and wear a mask. The second focuses on closure and lockdowns in various sectors such as education, commercial activities or culture but also restrictions to national and international travels. Two classes—mobilization of the army and of the police—were added by board members specialized of security public policies to identify exceptional implementation modalities. Collecting data on implementation modalities is central to have a more fine-grained view of the stringency of the exceptional measures adopted. In some countries, such as Denmark, the state of emergency was declared but not implemented. In others, such as initially the Netherlands, the police largely played a mediation role and raised awareness among citizens about the importance of complying with exceptional measures. Other countries—such as France, or Poland—have seen a large deployment of the police and the army to support public hospitals and sanction non-compliance.

A more bottom-up inductive approach was followed to complement the initial identification of measures. This allowed us to compensate for literature gaps as well as to mitigate an initial biased focus on restrictive measures. Documenting exceptional measures aiming at granting exceptional rights to citizens—such as the possibility of attending court hearings online or the extension of legal and administrative deadlines—is equally important to uncover how governments navigate the dilemma between protecting the life of their citizens and preserving the functioning of democracies in pandemic times. To do so, the scientific board, supported by a researcher specifically hired for the project manually analysed a random sample of 50 legal documents focusing as much as possible on general COVID-19 law and containing at least one document per country. This process not only enabled us to refine the taxonomy of the subclasses identified but also to come up with a new class, focusing on government oversight.

Third, we leveraged computational text analysis methods to apply this taxonomy to our legal corpus. We experiment with a large array of supervised classifier models together with the support of a team of computational linguists (Tziafas et al., 2021). The automated pre-processing of the corpus performed by the most performant multilingual classifier was then provided to a multinational team of coders that further described the measures (duration, target groups, authority). The combination of both computational and close reading techniques allowed us to classify exceptional measures on a daily basis from January 2020 until the end of April 2021 in 32 countries of the European Economic Area at both national and subnational levels of governments.

The final EXCEPTIUS dataset (Egger et al., 2022) is structured as a longitudinal and cross-sectional dataset. Each entry in the dataset is an exceptional measure codified in a legal act and adopted on a specific day in a specific place (the national territory of a country or a subnational region based on the NUTS 2 typology). Each of the measures is allocated to a class and subclass based on the EXCEPTIUS taxonomy of measures (presented in Table 1.1 above). In addition, for each subclass, the modalities of enforcement of the measure, its duration, target groups as well as the sanctions foreseen for non-compliances are specified. Additional descriptive data include the authority which decided on the adoption of the measure, its legal source (type and URL) as well as the geographical coverage of the measure. The coverage of the dataset concerns 32 countries of the European Economic Area over 15 months (from January 2020 to April 2021).Each contribution to this volume leverages the EXCPETIUS dataset and sheds new comparative light on the patterns of variation of COVID-19 containment measures in Europe.

FACTS FIRST

Ideally, social scientists should be able to assess how effective various public policies are in containing a crisis. This is key not only to ensure that political accountability is informed by scientific evidence but also to trigger effective forms of policy learning. The COVID-19 pandemic offers a unique opportunity. The disease struck a large range of countries in a short and comparable timeframe and triggered very different policy responses. This context—akin to a natural experiment—provides counterfactuals, i.e., the opportunity to capture what would have happened if different policies had been implemented.

However, this unique opportunity is hampered by a lack of quality data. Current evaluations go in two different directions. Some rely on comparative data to analyse the impacts of COVID-19 policies but don't take the policies themselves as a central focus. For example, the study by Altiparmakis et al. (2021) uses surveys in 11 countries to predict citizens' positive or negative evaluations towards government responses as a whole. Other comparative studies are based on the Oxford COVID-19 Government Response Tracker (see Aknin et al., 2022; see Mendez-Brito et al., 2021 for a systematic review) which focuses on three core categories of containment policies (closures and lockdowns, economic and health response) but neglect changes compared to pre-crisis governance patterns. Yet, the way policies are decided upon is key to their legitimacy which in turn shape citizen compliance and ultimately the effectiveness of crisis response (Bargain & Aminjonov, 2020).

Other studies analyse a wider range of policies but limit their analysis to one country (see Knaul et al., 2021; in Mexico or Cramer et al., 2022, in the United States; Askim Christensen, 2022, in Norway). To the best of our knowledge, this volume is the first to provide a comparative and descriptive account of the way various governments handled the COVID-19 pandemic focusing on a large range of policies and countries.

The simple yet important aim of this book is, first and foremost, to precisely document the diversity of measures adopted across the European continent. Before evaluating the effectiveness of crisis governance, our ambition is to present in detail how each authority—at a national or subnational level—has governed. What everyone knows as lockdowns, compulsory vaccinations, wearing of masks, states of emergency or exceptional measures are in fact a set of rules that considerably vary from one country to another. Lockdowns were, for example, stringent in Europe and the depth of control used in enforcing them differed.

Each chapter focuses on a specific policy event to provide a detailed account of the differences across countries or so-called pandemic waves. This mapping comes with complementary data and attempts to assess the level of exceptionalism characterizing each country.

Prioritizing the establishment of the facts does not mean that the EXCEPTIUS dataset is immune from errors. Despite the attention and efforts of the many researchers involved in the project, the database will need to be corrected and expanded in the future. Some regulations may have been forgotten and the coding process, based on complex legislative texts, is not as mechanical as we would like it to be. Nonetheless, our project is the first to systematically record national and subnational regulations based on legal data and during the first three waves of the pandemic. The overall picture of pandemic management we draw from the data offers new and somewhat surprising insights.

First of all, the extent to which individual rights have been curtailed varies. 'Lockdowns' have been declared in almost all European countries, with the notable exception of Sweden. However, the experience of European citizens living under lockdown differed depending on the country they lived in. Chazel's contribution in this volume shows that the most severe lockdowns are reported in France, Italy, Romania, Austria and Spain. Such strict lockdowns persist over time, across the different waves of the pandemic. Some Northern European countries, such as the Netherlands, relied on a rather light lockdown compared to their European counterparts. In addition to lockdowns, freedom of movement was also curtailed by limitations on international and domestic travel. Conde Belmonte, Huesca González and Villacián Goncer confirm that Spain and Romania have taken a particularly radical approach, banning almost all forms of travel, including for asylum seekers. Italy stands as a notable exception as the country maintained a certain degree of openness during the different waves. On the other hand, Finland and Switzerland closed their external borders but allowed internal travel.

The management of the COVID-19 has raised concerns about freedom of speech, freedom of the press and freedom of religion. The spread of critical opinions against the lockdown or COVID-19 vaccines, especially if supported by disinformation strategies, could have a negative impact on the management of the pandemic by reducing compliance with COVID-19 measures and trust in the government. Restricting the expression of these opinions during crisis times could increase the effectiveness of crisis-management strategies but also create a disproportionate burden on fundamental liberties. Neves, Merrill, Miguel and Forte explain that such blanket have rarely been observed in Europe to the notable exception of Romania. Indirectly, however, the lack of transparency, limitations faced by journalists to access information and restrictions on press conferences have negatively impacted the quality of public debates. While such restrictions have been experienced in many countries, they are particularly prevalent in Southern Europe.

Another typical pattern of the management of the pandemic is the disruption introduced to pre-crisis democratic governance and, in particular, the balance of power. In almost all European countries, the executive played a dominant role during the pandemic. Poyet demonstrates that this trend was almost absent in the Scandinavian countries, Austria and Ireland. In Germany, Norway and Austria, the parliament stayed very active. In contrast, in new and fragile democracies such as Hungary and Poland, members of parliaments have been hardly consulted over crisis-management modalities and these countries experienced the strongest concentration of power in the hands of the executive. Egger shows that the declaration of the state of emergency only partially accounts for such differences as countries that relied on constitutionally or legally enshrined exceptional provisions were not characterised by a stronger role of executive but did derogate more heavily on fundamental rights. Crises are often associated with the centralisation of power because of the need for a rapid and coordinated response. Magni-Berton does not find convincing evidence for such a rationale and shows that many countries have opted for managing the pandemic in a decentralised way. In federal countries, such as Germany, Switzerland and Belgium, much of the decision-making was located at the subnational level, while in Austria, power was highly centralised. In regionalised countries, crisis-management was implemented at regional level (Italy) or regions were granted additional capacities during the second wave of the pandemic (Spain). France and the United Kingdom also increased their local management over the waves. Finally, Portugal and Finland only opted for a more decentralised approach in the third wave. The other (unitary) countries maintained a centralised approach.

Finally, Ehin and Talving document that many local elections were postponed because of the pandemic. The only exception was the Polish presidential election, which was postponed by 49 days. When they were held on time, the turnout was much lower than usual. Throughout Europe, referendums were suspended, although in Switzerland people were allowed to vote in two suspensive referendums on pandemic preparedness, with high turnout and a recorded positive effect on social cohesion. The integration of special voting arrangements into regular electoral law before the onset of the pandemic increased the opportunities for people to cast their votes other than in person at the polling station.

Towards New Avenues to Explain and Evaluate Pandemic Policy-Making in Europe

The priority given to describing the public policies adopted in Europe is followed, in some chapters, by exploratory efforts to explain and evaluate these policies.

Explaining the options followed by governments is important to understand the institutional, cultural and ideological context in which the COVID-19 pandemic was handled. Past large-scale crises—such as the jihadist attacks in Paris in November 2015 or the L'Aquila earthquake in 2009—often draw public attention to government (Boin et al., 2016). This attention is associated with high expectations about the ability of leaders to manage the crisis effectively and strong demands for accountability. The visibility on public authorities has fuelled academic interest in the patterns and dynamics of crisis leadership, such as charisma (Pillai, 1996; Halverson et al., 2004) or personality traits (Fredrickson et al., 2003).

Personality traits were also used as predictors of specific policy responses in COVID-19. Medeiros et al. (2022) found that world leaders scoring high on 'plasticity' (extraversion, openness) were quicker to implement travel restrictions and provide financial relief, and generally offered a stronger response. In contrast, leaders who scored high on "stability" (conscientiousness, agreeableness, emotional stability) offered both faster and greater financial relief. On the other hand, some studies have focused on the strategic role played by leaders in times of crisis. Boin et al. (2016: 15) identify five central tasks that leaders perform for an effective crisis-management strategy in democratic settings: (1) sense-making: gathering and processing information that helps to identify a crisis and understand its significance; (2) decision-making and coordination; (3) meaning-making: proposing a narrative that mobilises crisis managers and citizens; (4) accounting for the way the crisis has been managed in public forums; and (5) learning from the crisis and its resolution. In analysing these tasks, the authors note that crises often trigger "situational leadership," i.e., the emergence of individuals who take actions, make decisions and assume authority roles that are not necessarily foreseen. In a similar vein, Demiroz and Kapucu (2012) provide an analytical framework that allows for the comparison of the competencies of leaders in a crisis, linking the tasks identified by Boin et al. (2016) to concrete skills.

Although such a literature provides relevant insights into different levels of leaders' performance in crises, leaders' personality traits and skills can be considered as an endogenous feature of crisis-management institutions. As Janis (1989) points out, leadership traits and skills are determined by the specific procedures of crisis decision-making. A more cynical interpretation sees crises as perfect times for leaders—usually constrained by democratic checks and balances—to seize absolute power (Voigt, 2022). In this volume, we move away from a focus on leadership in crisis to one on the institutional configurations of decision-making and policy-making in crises.

A pattern of concentration of power in the hands of the executive was observed in many countries during the COVID-19 pandemic (Dostal, 2020; Kühn et al., 2021; Turnbull & Bernier, 2022). The chapters by Egger and Kuebler in this volume document a similar trend but show variations in the intensity of such concentration of power based on emergency legislation (Egger) and pre-crisis levels of democratic quality (Kuebler). At the same time, our volume also highlights minority tendencies to decentralize crisis decision-making to the benefit of parliaments (Poyet) and local authorities (Magni-Berton). Such an important—but neglected—role of decentralization in crisis-management was already observed by Hart and his co-authors in 1993.

The extent to which the role of the executive was strengthened during the pandemic depends on how strong the role of the executive was before the pandemic. The increase in executive power is particularly weak in consensual countries (in Lijphart's classification) or in countries with many veto players (in Tsebelis's classification). Similarly, powers are least centralised in federal countries and, more generally, the degree of centralisation of decision-making before the pandemic is associated with the degree of centralisation during the pandemic. However, this institutional inertia is not universal. Austria sits oddly in this list, as it adopted exceptionally stringent measures, given its consensual and federal institutions.

While this could reflect a weak capacity of consensual and federal states to quickly respond to a pandemic (Hegele and Schnabel 2021), this conclusion is not consistent with the data. While the restrictions in these countries were globally less severe, the first measures to combat the pandemic were implemented early and, after two years, they still experienced fewer deaths and higher levels of political trust.

However, this does not mean that consensual and federal institutions are more effective, as other confounding factors may explain these results. These institutions are more prevalent in wealthier countries and in countries where political trust was higher before the pandemic. Many contributions confirm that these factors contribute to a less severe response to the pandemic (see Egger et al., 2021). Prosperity allows governments to find alternative ways to reduce the spread of the virus, such as identifying epidemic outbreaks or implementing rules. Political trust helps to achieve compliance without formal restrictions. In her paper, Vulcano shows that mobility is significantly reduced not only by the stringency of restrictions, but also by trust and the ability to enforce the law. However, EXCEPTIUS data also show that, in the long run and after an initial rally-around-the-flag effect, strict restrictions have a strong negative impact on public trust. This can lead to a vicious circle: in times of crisis, when public trust is low, policies need to be stricter to induce compliance, which in turn exacerbates the lack of trust. In the long run, this vicious circle weakens the ability of societies to respond to crises. More broadly, the observed and robust statistical relationship between the quality of democracy before the pandemic and the level of concentration of power during the pandemic is likely to reveal a reinforcing mechanism in which each factor reduces the other.

However, other exogenous factors should also be considered. For example, Conde Belmonte and co-authors show, in this volume, that interregional domestic travel bans and checkpoints have been introduced both South-Western and some Eastern European countries. Such a high level of restrictions can be understood as a protection against internal and external tourist travel, as they systematically occur in tourist destinations. Similar patterns can be observed in the case of COVID-19 passes that got introduced in the peak touristic season and later on in Northern European countries. Contexts of high affluence typically increase the potential spread of the virus and therefore the need for stringent measures. These factors suggest that some countries need to be more legally prepared for a pandemic than others. Specific institutions can be put in place to minimise changes in governance. An example can be found in the contribution of Ehin and Talving on special voting arrangements such as early voting, postal voting, proxy voting, remote internet voting and the mobile ballot box. Countries that had such arrangements in place before the pandemic were better able to maintain electoral continuity.

Although the study of legal preparedness and crisis-management after COVID-19 is still in its infancy, the EXCEPTIUS data will certainly expand the evidence base of such evaluation exercises. Managing a pandemic should not be a matter of feeling and intuition. Social engineering, based on experience and rigorous evidence, should be able to provide governments and citizens with standard policies capable of effectively combining health protection and political legitimacy. In contrast to long-term policies, which are expected to be driven by debates and values, emergency policies are paradoxically less challenging because they only aim at introducing efficient instrument to tackle a time-bounded emergency without upsetting the status quo. In an emergency, exceptional policy choices should be minimised so as not to interfere with the path chosen by each country in normal times. To minimise these choices, data, and analysis on the effectiveness of crisis-management are crucial. For the pandemic we have recently suffered, this book aims to support such crisis preparedness exercises.

References

Aknin, L. B., Andretti, B., Goldszmidt, R., Helliwell, J. F., Petherick, A., De Neve, J. E., et al. (2022). Policy stringency and mental health during the COVID-19 pandemic: A longitudinal analysis of data from 15 countries. *The Lancet Public Health, 7*(5), e417–e426.

Altiparmakis, A., Bojar, A., Brouard, S., Foucault, M., Kriesi, H., & Nadeau, R. (2021). Pandemic politics: Policy evaluations of government responses to COVID-19. *West European Politics, 44*(5–6), 1159–1179.

Askim, J., & Christensen, T. (2022). Crisis decision-making inside the core executive: Rationality, bureaucratic politics, standard procedures and the COVID-19 lockdown. *Public Policy and Administration, 0*(0). https://doi.org/10.1177/09520767221129676

Bargain, O., & Aminjonov, U. (2020). Trust and compliance to public health policies in times of COVID-19. *Journal of Public Economics, 192*, 104316.

Bjørnskov, C., & Voigt, S. (2018). The architecture of emergency constitutions. *International Journal of Constitutional Law, 16*(1), 101–127.

Boin, A., Stern, E., & Sundelius, B. (2016). *The politics of crisis-management: Public leadership under pressure.* Cambridge University Press.

Cheng, C., Barceló, J., Hartnett, A. S., Kubinec, R., & Messerschmidt, L. (2020). COVID-19 government response event dataset (CoronaNet v.1.0). *Nature Human Behaviour, 4*(7), 756–768. https://doi.org/10.1038/s41562-020-0909-7

Cramer, E. Y., Ray, E. L., Lopez, V. K., Bracher, J., Brennen, A., Castro Rivadeneira, A. J., et al. (2022). Evaluation of individual and ensemble probabilistic forecasts of COVID-19 mortality in the United States. *Proceedings of the National Academy of Sciences, 119*(15), e2113561119.

Demiroz, F., & Kapucu, N. (2012). The role of leadership in managing emergencies and disasters. *European Journal of Economic & Political Studies, 5*(1).

Dostal, J. M. (2020). Governing under pressure: German policy making during the coronavirus crisis. *The Political Quarterly, 91*(3), 542–552.

Egger, C. M., Magni-Berton, R., Roché, S., & Aarts, K. (2021). I do it my way: Understanding policy variation in pandemic response across Europe. *Frontiers in Political Science, 3,* 622069.

Egger, C. M., de Saint Phalle, E., Magni-Berton, R., Aarts, C. W. A. M., & Sébastian, R. (2022). *EXCEPTIUS dataset v1.0.* DataverseNL, V2. https://doi.org/10.34894/TTS0MF

Egger, C., Caselli, T., Tziafas, G., Phalle, E. D. S., & Vries, W. D. (2023). Extracting and classifying exceptional COVID-19 measures from multilingual legal texts: The merits and limitations of automated approaches. *Regulation & Governance.*

Engler, S., Brunner, P., Loviat, R., Abou-Chadi, T., Leemann, L., Glaser, A., & Kübler, D. (2021). Democracy in times of the pandemic: Explaining the variation of COVID-19 policies across European democracies. *West European Politics, 44*(5–6), 1077–1102.

European Commission. (2020a). *European civil protection and humanitarian aid operations, what we do civil protection (consulted on September 18th 2021).* EU Health Policy. https://ec.europa.eu/echo/what/civil-protection/mechanism_en

European Commission. (2020b). *Health systems coordination.* EU Health Policy. https://ec.europa.eu/health/policies/systems_en

Ferejohn, J., & Pasquino, G. (2004). The law of the exception: A typology of emergency powers. *International Journal of Constitutional Law, 2*(2), 210–239.

Fredrickson, B. L., Tugade, M. M., Waugh, C. E., & Larkin, G. R. (2003). What good are positive emotions in crisis? A prospective study of resilience and emotions following the terrorist attacks on the United States on September 11th, 2001. *Journal of Personality and Social Psychology, 84*(2), 365–376. https://doi.org/10.1037/0022-3514.84.2.365

Grogan, J., & Donald, A. (Eds.). (2022). *Routledge handbook of law and the COVID-19 pandemic.* Routledge.

Gross, O., & Aoláin, F. N. (2006). *Law in times of crisis: Emergency powers in theory and practice.* Cambridge University Press.

Hafner-Burton, E. M., Helfer, L. R., & Fariss, C. J. (2011). Emergency and escape: Explaining derogations from human rights treaties. *International Organization, 65*(4), 673–707.

Hale, T., Angrist, N., Goldszmidt, R., Kira, B., Petherick, A., Phillips, T., et al. (2021). A global panel database of pandemic policies (Oxford COVID-19 Government Response Tracker). *Nature Human Behaviour, 5*(4), 529–538.

Halverson, S. K., Murphy, S. E., & Riggio, R. E. (2004). Charismatic leadership in crisis situations: A laboratory investigation of stress and crisis. *Small Group Research, 35*(5), 495–514.

Hegele, Y., & Schnabel, J. (2021). Federalism and the management of the COVID-19 crisis: Centralisation, decentralisation and (non-)coordination. *West European Politics, 44*(5–6), 1052–1076. https://doi.org/10.108 0/01402382.2021.1873529

Janis, I. C. (1989). *Crucial decisions: Leadership in policymaking and crisis-management*. The Free Press.

Knaul, F., Arreola-Ornelas, H., Porteny, T., Touchton, M., Sánchez-Talanquer, M., Méndez, Ó., et al. (2021). Not far enough: Public health policies to combat COVID-19 in Mexico's states. *PLoS One, 16*(6), e0251722.

Kühn, D., Llanos, M., & Richter, T. (2021). Executive personalisation in the time of COVID-19. *Social Sciences Open Access Repository*. https://nbn-resolving. org/urn:nbn:de:0168-ssoar-71705-3

Massart, T., Vos, T., Egger, C., Dupuy, C., Morel-Jean, C., Berton, R. M., & Roché, S. (2021). The resilience of democracy in the midst of the COVID-19 pandemic. *Politics of the Low Countries, 3*(2), 113–137.

Medeiros, M., Nai, A., Erman, A., & Young, E. (2022). Personality traits of world leaders and differential policy responses to the COVID-19 pandemic. *Social Science & Medicine, 311*, 115358.

Mendez-Brito, A., El Bcheraoui, C., & Pozo-Martin, F. (2021). Systematic review of empirical studies comparing the effectiveness of non-pharmaceutical interventions against COVID-19. *Journal of Infection, 83*(3), 281–293.

Pillai, R. (1996). Crisis and the emergence of charismatic leadership in groups: An experimental investigation 1. *Journal of Applied Social Psychology, 26*(6), 543–562.

Porcher, S. (2020). Response2covid19, a dataset of governments' responses to COVID-19 all around the world. *Scientific Data, 7*(1), 423.

Rausis, F., & Hoffmeyer-Zlotnik, P. (2021). Contagious policies? Studying national responses to a global pandemic in Europe. *Swiss Political Science Review, 27*(2), 283–296.

Ritchie, H. (2020). *Coronavirus source data, our world in data*. University of Oxford. Available at https://ourworldindata.org/coronavirus-source-data

Rooney, B. (2019). Emergency powers in democratic states: Introducing the democratic emergency powers dataset. *Research & Politics, 6*(4), 2053168019892436.

Turnbull, L., & Bernier, L. (2022). Executive decision-making during the COVID-19 emergency period. *Canadian Public Administration, 65*(3), 538–546.

Tziafas, G., de Saint-Phalle, E., de Vries, W., Egger, C., & Caselli, T. (2021). A multilingual approach to identify and classify exceptional measures against COVID-19. In *Proceedings of the natural legal language processing workshop 2021* (pp. 46–62).

Viboud, C., Grais, R. F., Lafont, B. A., Miller, M. A., & Simonsen, L. (2005). Multinational impact of the 1968 Hong Kong influenza pandemic: Evidence for a smoldering pandemic. *The Journal of Infectious Diseases, 192*(2), 233–248.

Voigt, S. (2022). Contracting for catastrophe: Legitimizing emergency constitutions by drawing on social contract theory. *Res Publica, 28*(1), 149–172.

WHO. (2020). Coronavirus disease (COVID-19) pandemic), Health topics, health emergencies, Coronavirus disease (COVID-19) outbreak. Available at: https://www.euro.who.int/en/healthtopics/healthemergencies/coronavirus-covid-19/novel-coronavirus-2019-ncov

PART I

Patterns of Crisis Decision-Making

CHAPTER 2

What's in a Name? European Uses of States of Exception During COVID-19

Clara Egger

INTRODUCTION

At one point or another of the COVID-19 pandemic, most European governments declared that they were using "emergency" measures to fight it. However, behind the ostensive semantic proximity, there was considerable variation. Some countries relied on constitutionally enshrined state of emergency provisions, while others made use of more limited states of epidemic disease or sanitary emergency.[1] Yet others based their

---

[1] A variety of terms are used to cover different forms of extraordinary powers granted to governments in periods of crisis, such as "state of emergency," "state of exception," and "state of alarm" (as well as "state of siege," "martial law" or "state of war" in cases of threat of armed conflict). The authors have tried to closely follow each state's terminology. When generic terms have been necessary, we have used the terms of "emergency powers" and "state of exception."

C. Egger (✉)
Public Administration and Sociology, Erasmus University Rotterdam,
Rotterdam, The Netherlands
e-mail: egger@essb.eur.nl

© The Author(s) 2024   23
C. Egger et al. (eds.), *Covid-19 Containment Policies in Europe*,
International Series on Public Policy,
https://doi.org/10.1007/978-3-031-52096-9_2

measures on pre-existing ordinary laws on crisis-management (statutory regimes). Last, some states adopted new laws to tackle the spread of the disease. To complicate matters further, many European states used a combination of normative tools in a sequential or simultaneous manner.

This chapter asks: Does this matter? Or more precisely: Have countries that declared states of emergency (or other in principle more far-reaching and consequential exceptional states) seen more severe restrictions of human rights and freedoms and more extensive disruptions of democratic governance than those opting to rely on more limited provisions?

Theory would, at first glance, suggest a positive answer. The reason why states of exception are surrounded by so much weariness and caution is their pedigree. Looking back at European history, a proclamation of a state of exception has at times been the death knell for democracy. Between 1925 and 1929 for example, constitutional exceptional powers have been seized by the President of the Republic of Weimar 250 times. Hitler used such provisions upon his appointment as a chancellor in 1933 to suspend several constitutional protections on civil rights, paving the way for a totalitarian regime. Beyond such extreme cases, states of exception are moments of great danger for democratic rule and, consequently, for the political freedom of the citizenry (Ackerman, 2006; Gross & Aoláin, 2006). The theory is relatively simple: in an emergency, more power is vested with the executive, while the scope of decision-making of countervailing powers (the legislature and the judiciary) is curtailed. In addition, freedom of speech, of the press, of assembly and of movement are usually among the first to be restricted. The temptation of misusing emergency powers is hence great for political leaders and led constitutional drafters to set up different types of safeguards to constrain the activation of emergency powers.

The first such safeguard ensures that the key aspects regulating states of exception are put down in the constitution rather than in ordinary law, which can be more easily amended. The second key safeguard includes ensuring that parliament takes decisions regarding the prolongation of exceptional states and that it continues to function throughout the emergency. The third and fourth safeguards are that the constitution cannot be amended in such situations and the court system continues operating independently. Moreover, crucial human rights are ring-fenced. Another safeguard is to ensure that governments have an adequate toolbox to choose from by instituting more than one type of exceptional state. Thus, for instance the Central European states, which tend to have the most

recent constitutions, as a rule have several forms of exceptional state regulations constitutionally: a state of war/siege, a state of emergency (usually
meant to be activated in case of a severe threat to the constitutional order)
and a state of natural disaster. The latter also, at least in some cases, explicitly cater for epidemics. The consequences of the different exceptional
states are calibrated, so that the state of siege has the most severe repercus-
sions on the functioning of the state institutions and human rights and
freedoms; the government cannot restrict these to nowhere near the same
extent in the case of a state of natural hazard.[2]

So, if constitution-makers have attempted to shield democracy and
human rights from the dangers of emergency rule, we might find that
states relying on emergency constitutions end up disrupting state institutions and individual human rights less than predicted, and that the differences between countries that have declared states of emergency and those
relying on more limited provisions are not so great. It might even be that
such rules are less disruptive than new legislation, taken in a hurry amid a
pandemic.

Such a finding would be consistent with insights from empirical research
that shows that the design of emergency constitutions matters to explain
their varied impact on democratic governance and human rights. When
emergency powers are relatively easy to activate and lead to a substantial
increase in the powers of the executive compared to non-crisis times, they
are more likely to trigger unnecessary restrictions of democratic rule and
human rights (Bjørnskov & Voigt, 2018a, b). However, research has also
shown that the likelihood of emergency powers to negatively impact democratic governance and human rights is context-dependent. The use of
emergency powers after a natural hazard is more proportionate and limited than in the wake of a conflict (Bjørnskov & Voigt, 2018b; Rooney,
2019). This contribution looks at the effects of using emergency powers
during pandemics. The extant scholarship provides mixed answers to this
question. On the one hand, Bjørnskov and Voigt (2020) found that emergency powers were used to unnecessarily curtail media freedom in a large
number of countries. On the other hand, Ginsburg and Versteeg (2021)
show that executives were constrained by a large range of counterpowers
in their uses of emergency powers. The sizable literature on the relationship between COVID-19 measures, democracy and human rights has not

---

[2] Other countries have chosen to regulate the most severe form of exceptional state in the
constitution, leaving other types of emergencies to organic or ordinary law.

systematically examined whether the type of exceptional state/emergency regulation has had an impact on the extent and severity of restrictions. Instead, the focus has been elsewhere.

Unsurprisingly, several studies have found that human rights, and in particular the freedom of movement, assembly and association, the right to personal liberty and to a private life, the right to manifest one's belief or religion, the right to work and to education were severely affected during the pandemic (Spadaro, 2020; Chad Clay et al., 2022). Quantitative studies focusing on democratic governance during COVID have covered issues such as which types of states were most likely to declare a state of emergency (Grogan, 2020, Lundgren et al., 2020) and whether the characteristics of the COVID crisis is less conducive to a disruption in checks and balances than national security crises (Ginsburg & Versteeg, 2021).

This chapter intends to contribute to these various streams of literature by analysing whether the activation of constitutional emergency powers is associated with more constraints on the action of the executive, compared with emergency measures taken outside of the scope of constitutional safeguards. To analyse whether the type of emergency legislation matters, I rely on the EXCEPTIUS dataset that includes exhaustive information about how and to what extent COVID-19 measures restricted civil liberties, human rights and the normal functioning of state institutions in these countries.

The descriptive analysis reveals three core findings. First, the legal mapping of COVID-19 emergency measures reveals that less than half of the countries in our sample activated emergency powers to deal with the pandemic. I zoom into this group of countries and present the different emergency regimes introduced, their duration and the modalities of their activation. My analysis shows that, while the activation modalities and the scope of emergency powers display strong similarities in theory, in practice the role of counterpowers and the impacts of emergency powers vary strongly from one country to the next. To further analyse the relationship between the legal basis of COVID-19 emergency measures and their impacts, I focus on three areas: the concentration of powers in the hands of the executive, the protection of the freedom of movement and freedom of assembly. The descriptive comparison suggests that my initial intuition is only partly valid. Declaring a state of emergency creates more constraints on the executive than relying on disaster-management legal regimes. Yet, states of emergency are more detrimental to the protection of human rights and less responsive to the evolution of the pandemic over time.

Mapping the Legal Basis of Emergency COVID-19 Measures

Almost all European governments declared relying on "emergency measures" to tackle the spread of the COVID-19 pandemic. The following section presents three core dimensions of variation, namely: (1) the legal basis of emergency powers; (2) the decision-making process leading to their adoption; (3) the timing of the declaration and the duration of emergency measures.

The Legal Basis of Emergency Measures

As the COVID-19 pandemic spread over the European continent, governments relied on wide ranges of policy measures to contain it. Most of them were labelled as "emergency" responses aiming to tackle a fast-evolving public health crisis. Two types of emergency measures can be distinguished. On the one hand, governments can declare a state of exception based on national or, sometimes, subnational constitutional provisions. These so-called emergency constitutions are present in 90% of countries globally and are defined as "legal rules specifying who can declare an emergency, when they can do so, and what actors have what powers once it has been declared" (Bjørnskov & Voigt, 2018a, 1). Although the nature of emergency powers varies from one country to the next (see Table 2.1 below for a description), declaring state of exception typically leads to concentrating powers in the hands of one political actor (often the head of the executive) and derogating from some fundamental rights to protect the state's institutions and the population against a large-scale disaster. On the other hand, governments can adopt emergency measures without necessarily activating a state of exception. This is often the case when policy responses draw upon crisis-management legislation such as, in the case of the coronavirus pandemic, a legal act specifying the emergency measures to be taken in case of an epidemic. Figure 2.1 contrasts European countries which activated a state of exception with countries which relied on non-constitutional crisis-management legislation.

Ten states out of the 23 included in our sample relied on state emergency provisions to contain the spread of the COVID-19. Table 2.1 below details the list of countries concerned, the specific denomination of the provision as well as what the deviations from ordinary democratic governance they allow. This mapping allows us to distinguish between

Table 2.1 State of exception provisions

Country	Denomination	Legal basis	Deviations to pre-crisis governance introduced
Czech Republic	State of emergency (nouzový stav)	National constitution (Constitutional Act No. 110/1998)	Applicable to events threatening the health of the Czech Republic Further specified in Crisis Act No. 240/2000 Par.5 of the act details the rights and freedoms that can be impacted, such as the right to inviolability of a person and habitation; the right to property; freedom of movement and residence; right to free assembly; the right to operate the business that would endanger executed crisis measures or disrupt or preclude their realization; the right to strike
Estonia	State of emergency (eriolukord)	National constitution (clause 8 of § 87)	Specifically applies to "prevent the spread of an infectious disease" Declaration procedure specified in a State of Emergency Act Derogations to right to property, privacy, freedom of movement and association
Finland	Situations of emergency (poikkeusoloissa)	Ordinary law (Emergency powers act) National constitution (article 23) refers to Emergency Act for provisions authorizing provisional exceptions to fundamental rights in "situations of emergency"	No specific mention of disease/epidemic as a case of emergency situations Limited derogations foreseen: constitutionally protected freedoms shall not be restricted on the basis of this Act except in the event of an armed attack against Finland and in time of war

(*continued*)

Table 2.1 (continued)

Country	Denomination	Legal basis	Deviations to pre-crisis governance introduced
France	State of sanitary emergency (état d'urgence sanitaire)	Ordinary law (Act of March 23, 2020)	Derogations to the freedom of movement, freedom of assembly, property, freedom of entrepreneurship (article 2)
Greece	Imminent threats against national security	National constitution Article 44; 48	Applicable to war or "imminent threats to national security" (art. 48) Derogations possible to: inviolability of home, right to privacy (incl. protection of personal data); assembly, association, expression and freedom of the press, secrecy of correspondence, right to work and right to strike
Hungary	State of emergency (veszélyhelyzet)	National constitution (article 48)	Only foreseen in the "event of armed acts aimed at the overturning of the constitutional order or at the exclusive acquisition of power, and of serious mass acts of violence threatening life and property, committed with arms or in an armed manner" President allowed to pass any extraordinary measure for 30 days.
Italy	Emergency measures (misure urgenti)	Legislative Decree 1/2018 (article 14) Followed Decree Law n. 6 (23/02/2020) Consistent with constitutional notion of "extraordinary cases of necessity and urgency"	Some derogations explicitly foreseen by the Constitution (government decree power— 77; police specific authorization—13) Restrictions of freedom of movement, assembly + any other measures needed to contain the spread of COVID-19

(continued)

Table 2.1   (continued)

Country	Denomination	Legal basis	Deviations to pre-crisis governance introduced
Luxembourg	State of international crisis (état de crise internationale) (article 32.4)	National constitution + confirmation by ordinary law	Specifically focuses on the cases of "international crisis" (not defined). Grand Duke can take any regulations and derogations for a period of 3 months.
Portugal	State of emergency (article 19) (estado de emergência)	National constitution	Can be declared in cases of "actual or imminent aggression by foreign forces, a serious threat to or disturbance of constitutional democratic order, or public disaster" (39.2) but also in "less serious" cases (39.3) All rights and freedoms can be suspended except "rights to life, personal integrity, personal identity, civil capacity and citizenship, the non-retroactivity of the criminal law, defendants' right to a defence, or freedom of conscience and religion" (39.6) State of emergency provisions should not affect responsibilities and functioning of the bodies that exercise sovereign power or of the self-government bodies of the autonomous regions, or the rights and immunities of the holders of such offices.

(*continued*)

Table 2.1 (continued)

Country	Denomination	Legal basis	Deviations to pre-crisis governance introduced
Romania	State of emergency (article 53;89, 93, 73, 115; 152) (starii de urgenta) State of alert (as of May 15, 2020)	National constitution + detailed in organic law Ordinary law	Applicable to cases where public health needs to be protected Possibility for the government to issue emergency ordinances (art. 115) or suspend fundamental rights and freedoms by the means of law (in a proportionate and non-discriminatory manner; art. 53)
Spain	State of alarm (estado de alarma)	National constitution (article 116); modalities of state of alarm specified in an organic law (Organic Law 4/1981)	This organic law specifies that the state of alarm may be declared in instances of health crises No suspension or derogation of rights allowed under the state of alarm but limitations are possible on the freedom of movement at certain hours or under certain requirements, goods can be requisitioned, the intervention and transitory occupation of premises (except private homes) is possible, the use or consumption of services or essential commodities can be rationed or to the adoption of health and environmental protection measures. In any case, Art. 1.2 of this Organic Law establishes that the measures to be adopted in any of these situations, as well as their duration, will be "those strictly indispensable to ensure the reestablishment of normality"

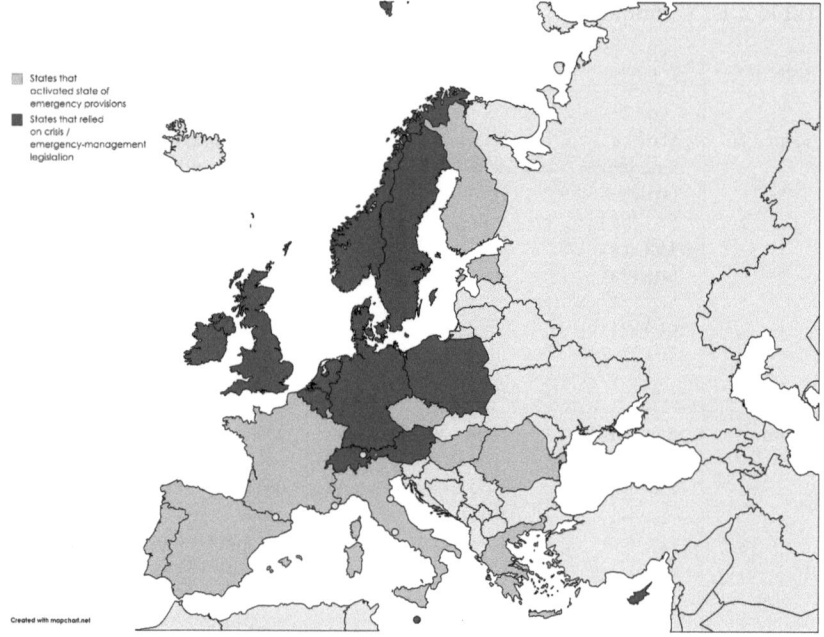

Fig. 2.1 Legal basis of emergency measures in Europe (from January 30, 2020 until April 30, 2021). Source: EXCEPTIUS, own rendering. Note: Countries in yellow activated state of emergency provisions based on their national constitutional framework. Countries in blue relied on crisis-management legislation. The map displays the list of countries that activated state of emergency provisions at least once during the first three waves of the COVID-19 pandemic (from January 30, 2020, until April 30, 2021)

emergency provisions that introduce considerable derogations from democratic governance and human rights—such as in the case of Spain—and provisions that have a more signalling purpose, aiming at alerting the public to the severity of the crisis at stake but without introducing strong deviation from non-emergency governance structures and procedures (Finland).

The table shows—consistently with the literature—that emergency constitutions allow derogations to a rather large range of fundamental rights and freedoms. In some cases, such rights are listed in a detailed manner while in others, the choice is left to the executive. Note that

Finland is the only country in our sample that only allows derogations from constitutionally protected rights in the event of an armed attack against the country in case of war. Only Czech Republic, Estonia and Romania explicitly mention public health crisis as an event qualifying for the activation of emergency powers. All the other countries rely on more ambiguous labels subject to interpretation.

The remaining countries in our sample relied on emergency-management legislation to tackle the pandemic. In most of these countries, the basis for action can be traced back to (sometimes old) laws governing the management of pandemics or contagious diseases, often adapted to the specifics of the COVID-19 crisis. In Austria, the government acted based on the Epidemic Management Act later amended by the Parliament to account for the COVID-19 crisis. The Cypriot government decided to "go back in time" and used the March 1932 Quarantine Law. Denmark relied on the law on measures against contagious or other transferable diseases which was amended twice in 2020, all amendments having a sunset clause. The legal basis for the control of infectious diseases in Germany was provided by the Federal Act to Prevent and Combat Infectious Diseases in Humans—Infection Protection Act of 2001. Malta and Ireland relied on a public health act to adopt emergency regulations. In the case of Ireland, the Act was substantially amended in 2020 to refer to the COVID-19.

In other cases—such as the Netherlands and the United Kingdom—governments relied on recommendations introducing COVID-19 containment measures while members of parliament were working on the adoption of COVID-19 legislation.

The Duration and Timing of Activation of the Measures

The duration of the measures also varied from one country to the next as shown in Fig. 2.2 below. Three groups of countries can be distinguished. The first is composed of countries with a long-lasting state of emergency. France holds the European record with 861 days, followed by Romania (718 days) and Hungary (673 days). Although the latter are much younger democracies than France, these three countries experienced a loss of democratic quality during the pandemic with Hungary backsliding into autocratic rule (Guasti & Bustikova, 2022). It is notable that Hungary is the only European country where the executive declared a state of emergency for an unlimited period of time on March 30, 2020 (Rácz, 2020). The

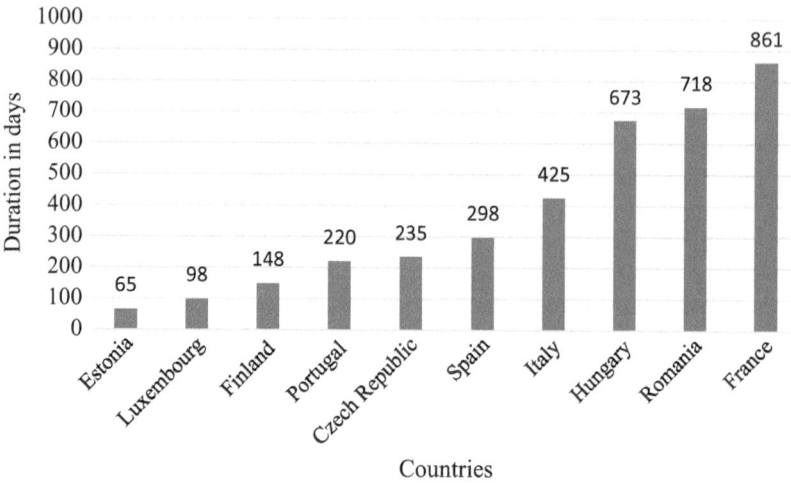

Fig. 2.2   Duration of state of exception provisions (in days, from January 2020 to April 2021). Source: EXCEPTIUS, own rendering

long-lasting nature of emergency provisions reflects the fact that, in these countries, the state of emergency was declared during the first wave of the pandemic and only revoked when the pandemic was considered as over by the authorities, in 2022. Italy falls in the same group, although the state of emergency provisions were withdrawn considerably earlier than in France, Hungary and Romania. The second group of countries activated their state of emergency provisions twice during the pandemic but each time for a limited period. This group includes states such as the Czech Republic, Finland, Portugal and Spain. The last group includes Estonia only, which was the only state that declared a state of emergency once, during the first wave of the pandemic.

Overall, these results suggest that very few countries adapted their crisis-management capacities during the pandemic and changed strategy from one COVID-19 wave to the next. Once activated, state of emergency provisions not only tend to be extended in time, but they are also considered as a default option to manage the pandemic.

When it comes to procedural matters, in all the countries in our sample, the power to declare the state of emergency lies in the hands of the executive. Yet, behind this apparent homogeneity, the modalities of declaration and the constraints placed on the executive highly vary from one country to the next consistently with the type of democratic system in place in such countries. In Finland, France and Portugal, the head of the government needs to be authorized to activate emergency powers. In France, in the case of law of sanitary emergency, the Parliament authorizes the government to act by ordinances for a duration of two months.

In the two other countries, parliamentary authorization follows the declaration of the state of emergency. Such a parliamentary veto exists in Finland where the Parliament has the power to repeal in part or in full the emergency provisions (see Chap. 3 of this volume) and in Greece the emergency provisions ceased to be enforceable if they are not ratified. In Spain, parliamentary approval is necessary if the government foresees an extension of the state of emergency after the initial legal period of 15 days. The Hungarian case is ambiguous. While in theory activating emergency powers falls under the jurisdiction of the Parliament, in practice the President is granted this power when the Parliament is considered "unable" to do so. During COVID-19, Victor Orbán declared the state of emergency but with the support of a majority in the national parliament.

In Estonia, Luxemburg, Italy and Romania the declaration of the stage of emergency must be countersigned by a member of government and the head of the state (the President or the Grand Duke, in the case of Luxemburg). Two findings emerge from this initial overview of the modalities and uses of the state of emergency in Europe. First, the design of emergency provisions is quite similar across European countries: they all allow the executive to enforce considerable restrictions and pass legislation for a restricted period of time. Yet, the duration of the measures and their monitoring by counterpowers display strong variation in Europe. In the next section, we explore whether such a variation has consequences for the level of stringency of adopted measures especially when compared with exceptional crisis-management measures embedded in other legal frameworks.

Do State of Emergencies Lead to More Draconian Measures?

This section departs from an exclusive focus on countries that did activate emergency powers during the pandemic to compare the effects of exceptional measures (whatever the types of emergency legal framework used) on the stringency of the restrictions adopted. To do so, I leverage

EXCEPTIUS comparative data which allow to trace, on a daily basis, the type and stringency of deviations from democratic governance introduced by exceptional measures. The analysis that follows focuses on three core dimensions. The first concerns the concentration of powers in the hands of the executive. Five types of changes are recorded by EXCEPTIUS in an ordinal manner, ranging from the changes that are the less detrimental to democratic governance to the ones that have the most consequences:

- Changes in the modalities of executive decision-making that don't alter the balance of power or the rule of law;
- Changes allowing the executive to derogate from fundamental rights;
- Changes allowing the executive to derogate from rule of law;
- Changes leading to restrictions in both fundamental rights and the rule of law;
- Extension of the powers and competences of the executive.

To assess whether emergency powers lead to a concentration of powers in the hands of the executive, we compared the average scores of this variable (labelled ExPow for executive powers) during the three waves of COVID-19 for all the countries of our sample. We however distinguish between the countries that relied on emergency powers (in orange in Fig. 2.3) and countries that based their action on pandemic or disaster management laws (in blue).

This descriptive analysis reveals that countries that relied on emergency powers have, on average, experienced a weaker predominance of the executive than countries that did not activate such powers. Such finding can be explained by the fact that state of emergency legislation is precisely designed to constrain the action of the executive during crises. Such constraints derive, for example, from a stronger parliamentary or judicial oversight. Our data suggests that, during COVID-19, state of emergency provisions achieved their stated goals of shackling the executive. In contrast, exceptional measures introduced through crisis-management law created stronger disruptions in democratic governance. They especially peaked during the second wave as Denmark and Belgium granted additional powers and competences to the executive to manage the pandemic. Figure 2.3 also shows that the powers of the executive got weakened as the pandemic unfolded. This may be due to the fact that, as state of emergency provisions, lasted in time, parliaments introduced restrictions in what the executive was entitled to do and to the adoption of COVID-19

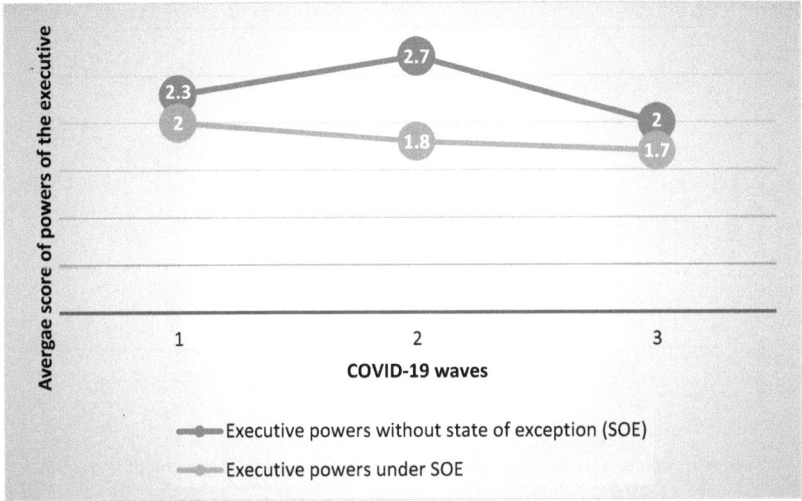

Fig. 2.3 COVID-19 exceptional measures and changes in executive decision-making. Source: EXCEPTIUS, own rendering

legislation giving a stronger role to parliamentary and territorial counterpowers.

To continue my investigation, I zoom into the relationship between the legal basis of exceptional powers and the derogations they allow on fundamental rights. EXCEPTIUS data allows tracing the impacts of COVID-19 containment measures on a large range of fundamental rights as defined and guaranteed by the European Convention on Human Rights. To get a clearer picture of the impacts of diverse emergency legislations, we focused on rights that (1) were restricted in a sufficiently large number of countries for the comparison to be meaningful and (2) were particularly vulnerable to derogations due to the specific nature of the crisis at stake (a pandemic). This leads us to focus on two core fundamental rights: freedom of movements (also analysed by Conde Belmonte and co-authors in this volume) and freedom of assembly.

The Europe Convention on Human Rights foresees in its article 2, par. 3 possibilities for European states to restrict freedom of movement in the interests of the protection of health. When activating emergency powers, governments have a duty to inform the European Court of Human Rights about the nature and duration of such restrictions. Figure 2.4 compares

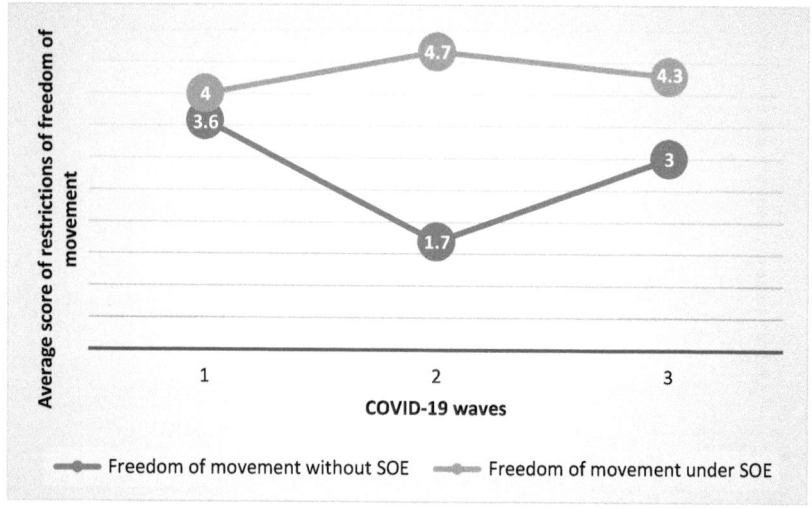

Fig. 2.4 COVID-19 emergency measures and restrictions of freedom of movement. Source: EXCEPTIUS, own rendering

the severity of restrictions in freedom movement between countries that declared emergency powers and countries that did not do so. Restrictions are coded based on the definition of the European Convention focusing on travel within and between European countries. EXCEPTIUS data record the following categories: travel restrictions and ban between countries; travel restrictions and ban within countries, all the possible combinations of the two and a ban on all forms of travels. The lowest possible score a country can get is 0 (for no derogation) to 8 for a ban on all forms of travels. Here again, the data is coded on an ordinal scale: the higher the score, the more stringent the restrictions.

Figure 2.4 shows that no countries implemented a full ban on travels during the pandemic. However, it displays a very different picture than Fig. 2.1 as EXCEPTIUS data reveal that countries that did rely on emergency powers to manage the pandemic implemented more stringent restrictions on freedom of movement than countries that did not activate emergency powers. The pattern is roughly stable over time, with a slight increase of restrictions during the second wave. In contrast, countries that relied on disaster-management legal framework implemented early on lower restrictions on freedom of movement and seemed to have reacted in a more proportionate manner to the evolution of the pandemic on their territories. Such countries also appear to be more responsive to the evolution of the public health situation with restriction measures being lifted and reintroduced throughout the different waves.

The analysis of the impacts of exceptional measures on the freedom of assembly and association (protected by article 11 of the ECHR) reveals a very close picture. EXCEPTIUS data record three core types of restrictions: the introduction of new regulations that don't necessarily restrict such right (such as, for example, the possibility for associations to hold online meetings); restrictions on either the right to assembly or to association; suspensions on either the right to assembly or to association and all possible combinations of restrictions and suspensions on both rights. The data is coded on an ordinal scale ranging from 0 (no restrictions introduced) to 9 (suspension of both rights). Figure 2.5 shows that states that activated emergency provisions also introduced more stringent restrictions on freedom of association and assembly than states that did not activate such provisions. The evolution of restrictions over the three waves of the pandemic is, however, less stable than for restrictions in freedom of movement. Governments using emergency powers only regulated such rights

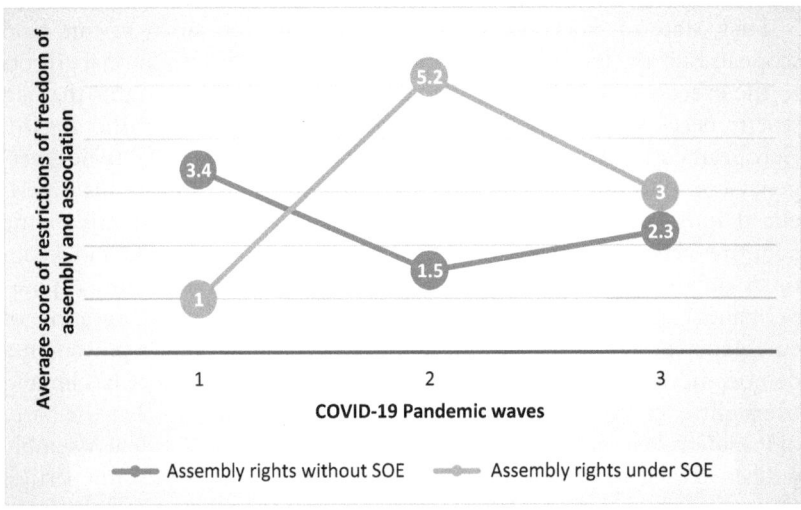

Fig. 2.5 COVID-19 emergency measures and restrictions of freedom of assembly and association. Source: EXCEPTIUS, own rendering

during the first wave of the pandemic. However, they strengthened the stringency of restrictions during the second and third waves. States that relied on crisis-management legal frameworks followed a different pattern: they initially implemented more stringent restriction to later adapt them to the evolution of the pandemic.

This is, however, not true for the first wave of the pandemic where states declaring the state of emergency mainly introduced new regulations to such freedoms.

CONCLUSION

The COVID-19 pandemic has seen the comeback of exceptional rule in Europe, taking the shape of either states of emergency (constitutionally regulated or not) or emergency measures derived from disaster-management legal frameworks. This chapter aimed at investigating whether activating emergency powers lead to more stringent restrictions in democratic governance and fundamental rights. Based on the literature on the impacts of emergency powers on democratic governance, we expected states of emergency to be associated with a stronger concentration of powers in the hands of the executive and more draconian restrictions of fundamental rights. This chapter yields three core findings.

First, state of emergency provisions considerably varied in time and scope in Europe. By design, emergency provisions grant additional powers to the executive and allow for derogations to fundamental rights that are strictly necessary to protect the health of a population. In this regard, European countries are rather homogeneous in the design of their emergency constitution or law. In practice, however, some Europeans experienced long-lasting exceptional provisions while others did not. Some countries activated emergency powers for a very limited period and sometimes only once during the pandemic while others lived under a quasi-permanent state of emergency during the pandemic. The duration of emergency powers is associated with the strength of counterpowers in a democratic system. In Hungary and Romania, the Parliament has limited oversight over emergency powers while in France, the fact that the party of President Macron enjoyed an absolute majority in the National Assembly weakened the role of parliamentary counterpowers and opposition parties. Other European countries took a different route and opted for relying on non-exceptional disaster management framework. In most cases, pandemic management frameworks were adapted to the case of COVID-19 and strengthened during the pandemic.

Second, this contribution shows that this difference matters for democratic governance and human rights. On the one hand, state of emergency provisions shield democracy against a concentration of powers in the hands of the executive better than disaster-management legislation does. This is in line with the theoretical arguments in favour of the adoption of emergency constitutions. Key to the defence of emergency constitutions is the fear of the action bias of the executive left without any guidance on how to proportionately manage a crisis and faced with societal demands to act, executive may be keen to abuse their power (Voigt, 2022). Our results support this fear and reveal that, if not planned properly, crisis-management legislation may concentrate powers in the hands of the executive to the detriment of parliaments and courts. On the other hand, the activation of emergency powers also coincides with more stringent restrictions of fundamental rights. This can be since state of emergency provisions allows for the introduction of blanket restrictions once activated. In contrast, each restriction introduced by disaster management law needs to be justified.

Coming back to the questions that aroused our initial interest (Is COVID-19 different from other crises in the (mis)use of emergency powers?), our contribution suggests two conclusions. It first confirms that the activation of emergency has strong and lasting consequences on human rights. Yet, our sample, mostly composed of consolidated democracies, reveals that the risks these regimes have for the concentration of powers are lower than expected. Second our descriptive account calls for paying more attention to the impacts of disaster-management framework—adopted during the pandemic—on democratic governance and human rights. Because their consequences are less spectacular—after all, activating disaster management tools does not come with specific constraints in terms of accountability and transparency—disaster management laws are considered less risky and suspicious. Yet, our initial findings show that they are no less detrimental to the quality of democratic governance. In strengthening legal preparedness to future crises, policy makers need to be particularly cautious in devising legal arsenals that maintain high levels of democratic governance and oversight in crisis times.

REFERENCES

Ackerman, B. A. (2006). *Before the next attack: Preserving civil liberties in an age of terrorism.* Yale University Press.

Bjørnskov, C., & Voigt, S. (2018a). The architecture of emergency constitutions. *International Journal of Constitutional Law, 16*(1), 101–127.

Bjørnskov, C., & Voigt, S. (2018b). Why do governments call a state of emergency? On the determinants of using emergency constitutions. *European Journal of Political Economy, 54,* 110–123.

Bjørnskov, C., & Voigt, S. (2020). *This time is different? On the use of emergency measures during the corona pandemic.* ILE working paper no. 36, University of Hamburg, Institute of Law and Economics (ILE).

Clay, K. C., Abdelwahab, M., Bagwell, S., Barney, M., Burkle, E., Hawley, T., et al. (2022). The effect of the COVID-19 pandemic on human rights practices: Findings from the Human Rights Measurement Initiative's 2021 Practitioner survey. *Journal of Human Rights, 21*(3), 317–333.

Ginsburg, T., & Versteeg, M. (2021). The bound executive: Emergency powers during the pandemic. *International Journal of Constitutional Law, 19*(5), 1498–1535.

Grogan, J. (2020). States of emergency: Analysing global use of emergency powers in response to COVID-19. *European Journal of Law Reform, 4,* 338–354.

Gross, O., & Aoláin, F. N. (2006). *Law in times of crisis: Emergency powers in theory and practice.* Cambridge University Press.

Guasti, P., & Bustikova, L. (2022). Pandemic power grab. *East European Politics, 38*(4), 529–550.

Lundgren, M., Klamberg, M., Sundström, K., & Dahlqvist, J. (2020). Emergency powers in response to COVID-19: Policy diffusion, democracy, and preparedness. *Nordic Journal of Human Rights, 38*(4), 305–318.

Rácz, A. (2020). *Hungary's 'coronavirus law': How power becomes unlimited?* International Centre for Defence and Security. https://icds.ee/en/hungarys-coronavirus-law-how-power-becomes-unlimited/

Rooney, B. (2019). Emergency powers in democratic states: Introducing the democratic emergency powers dataset. *Research & Politics, 6*(4), 2053168019892436.

Spadaro, A. (2020). COVID-19: Testing the limits of human rights. *European Journal of Risk Regulation, 11*(2), 317–325.

Voigt, S. (2022). Contracting for catastrophe: Legitimizing emergency constitutions by drawing on social contract theory. *Res Publica, 28*(1), 149–172.

CHAPTER 3

The Role of Parliaments in Exceptional Times

Corentin Poyet

INTRODUCTION

The chapter addresses the critical question of the role of Parliaments during the pandemic. In most consolidated democracies (Switzerland and the United Kingdom are two significant exceptions), the Parliaments have never been totally shut down (Waismel-Manor et al., 2022). Still, their role in managing the pandemic has been more or less limited. Pandemic-related policy-making was almost exclusively initiated by governments, but some Parliaments had the opportunity to review, amend and even vetoed some decisions. Parliaments that are considered as strong in the classic rankings (Chernykh et al., 2017; Fish & Kroenig, 2011) are also those that played a greater role during the pandemic, mainly when the government had to rely on multi-party majorities. Italy is a major exception since its Parliament—one of the most powerful in the world—has been sidelined mainly when the crisis started. Moreover, since the agenda was busy with the pandemic, the treatment of other issues has been

C. Poyet (✉)
Department of Government, University of Bergen, Bergen, Norway
e-mail: corentin.poyet@uib.no

© The Author(s) 2024
C. Egger et al. (eds.), *Covid-19 Containment Policies in Europe*,
International Series on Public Policy,
https://doi.org/10.1007/978-3-031-52096-9_3

temporarily suspended, leading to a de facto reduction of the work of Parliaments. To this, we can also add a type of self-censorship of members of parliaments (MPs) who tried to avoid overburdening the government with written questions. Hence, besides reducing the role of the Parliament, there is a rally round the flag as observed when major crises arise, although exceptions exist (Kritzinger et al., 2021). Moreover, at least at the beginning of the pandemic, the Parliaments have also been the collateral victims of other regulations mainly related to the limitation of indoor gatherings and social distance. At later stages, parliaments and committees were, however, allowed to gather mainly because the regulations and restrictions were more targeted towards specific sectors of societies and with the generalisation of mask mandates in indoor settings.

Measuring the power of Parliaments during the pandemic has been at the core of a large body of literature (Griglio, 2020; Hájek, 2021; Pedersen & Borghetto, 2021; Waismel-Manor et al., 2022). There is a broad agreement about the negative consequences of the pandemic on legislatures and the eventual impact on democracy as a whole (Kolvani et al., 2020; Lührmann et al., 2020; Engler et al., 2021). Legislatures have found themselves in a position where they had to redefine their role or, paraphrasing Merkel and Lührmann (2021), to adapt to the situation. It is on this aspect that the literature offers various perspectives depending on what is studied. Unlike previous studies that only aimed to understand the place of the Parliament in the daily management of the pandemic, this chapter ambitions to also understand how the decisions and policies implemented during the pandemic impacted the work of legislatures. It thus does not only focus on the decision-making and what role was granted to Parliaments. It also aims to highlight the consequences for the institutional arrangements and the daily work in the Parliament. It shows that Parliaments that were involved in the decision-making are also those that have been the most untouched thorough the pandemic.

EUROPEAN PARLIAMENTS AND THE DAILY MANAGEMENT OF THE COVID-19 PANDEMIC

During the first wave of the pandemic, from March to May 2020, the media coverage primarily focused on the executive and health authorities. From this point of view, the Parliaments seem to play, at best, a limited role, if no role at all (Waismel-Manor et al., 2022; Hájek, 2021). Indeed, the state of emergency offered little room to the Parliament in many countries. For example, in Italy the work of committees has been limited (both in time and scope) on the bills deemed urgent by the government that favoured the use of decrees. Similarly, Pedersen and Borghetto (2021) explain that the government regularly attached confidence vote to the projects requiring a Parliamentary support in order to circumvent the debates and displace the decision away from the topic of the bill itself. In Hungary, the government managed the pandemic exclusively by decrees and the absence of a sunset close in the state of emergency law made it difficult for the Parliament to assess the government action in due time.

The Role of Parliament in the Management of the Pandemic

In Fig. 3.1, I display the percentage of decisions that the Parliament has issued (including regional and local assemblies) per country.

The figure shows that Parliaments rarely are the leading actors in managing the pandemic, that is, rarely the responsible authority. Five per cent of all documents included in EXCEPTIUS dataset were issued by a Parliament. Only Austria and the United Kingdom display a relatively high

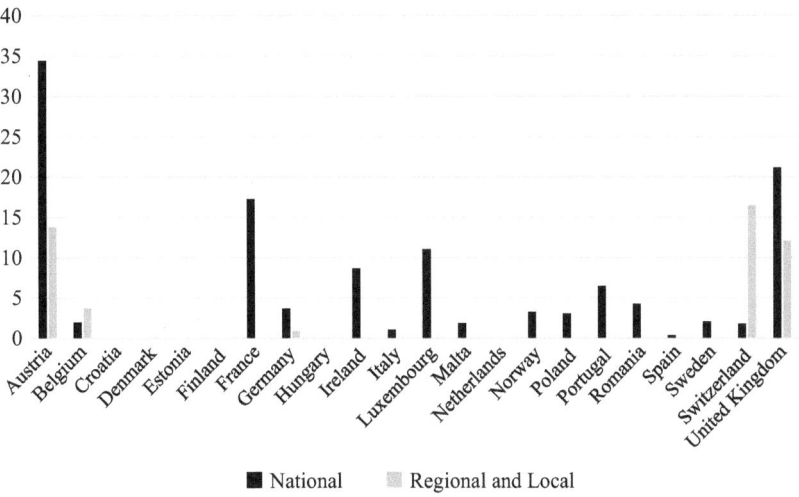

Fig. 3.1 Percentage of documents issued by national and subnational legislative bodies. Source: EXCEPTIUS data, own rendering

share of legislation issued by legislative authorities. As far as I know, only the Swiss Parliament has the power to declare a state of emergency. Elsewhere, it is a governmental prerogative, although a parliamentary approval may be needed (see Egger's contribution in this volume for a description of the procedures preceding to the declaration of the state of emergency). This country also stands out thanks to its comparatively high share of regulations issued by regional (i.e., cantonal) legislatures. Yet, even at the regional level, an executive dominance is observed even though such prominence is less marked at the subnational than at the national level. Most decisions regarding daily life restrictions were issued and supervised by the executives or administrative authorities. It does not mean that, in other countries, the Parliament was not involved in the decision-making. However, the decision (a bill, a restriction, etc.) is originating from and enacted by the government (or an administrative authority). For example, in Finland, the government played a major role in enacting legislation and, during the first wave, almost all pandemic-related acts originated from it. Yet, the Parliament still played a role in discussing and validating them.

In many countries—notably consensus democracies—collaboration between the political authorities has been the rule (Christensen & Lægreid, 2020; Saunes et al., 2022), but at the end, the government is the responsible authority. Interestingly enough, this decision-making process is correlated with a more successful fight against COVID-19 (Freiburghaus et al., 2023). Similarly, the Parliaments rarely initiated policies. Parliaments were the authority in charge only in a handful of cases and were limited to certain countries. This situation is not exceptional since implementing procedures is the essential role of executive bodies and state agencies. However, the question of executive dominance in policy-making is new in many countries known for their powerful Parliaments (Rasch & Tsebelis, 2013). In Italy, for example, the Parliament is considered one of the most potent legislatures, mainly regarding MPs' power of amendment and control over the agenda (Chernykh et al., 2017).

However, during the pandemic, its role was minimal. If it can amend the decrees, it had no role in the declaration of a state of exception or the possibility to end it. In the case of the pandemic, the situation is more problematic because of the legal instruments used. State of emergencies allowed the use of fast-track legislation and specific procedures characterised by the limited powers given to the Parliaments. The emergency powers were thus a priori detrimental to Parliaments. Yet, in many countries (e.g., United Kingdom, Germany, Finland, France or Ireland), state of emergencies came with a sunset clause meaning that they would expire at a given date. It means that government would need a new parliamentary approval to extend the state of emergency. In France, a parliamentary approval was not required to initiate the state of emergency, but any extension should be scrutinised and approved by the legislature. In Germany, these laws can last only 90 days and the Bundestag approval is needed for any extension. In some instance (e.g., in Denmark), these sunset clauses also allow the Parliament to exercise its oversight capacity and evaluate the decisions made by the government.

The Role of Parliamentary Oversight

In most countries, the Parliament was involved at least at the initial stages of the decision-making when governments drafted laws. These laws generally mean transferring a large part of the powers to the government and public agencies in charge of the daily pandemic management. Most of the restrictions are, of course, legally bound to a Parliamentary decision. If a legal basis already existed before the pandemic—like a public health code or communicable disease act—the Parliament was involved in the decision-making at some point in the past. Still, their timing and scope are generally set without the legislature. Also, the way the decision-making was organised is exceptional since most countries used emergency powers which, in most cases, ensure additional capabilities to the executive and sometimes without an act of Parliament. In addition, many countries made use of fast-track legislation, as evidenced by the meagre number of decisions that have been subject to a pre-check or reviewed by the Parliament or a judiciary body before the implementation.

In most countries, legal checks (either by the Parliament or a constitutional court) are not mandatory for all bills. However, for bills that introduce significant changes, the practice is, in many countries, to proceed with the checks, nonetheless. The Netherlands, Finland and Sweden, for example, have parliamentary committees in charge of the constitutional review when deemed necessary. In France, the chair of the Senate and National Assembly may also ask for a constitutional review by the *Conseil d'État*. One example illustrating the importance of these checks occurred in March 2021 in Finland when the governmental project of a strict lockdown was deemed too vague by the Constitutional Laws parliamentary committee   and   subsequently   withdrawn   by   the   government.

Pandemic-related legislation and decisions can be included in this group due to their impact on daily lives and the economy. However, the number of decisions per country that underwent ex ante legal checks is limited.

Again, in many countries, the legal framework was pre-existing, and these legal checks may have been done at the time of its acceptance, making any new reviews redundant. In this case, the most problematic is the lack of participation of the Parliament in the definition of the content of the bills. Without being necessarily involved in a legal or constitutional check, the Parliament generally contributes to the checks and balances, which eventually improve the quality of the bills. It is difficult to assess the quality of legislation, mainly when it comes to those related to the pandemic. A parliamentary vote contributes to the legitimacy of the law and may improve its acceptance by citizens. There is already a rich literature on trust in politics in times of COVID-19 (Baekgaard et al., 2020; Esaiasson et al., 2021; Kestilä-Kekkonen et al., 2022) with a focus on compliance with COVID measures (Wong & Jensen, 2020; Kritzinger et al., 2021). It could be interesting to assess better the impact of the decision-making on both trust and compliance with the restrictions. A reasonable expectation would be to observe higher levels of trust and compliance with measures when the Parliament has shown that perceived competence of decision-makers matters (Kestilä-Kekkonen et al., 2022). More generally, research on Nordic countries show a correlation between a governance based on individual responsibility and use of regular decision-making process. For example, in Norway, the collaboration between political authorities and actors at various levels of government has been highlighted as an important factor explaining the high trust in government's decision and general compliance with the decisions (Christensen & Lægreid, 2020).

Speeding Up the Law-Making Process: Detrimental to Parliaments?

However, fast-track legislation does not necessarily mean overriding the Parliament. In most cases, it "only" delays its work. In the United Kingdom, for example, the Parliament is still engaged, and the basic decision-making norms must be followed. Where a "regular" bill takes months to become a law, the 2020 Coronavirus Act was approved in five days. In Scotland, the whole process has been finalised in a bit more than 24 hours (Molloy, 2021). A fast pace offers a minimal opportunity for

MPs to amend and control the bill, but it offers a certain legitimacy to it. Similar observations can be made in other countries. In Switzerland, the COVID-19 act was accepted by the Parliament a bit more than one month after the message from the Federal Council (submission of the bill by the government for parliamentary scrutiny) when this process can generally last a year or even more. Some of the committees proceeded in less than a day. The Parliaments have thus the capacity to make quick decisions even in a country known for its slow legislative process. More generally, it also shows that emergency situations and exceptional powers granted to the executives may not be needed to ensure a quick decision-making. To paraphrase, the emergency does not justify overriding Parliaments or making use of specific legislative instruments (Voigt, 2022). In France, the bill was accepted five days after the government proposal. Yet, parliamentary approval was not necessary to implement the first restrictions. The government decided about the lockdown one day before submitting the bill proposal to the Parliament. The role of the Parliament is thus paradoxical. On the one hand, the governments cannot proceed without it. On the other hand, it may implement the act before the Parliament's approval, making it a formality. Even more paradoxical was the necessity for MPs to travel from their district to Paris (and back) to deliberate on the project when the whole country was in a lockdown and intercity travels, banned.

The question that arises is about the institutionalisation of such features. The pandemic has somewhat displayed a pessimistic picture of the Parliament. Still, new law-making patterns may appear, for some, more efficient in addressing problems, mainly when they require a quick response. In some countries, the relative establishment of the fast-track procedures started before the pandemic, but the emergency gave credit to them and introduced a reason for further using them. Moreover, there are examples of migration of emergency procedures in the standard legal system, reducing the role of Parliament in policy-making (Bolleyer & Salát, 2021). Bolleyer and Salát (2021) cite the examples of Hungary and the United Kingdom, where some elements of the emergency procedures were included in the common laws on catastrophe management and public health. The authors cite the case of the "negative procedure" in the United Kingdom that allows a minister to set a law unless the legislature agrees to reject it (Bolleyer & Salát, 2021, 1116). In Slovakia, the government made use of the emergency situation to reform other laws using fast-track legislations and decree.

The scholarship acknowledges this trend but also highlights the transformation of the role of the Parliament. Its position in drafting legislation has decreased, but, at least in theory, this should be compensated by stronger oversight powers. Ex post controls are among the most frequent, and COVID bills have been subject to these checks in many countries. In the United Kingdom, the Coronavirus Act included a sunset provision which ensures that the law ceases after a set period and cannot be extended without a new act. However, in the British case, this provision also includes additional powers for the Parliament to review the legislation later, generally once the emergency is gone. In Denmark, the legislation went even further. Like elsewhere, the Parliament did not play a vital role in the daily management of the pandemic, and fast-track procedures were used for virtually all COVID-related bills, limiting the duration of hearings, an essential feature of this working Parliament (Pedersen & Borghetto, 2021). Sunset provisions were also included, but in addition to this, the Parliament was able to extend its oversight powers. A special committee composed of representatives from all parliamentary groups was set to scrutinise the act's implementation (Pedersen & Borghetto, 2021). As far as I know, such a post-legislative control committee is a unique case, but it shows that even in an emergency, Parliaments can transform themselves to fit a new "state of the world." In other words, although it is undoubtedly a unique occurrence, the pandemic can also be a trigger for reforms that are not necessarily going in the direction of a declining Parliament. In France, the emergency also incited the government to delay the parliamentary procedure, but without a proper sunset procedure requiring a parliamentary evaluation. In this case, the Parliament can reject the decrees after a month. However, the addition of a rally round the flag, strong party discipline and support to the government and president clearly limited the impact of the procedure.

As underlined in other chapters, there are various situations behind the idea of emergency powers. This variety also impacts the role of Parliament in managing the pandemic. Exceptions are observed, and in some countries, the Parliament was able not only to play a crucial role but also to expand its capacity or transform its role. One event illustrates this process. It happened in Finland in March 2021 when the number of daily cases was on the rise. The government and president had declared a state of emergency for the second time in the pandemic to allow the government to lead the fight. However, in this country, each new decision (e.g., closure of public facilities or schools), including those made during a state of emergency, requires parliamentary approval. The Parliament (mainly the standing committee for constitutional laws) has to proceed with the legal review. In March 2021, a project to implement a strict lockdown was drawn by the government and submitted for review. The committee assessed the project as being too vague, which led the government to withdraw it. The parliamentary agreement was also necessary before implementing the most stringent measures in March and April 2020 (closure of schools and isolation of the capital region from other Finnish regions).

Although it is difficult to find a causal mechanism here, one explanation could be the level of preparedness of a political system (Saunes et al., 2022). Finland (and other countries) clearly set emergency powers and communicable diseases acts. Pre-existing legal frameworks set the responsibilities of each actor. In Finland, for example, the emergency powers do not directly force the Parliament to step down. The law-making process was similar to normal, although MPs decided to speed up the process. The episode of March 2021 shows that when needed, the Finnish Parliament knows how to keep its prerogatives and the government has no choice but to withdraw its bill. In other countries, the pattern is more concerning. When the legal framework regulating emergency powers granted discretional powers to the executive, the Parliament was de facto put on the back burner. In addition to the legal framework regulating the management of the pandemic, there are political features that also intervene. Bolleyer and Salát (2021) highlighted the negative impact of unified and single-party governments. When the government does not need to make agreements with coalition partners or the opposition, the number of possible gridlocks is relatively low, facilitating quick decisions and government empowerment in emergencies (Olsson, 2009). The nature of coalition governments makes it necessary for the quest of agreements and intra-government check-and-balance to apply still. In other words, the less concentrated the power, the less weakened the Parliament.

To sum up, a state of emergency was declared in many European countries without the immediate support of the Parliament. Besides, the role of Parliament remains limited once the state of emergency is implemented. Most decisions are made by the executives and/or administrative authority without parliamentary oversight. This should not, however, hide that situations are very diverse. Some parliaments were able to regain their powers or transform their role, mainly thanks to sunset clauses that offer the opportunity for Parliaments to exercise an ex post control over the government's actions.

Daily Work During the Pandemic

The EXCEPTIUS data display no evidence of pandemic-related legislations directly targeting the Parliament. As explained in the previous section, the Parliaments have sometimes been the collateral victims of the policies made by executives. Complete closure of Parliaments was very exceptional even during the uncertain times of the first wave.

However, this does not mean that the work in legislatures remains untouched. Like other types of assemblies, the Parliament was impacted by the restrictions of gathering and regulations about social distancing, as well as other policies applying to indoor settings. Some assemblies also implemented some work-from-home policies not only for their administrative staff but also for legislators. Similarly, the public could not access the Parliament anymore due to the closure of indoor spaces. In virtually all countries, the Parliament was, thus, not treated differently from other public venues. EXCEPTIUS data do not, for example, display any illustration of an exception granted to a parliamentary building to continue hosting the public.

In some cases, the physical closure of the building occurred even before the first significant measures were voted (Pedersen & Borghetto, 2021). Also, in some instances, members of Parliaments were subject to travel restrictions. They were prevented from travelling between their district and the capital but also within their constituency. Although they were not directly targeted, they were not granted any exceptions either. For example, such travel restrictions have been reported in Italy (Pedersen & Borghetto, 2021). Elsewhere, although regulations applied, MPs were granted exceptions (as other public officials) and were not directly prevented from fulfilling their duties. For example, in France and Finland, a fixed share of MPs could be in the plenary simultaneously (the number varies over time), and online meetings were organised mainly for the work in committees.

There are also some instances of Parliaments gathering in new venues to respect the physical distance or to fit all members in a closed space. We have observed such delocalised meetings in Liechtenstein, where plenary sessions took place in the *Vaduzer Saal* and Switzerland. The federal Parliament convened at the Bern Expo exhibition centre in the latter case.

Some cantonal Parliaments also set meetings in delocalised manner. For example, the Neuchâtel Grand Conseil convened in La Chaux-de-Fonds' sport centre (*pavillon des sports*).

One of the most striking evolutions is observed in Latvia with the creation in May 2020 of the *e-Saeima* platform (literally the e-Parliament). It allowed all parliamentary meetings (including plenary sessions) to take place remotely and offered MPs the opportunity to cast their votes securely. Such an online voting tool is exceptional in European legislatures, although many at least thought about setting it. Safety issues have been raised in many cases to explain the lack of an online voting system. As a result, beyond Latvia, as far as I know, only Belgium and Ukraine set some online voting procedures, even though they did not go as far as Latvia. Other countries set other arrangements. In Greece, there was an option to cast a ballot by post while the Parliament convened at a limited capacity. In that sense, the pandemic may have had positive consequences mainly because these tools did not exist before. Some countries were thus able to adapt very quickly to the new situation and to develop instruments to facilitate the parliamentary work during hard times.

Elsewhere, although online meetings were possible in other countries, they were scarcer. In some legislatures like Germany, Estonia and Hungary, only urgent matters were considered, mainly in a remote way. Online voting had been an issue in most countries, during the first stages of the pandemic, at least essential matters (the definition varies from country to country) were handled and most Parliaments resumed their normal activities very quickly in 2020.

The pandemic triggered or accelerated the pace of some transformations that are not necessarily negative. Many Parliaments experienced significant changes, and the move to a fully online setting as in Latvia may be an extreme example. However, procedural changes in Finland allowed committees to organise remote meetings and remote hearings. In a country where these meetings are crucial, it constitutes a major change. Although they were first temporary, they have been made permanent in 2021. In Ireland, the pandemic triggered the use of roll-call votes instead of manual votes. These transformations may enhance the transparency of the decision-making, since it may allow citizens to follow the debates and know how their MPs behave in Parliament. Before the pandemic, following the discussions would require going to the Parliament since only a few legislatures had their work broadcasted live on TV or their website. To a certain extent, the closure of parliamentary buildings to the public also enhances the visibility of the parliamentary work. It somewhat forced the Parliament to adapt to a new type of demand, and some chambers succeeded while others returned to their old practices.

The role of Parliaments in the management of the pandemic and its daily work has changed over time and across waves. The development of online tools and the wide use of personal protective equipment allowed MPs to go back to work already in the fall 2020 in most countries. This trend mainly impacted the management of all issues that were on standby during the first wave, but it also allowed them to work on pandemic-related legislations. First, since many governments introduced a sunset clause in the laws, it was required for the Parliament to deliberate and review the implementation of the bills. In some countries (e.g., France and Germany), it was also the moment for the Parliament to discuss a possible extension of the state of emergency. It is also during this period that governments and Parliaments started to revise the existing legislation to better handle upcoming emergencies. Finland revised it Communicable Diseases Act, and Norwegian Parliament worked on both the Infection Control Act and the Health Preparedness Act. In the two countries, the goal was to manage the pandemic with normal laws and avoid using exceptional powers. Parliaments played a major role in both cases and the regular law-making process was used mainly when it comes to committee hearings, an important element in these two Nordic countries.

Second, although Parliaments were not totally shut down during the first wave, they hardly functioned as normal. Both personal protective equipment (mainly face masks) and online tools allowed Parliaments to come back to an almost normal setting. Already in the fall 2020, most Parliaments started to gather in plenary sessions (some with a limited number of MPs) and to deal with the topics that were put on hold during the spring. In 2021 and 2022, the Parliaments worked almost as normal thanks to many adaptations. Procedural changes have been made to organise remote meeting when the risk of contamination was deemed too high (mainly committee meetings). Also, Parliaments benefited from a better knowledge of the virus and of more targeted measures to avoid being closed or restricted in 2021 and 2022. One major exception to this trend is the temporary vaccine mandate for MPs in Lithuania from November 2021 to July 2022. However, it must be noted that the Parliament itself voted in favour of this restriction. It is nevertheless a unique case in Europe, since no other Parliaments experienced those strict restrictions after the first wave. Maybe paradoxically, the fact that vaccine mandate (or test-mandate) does not apply to Parliaments has also been subject to some criticism.

CONCLUSION

The pandemic has had a massive impact on daily life and political institutions. Parliaments are no exceptions. The pandemic has undoubtedly reinforced the executives mainly due to the wide use of emergency powers. In managing the pandemic, Parliaments were put on the back burner. It must, however, be noted that most Parliaments conscientiously agreed to let the executive manage the pandemic since, in most countries, the emergency powers were subject to a preliminary vote in Parliament. So, executives benefited from an exceptional legal framework and a rally around the flag effect that encompassed most political actors and citizens. The opposition to these arrangements was thus limited at the early stages of the pandemic. Besides, there was a tacit agreement between parties not to overburden the government with non-urgent matters. All in all, it gave the impression that the legislature was shut down.

The reality is more complex and, more crucially, varies from country to country. It is difficult to highlight a pattern here, but two key elements make a difference: the emergency powers and their duration. Regarding emergency powers, not all countries have a similar legal framework, and it influences what role the Parliament plays. In all cases, there is a delegation process made by the Parliament in favour of the executive. The nature of this delegation does, however, differ, and some Parliaments were able to retain or recover remarkably well. In some cases, the emergency powers did not imply any weakening of the Parliament. Still, they allowed the government to make decisions on policy areas that it should not in regular times. Elsewhere, the Parliament agreed to transfer some competencies to the government and administration. In this case, the role of the legislature mainly depends on what is included in the state of emergency. Most countries added a sunset clause to make sure the legislation ends automatically. In some cases (the United Kingdom and Denmark, among others), it also stipulates the role of Parliament, which oversees the evaluation or even supervises the implementations. One key element for a democracy to keep working is its ability to recover from a crisis (Merkel & Lührmann, 2021).

In this aspect, the situation is not black or white. In most countries, the Parliaments recovered entirely and now work as usual. It is mainly the case in countries where the pandemic did not impact the parliamentary procedure, which could "get back to work" as soon as the restrictions on gatherings were dropped or amended. The pattern is less optimistic in the countries where emergency procedures were integrated into the customary laws. Hungary is the most striking case (Bolleyer & Salát, 2021). Still, it is essential to note that it is only one element of a broader trend towards democratic backsliding that started way before the pandemic (Bánkuti et al., 2012). More surprising are the positive developments that have been observed, for example, in Denmark and Latvia.

Hence, although Parliaments were not shut down during the pandemic, their role in managing it was not substantial. The state of emergency offered strong powers to the executives, and although most of the legislatures were able to regain their abilities, there were exceptions. Also, Parliaments had to adapt or redefine their procedures and work standards to fit the regulations. In some countries, it has been done by prioritising the tasks related to the pandemic and limiting the meetings and votes on other issues. Elsewhere, the Parliaments developed new tools (mainly online), allowing them to continue working. Some of the devices could even enhance the transparency of the law-making and, thus, the involvement of citizens in the policy-making.

An important role is also played by the institutional design and the general power of Parliament in the policy-making. Except for Italy, countries with a strong Parliament before the pandemic also had a strong Parliament during the pandemic. As a result, Parliaments played a greater role in parliamentary systems rather than in semi-presidential regimes. They were also the ones that went back to normal the quickest. Having an executive that is directly accountable to the legislatures is an important element against democratic backsliding (Boese et al., 2021) mainly because it ensures a broad democratic legitimacy to the decisions. The pandemic tends to confirm this trend. The best examples are Nordic countries— thanks to multi-party governments—that came across the crisis almost untouched and with Parliaments invested in the management of the pandemic. In countries with stronger executives, the situation is more varied. In Western Europe (e.g., France and Spain), the Parliaments did not play a great role in the daily management of pandemic mainly because of governments with single-party majorities limiting the need for cross-parties' agreements. A return to the normal settings occurred later than in the Nordic countries, but, at the end, they remain largely untouched. In Central Europe, the situation is more complex. Trends towards weakening Parliament were pre-existing mainly in Poland and Hungary and the pandemic did not alter them. This is the case in Poland and, mainly, in Hungary. Weak institutions also limited the ability of Parliaments to fulfil their duty. The lack of proper online settings made difficult for the Slovakian Parliament to extend the state of emergency (COVID-positive MPs were finally allowed to leave from quarantine). Also in Slovakia, the use of fast-track legislations literally exploded after the pandemic also for revising laws completely unrelated to the crisis. Czech Republic is an exception mainly thanks to the inability of two successive governments to hold a single-party majority.

Hence, (1) a strong Parliament in an established democracy leads to a legislature that is involved in the management of the pandemic and whose daily work has hardly been impacted by the pandemic. It is particularly true in Nordic countries, but also Germany and the Netherlands. Italy, on the other hand, is a major exception. (2) A strong executive in an established democracy leads to an executive dominance and temporary disruptions of the work of the Parliament. Yet, the legislature regained the lost powers over time and played a great role in reviewing governments' work. France, Spain and the United Kingdom illustrate this situation. (3) In countries with weaker democratic institutions, Parliaments sometimes struggled to play a role beyond the validation of government projects. In this situation, the consequences went beyond the pandemic with a use of emergency powers for projects unrelated to the crisis. Central European countries such as Poland, Hungary and Slovakia are in this situation.

The pandemic has shown the necessity of clearly defining the roles of each actor, Parliament included. Crises should not be immune of accountability and, more importantly, should not be used to increase one's powers (Boese et al., 2021), making crucial to anticipate them. Parliaments ensure the democratic legitimacy of the decision-making and constitutes a barrier to possible abuses. Laws regulating the use of states of emergencies should also come with guarantees against concentration of powers mainly by limiting the ability of government to use confidence vote to ensure the parliamentary approval, fast-track legislations and decrees. The pandemic has shown that Parliaments are able to make quick decisions without jeopardising the answer to the crisis. Hence, inciting governments to make use of "normal" legislative instruments and passing bills through the regular legislative process (even accelerated) does not mean the emergency would be inefficiently fought, quite the contrary. It would also contribute to legitimise the decision and limit the consequences for the democratic institutions. Power sharing appears to be the key (Christensen & Lægreid, 2020).

References

Baekgaard, M., Christensen, J., Madsen, J. K., & Mikkelsen, K. S. (2020). Rallying around the flag in times of COVID-19: Societal lockdown and trust in democratic institutions. *Journal of Behavioral Public Administration, 3*(2) https://www.journal-bpa.org

Bánkuti, M., Halmai, G., & Scheppele, K. L. (2012). Hungary's illiberal turn: Disabling the constitution. *Journal of Democracy, 23*(3), 138–146.

Boese, V. A., Edgell, A. B., Hellmeier, S., Maerz, S. F., & Lindberg, S. F. (2021). How democracies prevail: Democratic resilience as a two-stage process. *Democratization, 28*(5), 885–907.

Bolleyer, N., & Salát, O. (2021). Parliaments in times of crisis: COVID-19, populism and executive dominance. *West European Politics, 44*(5–6), 1103–1128.

Chernykh, S., Doyle, D., & Power, T. J. (2017). Measuring legislative power: An expert reweighting of the Fish-Kroenig Parliamentary powers index. *Legislative Studies Quarterly, 42*(2), 295–320.

Christensen, T., & Lægreid, P. (2020). Balancing governance capacity and legitimacy: How the Norwegian Government handled the COVID-19 crisis as a high performer. *Public Administration Review, 80*(5), 774–779.

Engler, S., Brunner, P., Loviat, R., Abou-Chadi, T., Leemann, L., Glaser, A., & Kübler, D. (2021). Democracy in times of the pandemic: Explaining the variation of COVID-19 policies across European democracies. *West European Politics, 44*(5–6), 1077–1102.

Esaiasson, P., Sohlberg, J., Ghersetti, M., & Johansson, B. (2021). How the coronavirus crisis affects citizen trust in institutions and in unknown others: Evidence from 'the Swedish experiment'. *European Journal of Political Research, 60*(3), 748–760.

Fish, M. S., & Kroenig, M. (2011). *The handbook of national legislatures: A global survey*. Cambridge Univ. Press.

Freiburghaus, R., Vatter, A., & Stadelmann-Steffen, I. (2023). Kinder, gentler – And crisis-proof? Consensus democracy, inclusive institutions and COVID-19 pandemic performance. *West European Politics*, 1–27. https://doi.org/10.108 0/01402382.2022.2156164

Griglio, E. (2020). Parliamentary oversight under the COVID-19 emergency: Striving against executive dominance. *The Theory and Practice of Legislation, 8*(1–2), 49–70.

Hájek, L. (2021). Legislative behaviour of MPs in the Czech Republic in times of COVID-19 pandemic. *Parliamentary Affairs*, gsab057.

Kestilä-Kekkonen, E., Koivula, A., & Tiihonen, A. (2022). When trust is not enough. A longitudinal analysis of political trust and political competence during the first wave of the COVID-19 pandemic in Finland. *European Political Science Review*, 1–17.

Kolvani, P., Lundstedt, M., Maerz, S. F., Lührmann, A., Lachapelle, J., Grahn, S., & Edgell, A. B. (2020). *Pandemic backsliding: Democracy and disinformation seven months into the COVID-19 pandemic.* V-Dem Policy Brief 25.

Kritzinger, S., Foucault, M., Lachat, R., Partheymüller, J., Plescia, C., & Brouard, S. (2021). 'Rally round the flag': The COVID-19 crisis and trust in the national government. *West European Politics, 44*(5–6), 1205–1231.

Lührmann, A., Edgell, A. B., Grahn, S., Lachapelle, J., & Maerz, S. F. (2020). *Does the coronavirus endanger democracy in Europe?* Carnegie Europe.

Merkel, W., & Lührmann, A. (2021). Resilience of democracies: Responses to illiberal and authoritarian challenges. *Democratization, 28*(5), 869 884.

Molloy, S. (2021). Approach with caution. Sunset clauses as safeguards of democracy? *European Journal of Law Reform, 23*(2), 147–166.

Olsson, S. (2009). Defending the rule of law in emergencies through checks and balances. *Democracy and Security, 5*(2), 103–126.

Pedersen, H. H., & Borghetto, E. (2021). Fighting COVID-19 on democratic terms. Parliamentary functioning in Italy and Denmark during the pandemic. *Representation, 57*(4), 401–418.

Rasch, B. E., & Tsebelis, G. (Eds.). (2013). *The role of governments in legislative agenda setting.* Routledge. https://www.taylorfrancis.com/books/9781136870460

Saunes, I. S., Vrangbæk, K., Byrkjeflot, H., Jervelund, S. S., Birk, H. O., Tynkkynen, L. K., et al. (2022). Nordic responses to COVID-19: Governance and policy measures in the early phases of the pandemic. *Health Policy, 126*(5), 418–426.

Voigt, S. (2022). Contracting for catastrophe: Legitimizing emergency constitutions by drawing on social contract theory. *Res Publica, 28*(1), 149–172.

Waismel-Manor, I., Bar-Siman-Tov, I., Rozenberg, O., Levanon, A., Benoît, C., & Ifergane, G. (2022). Should I stay (open) or should I close? World legislatures during the first wave of COVID-19. *Political Studies,* 00323217221090615.

Wong, C. M. L., & Jensen, O. (2020). The paradox of trust: Perceived risk and public compliance during the COVID-19 pandemic in Singapore. *Journal of Risk Research, 23*(7–8), 1021–1030.

CHAPTER 4

Elections and Special Voting Arrangements

Piret Ehin and Liisa Talving

INTRODUCTION

The COVID-19 pandemic has presented a major threat to elections—and, by extension, to democracy—worldwide. Authorities in democratic countries have faced the difficult task of figuring out how to protect the health of citizens and officials while ensuring "the continuity of our democratic life" (James, 2020) which entails holding free and fair elections at periodic intervals. Organising elections in the context of the pandemic raises a number of questions: under what circumstances should elections be cancelled or postponed? If elections are held, how can risks arising from the pandemic be minimised while ensuring compliance with international standards and global norms governing the appropriate conduct of elections? Specifically, should special voting arrangements, such as early voting, postal, proxy or remote internet voting be introduced or expanded?

The chapter examines policy responses to the coronavirus pandemic in the realm of elections in 27 EU member states, focusing on two main choices—whether to hold or postpone elections and whether and how to modify the way elections are run. With regard to the latter question, we

P. Ehin (✉) • L. Talving
Johan Skytte Institute of Political Studies, University of Tartu, Tartu, Estonia
e-mail: piret.ehin@ut.ee; liisa.talving@ut.ee

© The Author(s) 2024   63
C. Egger et al. (eds.), *Covid-19 Containment Policies in Europe*,
International Series on Public Policy,
https://doi.org/10.1007/978-3-031-52096-9_4

focus on special voting arrangements (SVAs). This term refers to voting modes other than conventional in-person voting at the polling station on election day. There are five main SVAs, including early voting (voting before election day), postal voting (voting by mail), proxy voting (ballot cast by one person on behalf of another), remote internet voting (casting an electronic vote over the internet) and the mobile ballot box, which means that members of the election administration bring the ballot box to a voter's home or to the institution in which they reside in order to facilitate their vote. The analysis covers national as well as subnational elections scheduled to take place between February 2020 and February 2022 (i.e., within two years from the onset of the pandemic in Europe).

The chapter is structured in five parts. The first describes the challenges associated with the "health versus democracy" dilemma and outlines the basic choices available to policymakers (hold, postpone or modify elections). The second section focuses on different initial conditions, mapping the use of special voting arrangements in EU-27 before the health crisis. The third section examines the postponement of elections during the pandemic, highlighting patterns and describing associated debates and difficulties. The fourth section focuses on the introduction and expansion of special voting arrangements during the pandemic. The fifth section discusses the implementation of policy responses, as well as the impact of the pandemic and associated restrictions on electoral behaviour. The concluding section summarises lessons learned and identifies a number of promising avenues for further research.

This analysis shows that in the realm of election organisation, policy responses to the COVID-19 pandemic varied extensively across 27 EU member states. Some countries postponed elections while others held them on schedule; some implemented extensive electoral reforms, introducing or expanding alternative voting modes, while in other countries, changes were limited to preventive health and social measures at polling stations. These differences in the national responses can be attributed to two main factors, including the timing of the elections relative to the onset of the pandemic as well as the extent to which SVAs were in place before the start of the health crisis. Our analysis highlights the importance of legal certainty and clarity in organising elections, as well as the difficulties and risks of changing electoral laws in haste. It shows that countries that had well-developed remote voting and early voting procedures in place were much better prepared for organising elections in the context of the pandemic than those that did not.

PANDEMIC MANAGEMENT IN THE CONTEXT OF ELECTIONS

The Challenge

Preventing the transmission of an infectious disease requires the minimisation of social contacts; yet, representative democracy depends on elections which rely on social contact throughout the electoral cycle, from campaigns to voting and vote counting (Landman & Di Gennaro Splendore, 2020). Not surprisingly, the pandemic has had a highly disruptive effect on elections (International IDEA, 2022). This has given rise to concerns about the resilience of democracies, including the threat of democratic backsliding and the rise of authoritarianism, especially in the context of a global decline of democracy, and in countries where democracy was eroding already before the pandemic (Rapeli & Saikkonen, 2020; Guasti, 2020; Repucci & Slipowitz, 2021).

From the perspective of disease transmission, elections are a type of public event characterised by the congregation of large numbers of people in a confined space. Going to the polling station to cast a vote has the potential to increase both infection rates and mortality from the coronavirus, especially among high-risk individuals including the elderly and those with pre-existing health conditions (Bertoli et al., 2020; Santana et al., 2020). Holding large-scale in-person elections has been shown to cause a viral spread of COVID-19 (Palguta et al., 2022) and significantly increases death counts (Bertoli et al., 2020). The risks are not limited to election day: participation in assemblies, rallies and other campaign events may equally contribute to the spread of the virus (Bach et al., 2021; Cipullo & Le Moglie, 2021). In addition to voters, political candidates, election administrators, poll workers, and observers are also at risk, notably because election organisation typically entails meetings attended by large numbers of people (e.g., poll worker training, vote counting, etc.). In sum, among public events, elections are uniquely risky in terms of the spread of the coronavirus, as they entail mobility and social contacts on a massive scale, as voting age citizens flock to polling stations on election day.

Despite the risks they entail, elections—in contrast to many other types of events—cannot be easily suspended, postponed or re-organised. Regular, periodic elections are a defining characteristic of democracy, enabling citizens to select leaders and to hold them accountable, serving as forums for the discussion of public issues, and reinforcing the stability and legitimacy of a political system and the political community. In democratic countries, elections are constitutionally mandated and extensively legally regulated. Furthermore, the conduct of elections is governed by a wide set of international standards and global norms. Electoral integrity depends on compliance with laws, norms and procedures associated with the appropriate conduct of elections. Thus, postponing or modifying elections has the potential to produce "legal quagmires" (Ellena, 2020) and undermine regime legitimacy and stability.

Amid the COVID-19 pandemic, the authorities in democratic countries faced two key choices concerning elections—whether to hold elections on schedule or to postpone them, and whether and how to modify the way elections are run. Both questions fall under the broader rubric of the practice of democracy during emergency situations (caused by natural or man-made hazards). There is a limited but growing literature focusing on the question of when and under what circumstances the postponement of elections can be regarded as justified. Distinguishing among various reasons and motivations for delaying elections (such as humanitarian reasons, political crisis, regime transition, death of a candidate, authoritarian power grab, and technical reasons), James and Alihodzic (2020, 345) highlight the postponement paradox which stems from the fact that postponing elections breaks institutional certainty, which, in turn, "may lead to partisan scrobbling which could trigger democratic breakdown and undermine trust in the system," especially in presidential systems and in countries with low levels of political trust.

All in all, there is no universally applicable formula for deciding whether elections should be held on schedule or postponed. Decision-makers need to assess the magnitude of risks, consider relevant constitutional, legal and institutional constraints and opportunities, and evaluate the effect of holding or delaying the contests on electoral integrity, including on the prospect of realising core democratic principles such as deliberation, participation, fair contestation, quality of electoral management and the institutionalisation of rules (James & Alihodzic, 2020, 345). Specifically, it is important to consider the implications for turnout as well as for the representation of different social groups, as well as the prospect that postponement—or holding elections in the context of an emergency—could hamper political competition, advantage political incumbents or enable an autocratic consolidation of power (Quarcoo, 2020).

Pandemic-related modifications of the way elections are run fall into two main categories. First, authorities and election administrators can introduce various health safeguarding measures without providing alternatives to the conventional voting mode: casting a paper ballot at the polling station in person. There is a wide variety of measures at multiple levels that can be implemented to make polling safer in the context of the coronavirus outbreak, such as sanitising polling stations, enforcing social distancing measures, mask-wearing and temperature screening, opening more polling stations, extending the voting period or opening hours to reduce crowding, training poll workers, expanding interinstitutional cooperation, including between election management bodies and national COVID-19 task forces (e.g., Birch et al., 2020; James, 2021).

The second category of modifications pertains to introducing or expanding special voting arrangements—i.e., arrangements that allow voters to exercise their right to vote by means other than casting a ballot in person at their respective polling station on election day. There is a lively debate in the literature about expanding SVAs in the context of the pandemic (Krimmer et al., 2021; Asplund et al., 2021). Most of this discussion focuses on five kinds of SVAs, including early voting, postal voting, proxy voting, remote internet voting and the mobile ballot box. These alternative voting modes have the potential to reduce the transmission of the virus because they reduce or eliminate social contacts, enable those infected with the coronavirus or required to self-isolate to exercise their right to vote, or help spread out the vote over an extended period, making polling stations less crowded and hence, safer.

While the introduction or extension of SVAs can appear as an appealing solution to the problem of managing elections during the pandemic, changing electoral legislation, procedures and practices can be a complicated, controversial and time-consuming process. SVAs pose new challenges in terms of electoral integrity: for instance, secrecy of the ballot could be compromised in the context of postal or remote internet voting (e.g., Vollan, 2006; Koitmäe et al., 2021). Any change in voting modes is susceptible to politicisation and can trigger partisan disputes with far-reaching consequences, as exemplified by the conflict surrounding the expansion of postal voting in the 2020 United States presidential election (Clinton et al., 2020).

The subsequent sections of this chapter analyse national-level policy responses to COVID-19 in the realm of election management in EU-27, focusing on choices regarding holding or postponing elections, as well as the introduction and expansion of SVAs. In order to understand the context for these choices, however, it is important to map the availability of SVAs before the onset of the pandemic.

Different Initial Conditions

There are vast differences among European countries in terms of how voting is organised. In some countries, the only way that citizens can exercise their right to vote is by going to the polling station on election day. In other countries, voters can mail in their ballots, vote by proxy, vote ahead of election day, order a mobile ballot box to their place of residence or cast a vote over the internet. Countries where SVAs were widely available already before the pandemic were better positioned to reduce health risks associated with voting during the pandemic. Table 4.1 summarises the availability of special voting arrangements in 27 EU member states before the onset of the health crisis.

Early voting was relatively uncommon in EU member states before the health crisis. Only six countries, most of them Nordic or Baltic (Denmark, Estonia, Finland, Latvia, Portugal, Sweden) offered the option of voting ahead of election day to all voters. Lithuania, Malta and Slovenia provided this option to some groups of voters (e.g., those out of the country on election day). The length of the early voting period varied from three days in Latvia and Slovenia to about a week in Estonia and Finland to several weeks in Denmark. In the majority of EU countries, voters could vote only on election day.

Provisions for postal voting varied extensively across the EU. In Germany and Luxembourg, any voter could apply for postal ballot documents without providing a reason. Postal voting is widespread in Germany: in the federal elections of 2017, 29% of votes cast were postal votes (Bermingham, 2020). Prior to the pandemic, 16 EU countries did not provide any form of postal voting, while 9 countries offered this option to selected groups of voters, typically those absent on election day as well as ill or disabled voters.

Before the pandemic, proxy voting—one voter casting a vote for another—was allowed in five countries: Belgium, France, the Netherlands, Poland and Sweden. Proxy voting is typically available only for specific groups of voters (e.g., elderly people, those who are ill or disabled, incarcerated or residing abroad). In most cases, voting by proxy must be requested ahead of election day.

Remote internet voting—a system where the voter casts an electronic ballot from any internet-enabled computer in the world—is rare. Estonia remains the only country in the world to provide all voters in all elections the option to cast an electronic ballot remotely. Introduced in 2005,

Table 4.1 Special voting arrangements in EU-27 before the onset of the COVID-19 pandemic

	Early voting	Postal voting	Proxy voting	Mobile ballot box	Remote internet voting
Austria	No	Yes	No	Yes	No
Belgium	No	No	Yes	No	No
Bulgaria	No	No	No	Yes	No
Croatia	No	No	No	Yes	No
Cyprus	No	No	No	No	No
Czechia	No	No	No	Yes	No
Denmark	yes	No	No	Yes	No
Estonia	yes	Yes	No	Yes	Yes
Finland	yes	Yes	No	Yes	No
France	No	No	Yes	No	Yes
Germany	No	Yes	No	No	No
Greece	No	No	No	No	No
Hungary	No	Yes	No	Yes	No
Ireland	No	Yes	No	Yes	No
Italy	No	Yes	No	Yes	No
Latvia	yes	No	No	Yes	No
Lithuania	yes	Yes	No	Yes	No
Luxemburg	No	Yes	No	No	No
Malta	yes	No	No	No	No
Netherlands	No	No	Yes	No	No
Poland	No	No	Yes	No	No
Portugal	yes	No	No	Yes	No
Romania	No	No	No	Yes	No
Slovakia	No	No	No	Yes	No
Slovenia	yes	Yes	No	Yes	No
Spain	No	Yes	No	No	No
Sweden	yes	No	Yes	Yes	No

Source: International IDEA. Note: Shaded cells indicate voting arrangements available to all voters

internet voting is widely trusted by the Estonian voters. Usage rates have grown rapidly: in the 2019 general and European elections, nearly a half of all votes cast were electronic votes (Ehin et al., 2022). France, the only other EU country to offer online voting, does so on a much more limited scale: internet voting is available only to voters living abroad, and only in parliamentary elections.

The mobile ballot box, brought by election administrators to the voter's home or to the institution in which they reside, is the most common

SVA, having been available in 17 EU countries before the pandemic. The option is reserved only for voters who are not capable of going to the polling station because of age, physical disability or health reasons. Similar to proxy voting, the mobile ballot box must be requested in advance.

In sum, this brief overview of SVAs in the EU before the pandemic reveals that the country with the most flexible voting arrangements was Estonia, which offered four out of five special voting arrangements, two of which (early voting and remote internet voting) were available to all voters. The availability of alternative arrangements has transformed the act of voting in Estonia. Already before the onset of the pandemic, in 2019, nearly half of all votes were electronic votes cast over the internet, and the share of early voters (which includes those who cast their vote online) exceeded 60% (Ehin et al., 2022). Other countries offering a variety of special voting arrangements included Finland, Sweden, Lithuania and Slovenia (three out of five SVAs available in each), although in most cases the alternative voting options were not available to all voters. On the other end of the scale, Cyprus and Greece were the only countries in the EU that did not provide any special voting arrangements before the pandemic.

POSTPONEMENT OF ELECTIONS

Of the 60 national, regional and local elections scheduled to be held in EU member states between February 2020 and February 2022, 45 were held on schedule and 15 (25%) were postponed. Table 4.2 provides a list of elections that were postponed in EU-27 within two years of the onset of the pandemic. Overall, the decision to hold or postpone elections is influenced by a number of considerations, including the severity of the public health situation and the magnitude of health risk; the phase of the crisis; constitutional and legal provisions; the type and importance of the elections concerned; the nature of the broader policy response to the pandemic, including whether a state of emergency had been declared or not; as well as considerations related to turnout, contestation, campaigning and the quality of electoral management. As evident from Table 4.2, many of the postponed elections in EU-27 during the first two years of the pandemic were subnational contests (with Polish presidential elections of 2020 as a notable exception). Out of 15 postponed elections, ten were local, four were regional and one was a national election. Also, the postponement of elections was more likely in the early phase of the pandemic (i.e., in 2020 as opposed to 2021 or 2022) when there was more

Table 4.2 Elections postponed due to the pandemic in EU-27 (February 2020 to February 2022)

Country	Election	Scheduled date	New date	Days delayed
Austria	Local election (Vorarlberg)	15 March 2020	28 June 2020	105
	Local election (Styria)	22 March 2020	28 June 2020	98
Czechia[a]	Senate by-election (Teplice, 1st round)	27–28 March 2020	5–6 June 2020	70
	Senate by-election (Teplice, 2nd round)	3–4 April 2020	13 June 2020	71
Finland[a]	Municipal election	18 April 2021	13 June 2021	56
France	Local election (2nd round)	22 March 2020	28 June 2020	98
	Regional and departmental elections	March 2021	20 June (1st round) and 27 June (2nd round) 2021	N/A
Germany	Local election (Hessen and Saxony)	April–October 2020	14 March 2021	N/A
Italy	Regional elections (Veneto, Campania, Tuscany, Liguria, Marche, Puglia, and Valle d'Aosta) and local elections (1149 *comuni* across Italy)	3 May 2020	20 and 21 September 2020	140
	Mayoral elections (Rome, Milan, Turin and Naples) and regional elections (Calabria)	15 April–15 June 2021	5 September and 15 October 2021	N/A
Latvia	Local election (snap elections, Riga)	25 April 2020	29 August 2020	126
Poland	Presidential election (1st round)	10 May 2020	28 June 2020	49
Romania[a]	Local election	June 2020	27 September 2020	N/A
Slovakia[a]	Local by-election	4 April 2020	3 October 2020	182
Spain[a]	Regional elections (Basque Country and Galicia)	5 April 2020	12 July 2020	98

Source: Egger et al., 2022; International IDEA, International Foundation for Electoral Systems, 2020. Notes: If elections were postponed several times, only the final date is indicated. N/A in the last column means that the exact number of days could not be determined

[a] State of emergency declared at some point during the first wave of the pandemic

uncertainty surrounding the coronavirus and when countries were struggling to devise a response to the new threat. The number of days by which an election was postponed varied from 49 days in the Polish presidential elections of 2020 to 182 in the Slovakian 2020 elections for local self-governing bodies. Five of the countries in which an election was postponed (Czechia, Finland, Romania, Slovakia, Spain) had declared a state of emergency at some point during the first phase of the pandemic (i.e., between February and June 2020).

The constitutional and legal constraints on the decision to hold or postpone elections deserve special emphasis. The Portuguese presidential election of 2021 serves as an example of constitutional provisions constraining the policy response. The election was held on schedule on 24 January 2021, despite that fact that a full lockdown had been enforced on 15 January due to a rapidly rising number of COVID-19 cases. Postponing the election was not an option because extending the president's mandate beyond five years would have required a constitutional amendment—which, in turn, would have been extraconstitutional if initiated during a state of emergency (Luís, 2021). Examples of legal complexities abound. In France, the decision to delay the second round of the 2020 local elections (see Table 4.2) led to the adoption of a new law to extend the term of 35,000 incumbent mayors (Quarcoo, 2020).

INTRODUCTION AND EXPANSION OF SPECIAL VOTING ARRANGEMENTS

Table 4.3 provides an overview of the introduction and expansion of SVAs in the context of national elections in EU-27 during the pandemic. According to our data, ten EU countries introduced or expanded alternative voting modes since February 2020. The introduction or increased availability of the mobile ballot box was the most popular pandemic-era modification of the voting process, implemented in seven countries. Three countries that did not have postal voting before 2020 introduced it in the context of the pandemic (the Netherlands, Poland, Romania) and one expanded this voting arrangement (Lithuania). Proxy voting was introduced in Croatia and expanded in Poland. Early voting was introduced in the Netherlands and expanded in Lithuania and Portugal. In Lithuania, early voting was facilitated by drive-by voting: voters who were

Table 4.3 Introduction and expansion of SVAs in EU-27 during the pandemic

Country	Election	SVAs introduced or expanded
Bulgaria	Parliamentary election (April 2021)	Mobile ballot box
	Parliamentary election (June 2021)	Mobile ballot box
Croatia	Parliamentary election (July 2020)	Proxy voting
		Mobile ballot box
Czechia	Parliamentary election (October 2021)	Mobile ballot box
Cyprus	Parliamentary election (May 2021)	Mobile ballot box
Lithuania	Parliamentary election (October 2020)	Early voting
		Postal voting
		Mobile ballot box
Netherlands	Parliamentary election (March 2021)	Early voting
		Postal voting
		Proxy voting
Poland	Presidential election (June, July 2020)	Postal voting
		Proxy voting
Portugal	Presidential election (January 2021)	Early voting
		Mobile ballot box
Romania	Parliamentary election (December 2020)	Postal voting
		Mobile ballot box

Source: Egger et al., 2022; International IDEA, International Foundation for Electoral Systems, 2020. Notes: National elections from February 2020 to February 2022. The list may be inexhaustive

self-isolating could submit completed ballot papers at a drive-in polling station prior to election day (Asplund et al., 2021). While we do not have systematic data on the use of SVAs in local and regional elections, there are reports on dramatic pandemic-induced changes to voting modes in some specific contexts. For instance, in the March 2020 local election in Bavaria (Germany), in-person voting was cancelled altogether—the only way to vote was to mail in ballots (Wagner, 2020).

While the pandemic triggered an expansion of alternative voting modes in Europe, the changes were, overall, fairly limited, and there is little evidence of policy convergence towards a single model or normative standard (see Fig. 4.1). As an example, only one of the 18 EU countries that did not practice early voting before February 2020 introduced it during the pandemic (the Netherlands)—even though early voting is regarded as the least controversial time-tested and low-tech SVA. In addition to early

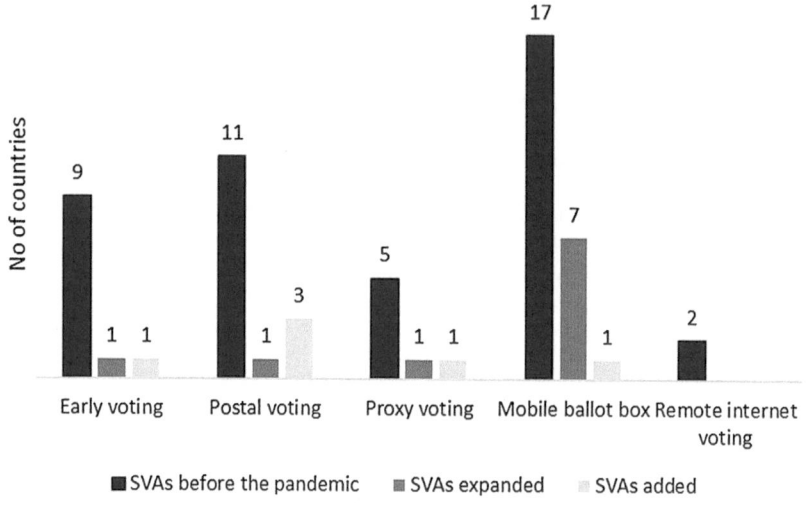

Fig. 4.1 The use of SVAs before and after the onset of the pandemic in EU-27. Source: International IDEA. Notes: Entries indicate the number of countries. Only national-level elections included. The list may be inexhaustive

voting, the Netherlands also introduced postal voting and expanded proxy voting to COVID-19 patients. New SVAs were also introduced in Poland (postal voting), Romania (postal voting for voters abroad), Croatia (proxy voting) and Cyprus (mobile ballot box). In other cases, existing SVAs were expanded, most commonly by making them available to COVID-19 patients. The reasons for a high degree of institutional continuity and inertia are understandable: elections are a highly regulated event, and changing electoral legislation and practices is a complicated and time-consuming process. Making last-minute changes to electoral legislation and operations has the potential to wreak organisational havoc and foment political controversy which could suppress turnout or undermine the legitimacy of elections. More sophisticated solutions, such as remote internet voting, cannot be introduced on short notice because they require technology development and testing, as well as extensive changes in electoral legislation and procedures (see Ehin et al., 2022).

IMPLEMENTATION AND IMPACT

During times of crisis, the way decisions are made and communicated is often as important as the content of these decisions. Norms governing the conduct of elections emphasise the importance of institutional stability and clarity of rules. The Council of Europe has recommended that electoral rules should not be changed less than one year before an election. It was not always possible to abide by this rule in the context of the pandemic, especially when elections fell into an early phase of the health crisis. In some countries, the question of how to proceed with elections in the context of COVID-19 caused extreme political controversy. This was the case in Poland, where the government's plan to hold the 10 May 2020, presidential election as scheduled, while changing electoral rules to allow the vote to take place exclusively by post, was criticised by a variety of actors. Less than two weeks before the scheduled election day, nine former Polish prime ministers and presidents urged voters to boycott the election, arguing that postal voting could be unconstitutional and does not guarantee voter confidentiality (Reuters, 2020). Following a series of conflicting messages from key political actors, including the ruling party, the parliament and the national electoral committee, the decision to postpone elections was finally taken only a few days before election day. The Polish case illustrates the dangers of proceeding with hurried, poorly conceived solutions of questionable legality that do not enjoy broad-based political support (Vashchanka, 2020).

The impact of the decision to hold or delay elections, and of various electoral amendments, can be assessed from different perspectives, including public health, legality and democratic norms and ideals. The literature about the effects of the pandemic on elections has been particularly concerned with voter turnout as "a crucial factor underpinning the legitimacy of an election, providing electoral mandates to leaders, and as a barometer for the health of democracy in general" (Landman & Di Gennaro Splendore, 2020, 1062). There are various ways in which turnout could be affected in the context of the pandemic. Voters could abstain because they fear the virus (Santana et al., 2020). Alternatively, voters could stay home because of restrictions, lockdowns, insufficient information about voting modalities in the context of COVID-19 or low trust resulting from poor election management in the context of the crisis. Studies examining the effect of the pandemic on turnout have shown that turnout decline was more pronounced in countries and areas with higher infection and mortality rates, as well as areas that are densely populated and have a high share of the elderly (Santana et al., 2020; Picchio & Santolini, 2022; Noury et al., 2021). Furthermore, the health crisis has accentuated patterns of social inequalities in political representation, as the disadvantaged have been more likely to abstain from voting (Haute et al., 2021).

Figure 4.2 graphs all nationwide elections held in EU-27 during the first two years of the pandemic on a plane defined by two axes, including turnout in presidential, parliamentary and nationwide regional/local elections held since the onset of COVID-19, as well as turnout in the most recent comparable election held before the pandemic. All cases located above the line of equality had higher turnout levels during the pandemic than before its outbreak, while the dots falling under the line represent elections where turnout declined compared to the most recent comparable pre-pandemic election. As evident from the graph, voter turnout declined in 18 cases and increased in 9 cases. For all the elections included in the analysis, the average drop in turnout during the health crisis was 2.7 percentage points. The largest decrease occurred in the French local elections of 2020, the Bulgarian presidential elections of 2021 and the Latvian local elections of 2021 where

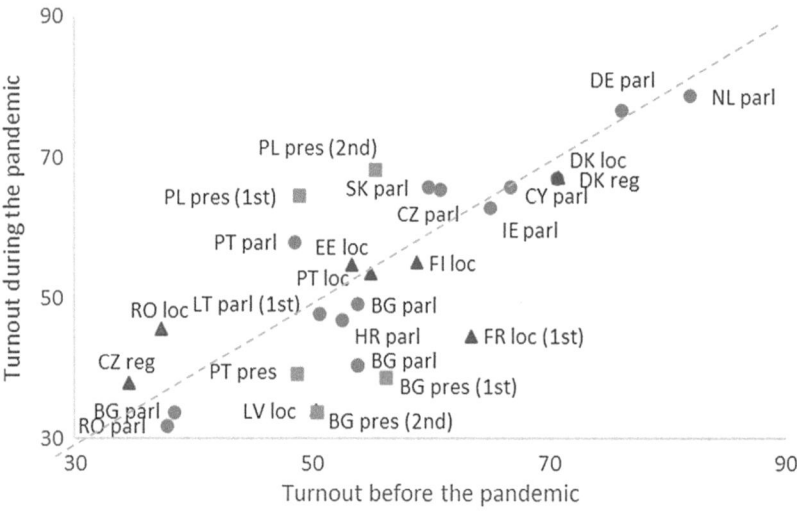

Fig. 4.2 Voter turnout in nationwide elections held during and before the pandemic. Source: International IDEA and Council of Europe. Notes: Only nationwide elections included. Circles represent parliamentary elections; squares stand for presidential and triangles for nationwide local or regional elections

turnout was more than 15 percentage points lower compared to previous similar elections. In contrast, turnout in the Polish presidential elections of 2020 increased by more than 10 percentage points compared to those held five years prior. There does not appear to be a clear correlation between turnout change and the phase of the pandemic, or between turnout change and whether an election was held as scheduled or postponed. However, in almost all elections that did not suffer from declining turnout levels amid the pandemic, SVAs had either been expanded or added.

Besides impacting turnout, the pandemic and the associated restrictions also have consequences for the electoral performance of parties and candidates. There is growing evidence that lockdowns and harsh restrictive measures increase, at least in the short run, electoral support for political incumbents (Bol et al., 2020; Leininger & Schaub, 2020; Giommoni & Loumeau, 2022). In healthy democracies, rallying around current leaders and institutions during a major crisis can be a positive, unifying phenomenon, especially if accompanied by improved trust in government and increased satisfaction with democracy (Bol et al., 2020). However, in polities characterised by democratic backsliding, lockdowns and restrictions appear to have contributed to the concentration of power in the hands of the dominant parties, while further depriving the opposition of a level playing field (Guasti, 2020).

CONCLUSION

Holding elections in the context of a pandemic entails a plethora of challenges revolving around the dilemma of "health versus democracy." These challenges were especially daunting for countries where elections were scheduled to take place shortly after the onset of the health crisis, in the first half of 2020. Proceeding with elections "as usual" could have contributed to the transmission of the virus and entailed the risk of low turnout and breaches of electoral integrity. Postponing elections or expanding special voting modes meant navigating constitutional and legal constraints, and conflicted with the norm of institutional stability and legal certainty. A key lesson from pandemic-induced electoral reforms is that major electoral changes cannot be prepared in haste, even in crisis context. Last-minute changes have the potential to wreak organisational and political havoc, and should be avoided. Legal clarity is of paramount importance, and any violations of the law have the potential to undermine the legitimacy of elections, and thus, of democratic governance.

Our analysis suggests that some EU countries were much better pre-pared to adapt elections to pandemic conditions than others. Countries with well-developed remote voting procedures, as well as those where the legal framework provides for early voting, could proceed with compara-tively minor revisions to existing laws and protocols. In settings where voters were already familiar with special voting arrangements, the legality and trustworthiness of such options were much less likely to be contested, and the risk that pandemic-related modifications undermine trust in elec-tions or reduce turnout, was significantly lower. In contrast, countries where the only way to exercise the right to vote was to cast a paper ballot at the polling station, the effect of the pandemic and associated restric-tions was much more disruptive and proposals to postpone elections or introduce new voting modes were more likely to raise constitutional, legal and political controversy.

This analysis points to a number of promising avenues for further research. Much is to be gained from a careful comparative analysis of elec-toral laws from the perspective of crisis readiness. More research is needed on the postponement of elections, including the question of when delays are justified. The pandemic has revealed the need for comparative research on special voting arrangements, including the development of technolo-gies, procedures and legal provisions for remote internet voting. While the prevalent attitude towards internet voting has been highly cautious, this may well change in the future as a result of technological advances, better protocols, and increased demand for location-independent voting ser-vices. There is also a need to better understand the politics of electoral reform, including the successes and failures of political consensus-build-ing. Future research should also cast additional light on the impact of the pandemic, as well as diverse policy responses to the pandemic, on voting behaviour, including turnout and electoral support for various political actors. Finally, given the central importance of elections in representative democracies, there is a need for evidence on how to maintain public trust in elections during crises, and how to ensure broad-based acceptance of the results of free and fair elections.

Acknowledgements The authors thank Sorcha Aniko Poirier Whitley for her valuable assistance with identifying sources and collecting data for this article.

Funding This research has been supported by funding from the European Commission under grant agreements 857622 and 822682.

REFERENCES

Asplund, E., Heuver, L., Ahmed, F., Stevense, B., Umar, S., James, T., Clark, A., & Wolf, P. (2021). *Elections and COVID-19: How special voting arrangements were expanded in 2020*. International Institute for Democracy and Electoral Assistance. https://www.idea.int/news-media/news/elections-and-COVID-19-how-special-voting-arrangements-were-expanded-2020

Bach, L., Guillouzouic, A., & Malgouyres, C. (2021). Does holding elections during a COVID-19 pandemic put the lives of politicians at risk? *Health Economics, 78*. https://doi.org/10.1016/j.jhealeco.2021.102462

Bermingham, P.-P. (2020). France split over 'American' mail-in ballots for 2021 regional elections. *Politico.* https://www.politico.eu/article/france-is-split-over-american-mail-in-ballots-2021-regional-election/

Bertoli, S., Guichard, L., & Marchetta, F. (2020). *Turnout in the municipal elections of March 2020 and excess mortality during the COVID-19 epidemic in France*. IZA discussion paper no. 13335. https://doi.org/10.2139/ssrn.3627035

Birch, S., Buril, F., Cheeseman, N., Clark, A., Darnolf, S., Dodsworth, S., Garber, L., et al. (2020). *How to hold elections safely and democratically during the COVID-19 pandemic*. The British Academy, COVID-19: Shape the Future. https://eprints.ncl.ac.uk/file_store/production/270392/517E0333-E4B4-4C11-B2B3-DE87CB4555D2.pdf

Bol, D., Giani, M., Blais, A., & Loewen, P. J. (2020). The effect of COVID-19 lockdowns on political support: Some good news for democracy? *European Journal of Political Research, 60*(2), 497–505. https://doi.org/10.1111/1475-6765.12401

Cipullo, D., & Le Moglie, M. (2021). To vote, or not to vote? Electoral campaigns and the spread of COVID-19. *European Journal of Political Economy, 72*(March) https://www.sciencedirect.com/science/article/pii/S0176268021001002

Clinton, J. D., Lapinski, J. S., Lentz, S., & Pettigrew, S. (2020). Trumped by Trump? Public support for vote by mail voting in response to the COVID-19 pandemic. *SSRN.* https://ssrn.com/abstract=3630334

Egger, C., de Saint Phalle, E., Magni-Berton, R., Aarts, K., & Roché, S. (2022). *EXCEPTIUS dataset v1.0*. DataverseNL. https://doi.org/10.34894/TTS0MF

Ehin, P., Solvak, M., Willemson, J., & Vinkel, P. (2022). Internet voting in Estonia 2005–2019: Evidence from eleven elections. *Government Information Quarterly, 39*(4). https://doi.org/10.1016/j.giq.2022.101718

Ellena, K. (2020). The legal quagmire of postponing or modifying elections. *International Foundation for Electoral Systems.* https://www.ifes.org/news/legal-quagmire-postponing-or-modifying-elections

Giommoni, T., & Loumeau, G. (2022). Lockdown and voting behaviour: A natural experiment on postponed elections during the COVID-19 pandemic. *Economic Policy*. https://doi.org/10.1093/epolic/eiac018

Guasti, P. (2020). The impact of the COVID-19 pandemic in Central and Eastern Europe. *Democratic Theory, 7*(2), 47–60. https://www.berghahnjournals.com/view/journals/democratic-theory/7/2/dt070207.xml

Haute, T., Kelbel, C., Briatte, F., & Sandri, G. (2021). Down with COVID: Patterns of electoral turnout in the 2020 French local elections. *Journal of Elections, Public Opinion and Parties, 31*(1), 69–81. https://doi.org/10.1080/17457289.2021.1924752

International Foundation for Electoral Systems. (2020). *Global impact of COVID-19 on elections*. https://www.ifes.org/publications/global-impact-COVID-19-elections

International IDEA. (2022). *Global overview of COVID-19: Impact on elections*. https://www.idea.int/news-media/multimedia-reports/global-overview-COVID-19-impact-elections

James, T. (2020). Should elections be postponed because of coronavirus? *The Conversation*. https://theconversation.com/should-elections-be-postponed-because-of-coronavirus-133819

James, T. S. (2021). New development: Running elections during a pandemic. *Public Money & Management, 24*(1), 65–68. https://doi.org/10.1080/09540962.2020.1783084

James, T. S., & Alihodzic, S. (2020). When is it democratic to postpone an election? Elections during natural disasters, COVID-19, and emergency situations. *Election Law Journal: Rules, Politics, and Policy, 19*(3), 344–362. https://doi.org/10.1089/elj.2020.0642

Koitmäe, A., Willemson, J., & Vinkel, P. (2021). Vote secrecy and voter feedback in remote voting – Can we have both? In *Electronic voting. E-vote-ID 2021* (pp. 155–169). Springer. https://doi.org/10.1007/978-3-030-86942-7_10

Krimmer, R., Duenas-Cid, D., & Krivonosova, I. (2021). Debate: Safeguarding democracy during pandemics. Social distancing, postal, or internet voting – The good, the bad or the ugly? *Public Money & Management, 41*(1), 8–10. https://doi.org/10.1080/09540962.2020.1766222

Landman, T., & Di Gennaro Splendore, L. (2020). Pandemic democracy: Elections and COVID-19. *Journal of Risk Research, 23*(7–8), 1060–1066. https://doi.org/10.1080/13669877.2020.1765003

Leininger, A., & Schaub, M. (2020). *Voting at the dawn of a global pandemic*. SocArXiv Papers. https://doi.org/10.31235/osf.io/a32r7

Luís, C. (2021). *Presidential elections in Portugal: From 'restrictions as usual' to unexpected lockdown*. International Institute for Democracy and Electoral Assistance, Case Study. https://www.idea.int/sites/default/files/2021-09-24-case-study-presidential-elections-in-portugal-from-restrictions-as-usual-to-unexpected-lockdown-en.pdf

Noury, A., François, A., Gergaud, O., & Garel, A. (2021). How does COVID-19 affect electoral participation? Evidence from the French municipal elections. *PLoS One, 16*(2). https://doi.org/10.1371/journal.pone.0247026

Palguta, J., Levínský, R., & Škoda, S. (2022). Do elections accelerate the COVID-19 pandemic? *Journal of Population Economics, 35*, 197–240. https://doi.org/10.1007/s00148-021-00870-1#Sec15

Picchio, M., & Santolini, R. (2022). The COVID-19 pandemic's effects on voter turnout. *European Journal of Political Economy, 73*. https://doi.org/10.1016/j.ejpoleco.2021.102161

Quarcoo, A. (2020). *Can elections be credible during a pandemic?* Carnegie Endowment for International Peace. https://carnegieendowment.org/2020/07/29/can-elections-be-credible-during-pandemic-pub-82380

Rapeli, L., & Saikkonen, I. (2020). How will the COVID-19 pandemic affect democracy? *Democratic Theory, 7*(2), 25–32. https://doi.org/10.3167/dt.2020.070204

Repucci, S., & Slipowitz, A. (2021). Democracy in a year of crisis. *Journal of Democracy, 32*(2), 45–60. https://doi.org/10.1353/jod.2021.0018

Reuters. (2020). Former Polish presidents, PMs call for presidential election boycott. *Reuters.* https://www.reuters.com/article/us-health-coronavirus-poland-boycott-idUSKBN22C30Q

Santana, A., Rama, J., & Casa Bértoa, F. (2020). *The coronavirus pandemic and voter turnout: Addressing the impact of COVID-19 on electoral participation.* https://osf.io/3d4ny/download

Vashchanka, V. (2020). *Political manoeuvres and legal conundrums amid the COVID-19 pandemic: The 2020 presidential election in Poland.* International Institute for Democracy and Electoral Assistance. https://www.idea.int/sites/default/files/political-manoeuvres-and-legal-conundrums-2020-presidential-election-poland.pdf

Vollan, K. (2006). Voting in uncontrolled environment and the secrecy of the vote. In *Electronic voting 2006 – 2nd international workshop* (pp. 155–169). Gesellschaft für Informatik e.V.

Wagner, R. (2020). *Responding to COVID-19 with 100 per cent postal voting: Local elections in Bavaria, Germany.* International Institute for Democracy and Electoral Assistance. https://www.idea.int/sites/default/files/responding-to-COVID-19-with-postal-voting-local-elections-in-bavaria.pdf

CHAPTER 5

Varieties of Democracies in the COVID-19 Pandemic

Daniel Kübler

INTRODUCTION

For democratic governments, the COVID-19 pandemic was a nightmare. Measures aiming to halt the spread of the coronavirus, such as contact restrictions, travel bans, lockdowns, curfews, certificate and vaccination requirements were not just inconveniences in everyday life. Some of these measures also led to restrictions on fundamental rights or affected the exercise of political rights that are central to democracy. Among the most obvious was the freedom of assembly, that was curtailed by the bans on gatherings adopted by many countries. Campaigning for elections was also made difficult by lockdowns and curfews, which is why some governments decided to postpone elections during the pandemic (see Ehin's and Talving's contribution). What is more, the dynamics of the pandemic, sometimes with its rapid waves of contagion, also forced governments to act rapidly. Decision-making processes were accelerated and shortened,

D. Kübler (✉)
Department of Political Science and Centre for Democracy Studies,
University of Zurich, Zürich, Switzerland
e-mail: Daniel.Kuebler@ipz.uzh.ch

C. Egger et al. (eds.), *Covid-19 Containment Policies in Europe*,
International Series on Public Policy,
https://doi.org/10.1007/978-3-031-52096-9_5

83

the separation of powers shifted in favour of the executive, sometimes resulting in a loss of democratic control and accountability. Many parliaments saw their role in law-making weakened as executives sought to forgo formal checks and balances in the interest of quick responses to the crisis.

Both these aspects—the free exercise of rights and the control of powers—are pillars of liberal democracy. The pandemic turned out to be a stress test for them. How did democracy, how did different democracies fare in the pandemic? What impact did the COVID-19 crisis have on the quality of democracy? Since the outbreak of the pandemic, these questions have been on the agenda of democracy researchers worldwide. The number of studies and publications on the relationships between the pandemic and democracy is therefore very large. The present chapter adds to this field of study by examining the relationship between the quality of democracy and legislative activities involved in policy responses to the pandemic, drawing, among others, on an analysis of the data compiled by the EXCEPTIUS consortium.

The chapter is structured as follows. The next section discusses the role of democracy in policy responses to the pandemic in an internationally comparative perspective. The following section then zooms in on a single case, namely Switzerland, to illustrate this role more particularly. Indeed, the Swiss case is interesting in that this is, until today, the only democracy in the world where a government's policy response to the pandemic was submitted to a popular vote.[1]

THE ROLE OF DEMOCRACY IN POLICY RESPONSES TO THE CORONA PANDEMIC

The Quality of Democracy

When the COVID-19 began to spread around the world in spring 2020, most governments took emergency measures to reduce the number of infections. The initial reaction revealed the first fundamental difference between regime types: dictatorships reacted more quickly and with more

---

[1] So far, Switzerland held three nationwide referendums on its COVID-19 legislation, the first one in June, the second one in November 2022, and the third one in June 2023. To the best of our knowledge, the only other state to have held a referendum about legislation related to COVID-19 was the principality of Liechtenstein in September 2022.

drastic measures than democracies (Cheibub et al., 2020). But significant differences were also observed between democratic countries, as the study by Engler et al. (2021) shows, investigating the variety of responses to COVID-19 in Europe during the first wave of the pandemic (see Fig. 5.1). On the one hand, using data from the Oxford COVID-19 Government Response Tracker (Hale et al., 2020), their analysis shows that restrictions on individual freedoms were far from the same everywhere. In Europe, during the first wave of the pandemic, there were countries such as Iceland, Sweden or Finland with relatively few binding restrictions, but also those with strict lockdowns, curfews, assembly bans and school closures, such as Serbia, Spain or Italy. On the other hand, there were also differences in the extent to which power was concentrated on the executive in the first wave of the epidemic, as can be shown on the basis of data from the V-Dem project on so-called pandemic backsliding (Edgell et al., 2021). While in

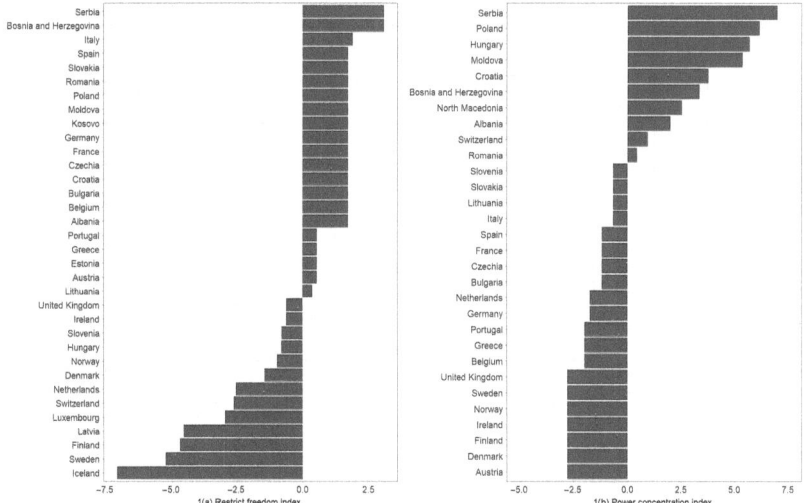

Fig. 5.1 Restrictions of freedom (left graph), and power concentration in favour of the executive (right graph) in European countries during the first wave of the pandemic. Source: Engler et al. (2021: 1088). Note: The index of restrictions on freedom is based on the Oxford COVID-19 Government Response Tracker (Hale et al., 2020), the index of concentration of power on the Pandemic Backsliding Index (Edgell et al., 2021). Both indices show the values for the respective country in comparison to the European average (value 0)

most countries of Northern and Western Europe—with the exception of Switzerland (see below)—parliaments continued to meet and were able to control the decisions of their governments, in many countries of Central and Eastern Europe there was an actual disempowerment of parliaments and even, as in Hungary, Serbia or Moldova, restrictions on the freedom of the press.

According to Engler et al. (2021), the differences between these countries are only partly attributable to the country-specific threat situation (such as the number of COVID deaths) or resources in the healthcare system (such as the number of intensive care beds). They find that the quality of a country's democracy—measured by indices taken from the Democracy Barometer project (Bühlmann et al., 2012)—strongly influences the policy responses to the pandemic. The stronger the democracy before the crisis, the fewer individual freedoms were restricted during the crisis, and the less the power of the executive was expanded (Fig. 5.2). Looking at different dimensions of democratic quality, the most important role is played by the protection of fundamental rights and the rule of law: where these are upheld and protected in normal times, governments were reluctant to impose drastic, open-ended and sweeping restrictions during the first wave of the pandemic.

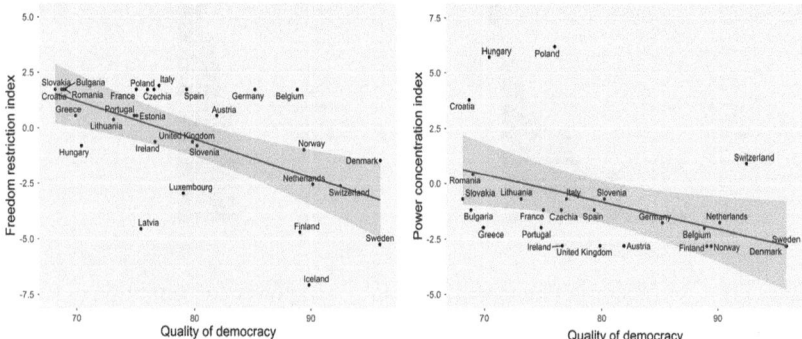

Fig. 5.2   Relationship between quality of democracy and restrictions of freedom (left graph), and power concentration on the executive (right graph) in European countries during the first wave of the Corona pandemic. Source: Engler et al. (2021: 1092)

COVID-19 Legislation and Varieties of Democracy

The EXCEPTIUS database[2] allows a closer look at the characteristics of the legislative activities behind these policy responses. More precisely, the version 2.0 of the dataset contains information on 1688 legal acts that were decided by national authorities in 24 European countries from mid-January 2020 to July 2021. As shown in Fig. 5.3, the number of legal acts varies strongly across countries, reflecting varying intensity of legislative action.

Most of those acts were decided by the government alone (89.2% overall), confirming previous evidence that the executive was clearly in the driver's seat in devising policies in the fight against COVID-19. Nevertheless, parliaments were involved as well, but this varies strongly across countries. On one end of the spectrum, we find countries such as Germany (40% of acts decided by parliament), Austria (32.8%), Norway (31.1%), the United Kingdom (14.3%), Switzerland (13.8%), France (13.5%), Portugal (11.6%) or Luxembourg (11.1%) where this share was

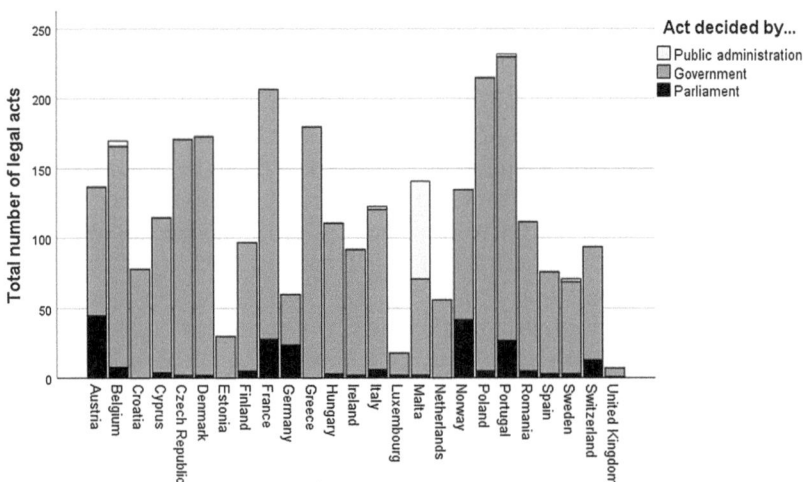

Fig. 5.3 Total number of legal acts per country, according to deciding authority. Source: EXCEPTIUS, own rendering

[2] In the following, we use the v.1.3 release of the EXCEPTIUS dataset from 2 September 2022.

above 10%. At the other end of the spectrum, there are a number of countries, where the entirety of the legal acts adopted in the period under study had been decided by the executive alone. This was the case in Croatia, Estonia, Greece as well as the Netherlands. In the remaining countries, the share of pandemic-related legal actors approved by parliament ranges between 1 and 5%. Finally, there are some countries in which a substantial share of legal acts was decided by the public administration (Malta: 49.6%; Sweden: 2.8%; Belgium: 2.4%; Italy: 1.6%, Portugal: 0.9%). In terms of the substantial content of these acts, no clear patterns emerge, meaning that measures of all sorts are found in an act independently from whether it was decided by the government alone or approved by parliament. There is one exception, however: decisions with measures related to the state of emergency as well as the design of crisis governance were more frequently decided by parliament (see Poyet's contribution to this volume).

These results echo the findings of Engler et al. (2021) suggesting that cross-national variation in the share of acts decided by parliament might be explained by the quality of democracy. Indeed, one can assume that the higher the quality of democracy in a country, the more likely that the parliament—as the primordial representative institution—is involved in legislative activities devising policy responses to COVID-19. To test this hypothesis, we explore the relationship between the share of legal acts with parliamentary involvement and a variety of established measures for the quality of democracy provided by the V-Dem project (Coppedge et al., 2022). The following figures (Figs. 5.4, 5.5 and 5.6) plot the share of legal acts decided by parliament in a country (on the y-axis) against this country's score on three macro-level indices describing features of democracy at an abstract level (x-axis) on a scale ranging from 0 to 1. First, the V-Dem index of electoral democracy (Fig. 5.4) measures the extent to which the principle of electoral democracy is realised in a country, i.e., making rulers responsive to citizens by electoral competition under circumstances of extensive suffrage. Second, the liberal democracy index (Fig. 5.5) measures the emphasis given to protecting individual and minority rights and against tyranny of the state and tyranny of majority. Third, the participatory democracy index (Fig. 5.6) gauges the extent of active participation of citizens in all processes, electoral and non-electoral.

All three graphs show a positive relationship between the share of legal acts with parliament involvement on the one hand, and the three macro-level indices of democratic quality on the other hand. It appears that this

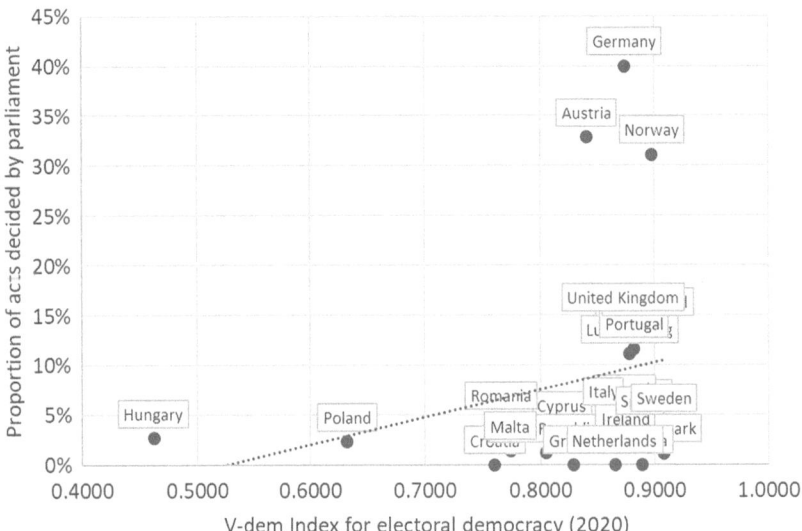

Fig. 5.4 Quality of electoral democracy and share of legal acts decided by parliament in EXCEPTIUS countries. Sources: V-Dem dataset 12 (Coppedge et al., 2022), EXCEPTIUS database, own rendering

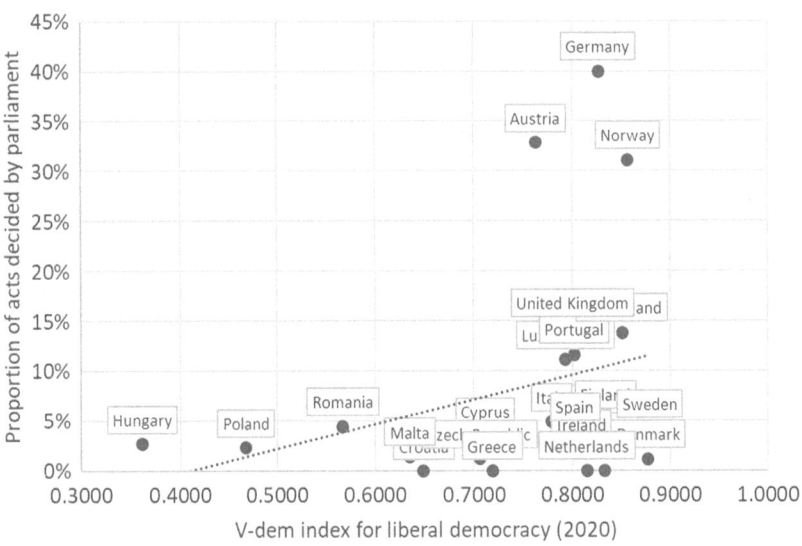

Fig. 5.5 Quality of liberal democracy and share of acts decided by parliaments in EXCEPTIUS countries. Sources: V-Dem dataset 12 (Coppedge et al., 2022), EXCEPTIUS database, own rendering

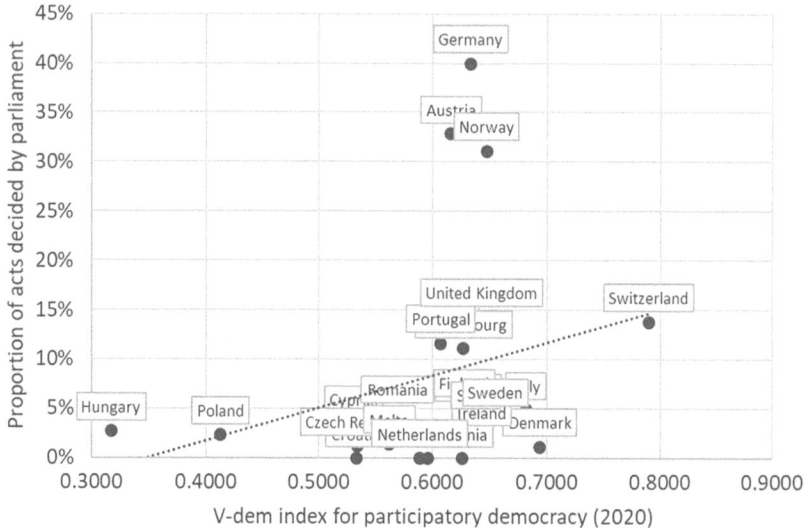

Fig. 5.6 Quality of participatory democracy and share of acts decided by parliament in EXCEPTIUS countries. Sources: V-Dem dataset 12 (Coppedge et al., 2022), EXCEPTIUS database, own rendering

result is driven not only by Central European low-quality democracies such as Hungary, Poland, Romania with low shares of parliament acts, but also by high-quality democracies such as Norway, Germany, Austria with very high shares of parliamentary acts. The overall trend is clear: higher quality democracies have a larger share of acts decided by parliament instead of government or the administration. In this sense, data from the EXCEPTIUS database complements the insights by previous studies: general quality of democracy—however measured—also came to bear in the COVID-19 crisis. High quality democracies were also those with larger shares of COVID-19 legislation legitimised by parliament.

Democracy and the Effectiveness of Measures Against COVID-19

Good democracies, thus, live up to democratic principles even in times of crisis. These findings are fundamentally welcome from a normative democratic perspective. However, when it comes to the goal of effectively combating the pandemic, the question arises as to potentially detrimental effects of democratic quality. Democratic checks and balances, it could be argued, slow down decision-making procedures and thereby hamper a government's capacity to act and specially to act quickly—which is particularly important in an acute crisis.

The study by Edgell et al. (2021) addresses this question based on a global comparative analysis. They first examine the spread of measures adopted in the fight against COVID-19 that violate democratic standards. By this they mean measures that can be described as "illiberal" (discrimination, denial of inalienable rights, unnecessary violent enforcement of measures) or "autocratic" (indefinite state of emergency, disproportionate restriction of checks and balances, disinformation campaigns), or that prevent the free circulation of information (restriction of media freedom). Their analysis reveals that a great number of countries have indeed violated democratic standards in the fight against COVID-19—this happened in both autocracies and democracies, but to a lesser extent in the latter (Edgell et al., 2021: 5). In a second step, Edgell et al. discuss whether the end, i.e., the most effective possible fight against the pandemic, justifies the means, i.e., the violation of democratic standards. For this purpose, they analyse the correlation between the adoption of such measures and the population-weighted number of COVID-deaths in the period from March to December 2020. However, they find this correlation to be far from statistically significant, even after taking into account a large number of control variables. This result shows, Edgell et al. conclude, "that illiberal and autocratic practices do not play a significant role in reducing COVID-19 deaths, contrary to claims made by actors engaging in such practices" (Edgell et al., 2021: 8). In other words: violating democratic standards is not worth it in epidemiological terms.

It needs to be emphasised, though, that this finding does not mean that the restrictions on individual freedoms imposed were ineffective in the fight against the pandemic. From a democratic point of view, it merely suggests that these measures should be adopted within the existing democratic and constitutional framework. Indeed, effective measures—even if they are of drastic nature—can be taken without violating democratic standards.

Participatory Democracy in the COVID-19 Crisis: A Tale from Switzerland

Switzerland provides an interesting illustration in this context. At the apex of the first pandemic wave in spring 2020, the federal government largely ruled alone. Based on the emergency powers provided for in the Epidemics Act it was competent to decide restrictions on its own—such as the first nationwide lockdown from mid-March to early May 2020. However, it was above all the indefinite interruption of the current parliamentary session on 15 March 2020 that resulted in a comparatively strong concentration of power in the hands of the executive (see also Fig. 5.1) and constituted a violation of democratic standards. Until the resumption of parliamentary business on 4 May 2020, the parliament—constitutionally the supreme power of the nation—was standing by, while the executive ruled the country on the basis of emergency law. Fortunately, Switzerland was spared a repetition of this democratically questionable self-suspension of parliament in the subsequent waves of the pandemic. In June 2020, the federal government ended the "extraordinary situation" and the measures to combat the COVID-19 pandemic were transferred to ordinary law. As part of the legislative process for the COVID-19 Act, these measures were submitted to public consultation as usual and were able to be discussed in detail by the parliament. And, as foreseen by the Swiss constitution, this legislation was also subject to referendum.

As a consequence, Switzerland was the only country in the world in which citizens were called to vote on COVID-19 legislation. This was the case even three times. After it had turned back to work after its self-inflicted pandemic recess, the Swiss parliament intensely debated the first COVID-19 Act and finally approved it in September 2020. The law provided the legal basis for government action to fight the spread of the virus through non-medical public health interventions (i.e., restrictions), but also to mitigate the impacts on the economy and society by providing financial support to businesses and/or individuals. Most importantly, it also defined the procedural rules specifying the implication of various institutions (notably the cantons, the Swiss federate states) prior to governmental decisions. Given the urgency of the situation, the act was declared an urgent federal decree which can enter into force immediately, with the possibility of holding an optional referendum being postponed by one year. Critics of the new law started to collect signatures in order to submit the law to a popular vote. A total of 50,000 signatures would have been necessary for an optional referendum—almost twice as much were collected. The law was put to vote on 13 June 2021, and accepted by a majority of 60.2% of voters.

But even before the June 2021 vote had taken place, the rapidly changing dynamics of the pandemic as well as its impact on society and economy made revisions to the law necessary. In December 2020, parliament debated a first revision, consisting in the specification and expansion of financial compensations provided not only to businesses, but also to sports clubs and cultural institutions. This first revision was largely uncontested. A second revision occurred in March 2021. It not only concerned further specifications regarding financial compensations, but also introduced new regulations regarding quarantine and vaccination, as well as the so-called COVID-certificate (informing on individual vaccination and/or test status), based on and compatible with EU regulations. Opponents to this second revision notably criticised the new quarantine regulations and the COVID-certificate. Again, declared an urgent federal decree by parliament, the revision entered into force immediately, with the possibility to hold a referendum postponed by 12 months. As with the original law, however, opponents successfully collected signatures (roughly 75,000 this time). The popular vote on the revised COVID-19 law was held on 28 November 2021. Turnout was exceptionally high for Swiss standards (65.7%), and the revision was accepted by a majority of 62.01% of the voters.

Approved in two popular votes during the pandemic, Swiss COVID-19 legislation can thus be considered to enjoy a rather high democratic legitimacy. Substantially, it allows for far-reaching measures to effectively combat the pandemic, as is shown by the second nationwide lockdown (from mid-December 2020 to mid-February 2021) which was decided according to the rules specified in the COVID-19 law. Apart from the parliamentary recess in the first lockdown, Swiss democracy has thus basically functioned as foreseen by the constitution during the pandemic. The role of the participatory instruments of referendum democracy, which are known to be strongly developed in Switzerland, is particularly noteworthy. As in numerous other countries, there were persistent demonstrations in Switzerland against the Corona measures of the authorities and numerous movements were founded to organise the protest. The first two successful referendums against the COVID-19 law of 2020 and its second revision of 2021 were mainly a result of the mobilisation by these groups. But in spite of this opposition and mobilisation against governmental measures, voters' support to the federal legislation even increased from the first (60.2% of yes votes) to the second referendum (62.01%). And this increase in governmental support occurred despite an exceptionally intense and emotional public debate and a voting campaign clearly dominated by the opponents of the law prior to the second referendum (Heidelberger & Bühlmann, 2021). After the second approval of government and parliament's COVID-19 policy by a majority of the citizens in the second referendum, protests against the measures to combat the pandemic decreased significantly and some of the protest movements disintegrated. The direct-democratic institutions were thus able to demonstrate one of their most important functions in the Swiss political system also during the COVID crisis: the integration of the opposition. Indeed, a classic argument of Swiss political science is that direct democratic institutions in this country contribute to the de-radicalisation of protest movements (Kriesi & Wisler, 1996). The possibility to collect signatures and conduct referendum campaigns to oppose a governmental decision makes opposition actors refrain from throwing stones or storming parliament to express their claims. By channelling protest institutionally, Swiss direct democracy contributes to stabilising the political system.

However, opposition against the Swiss COVID-19 law had not disappeared entirely after the pandemic. Although the government considered the pandemic as requiring no more specific attention in April 2022, parliament again debated the COVID-19 law in December 2022, and decided to extend its validity, in order to be prepared for an eventual pandemic surge. This most recent change of the law was, again, opposable by referendum. In a last effort, the already weakened opposing groups managed to collect the required number of signatures and Switzerland had its third popular vote on the COVID-19 law on 18 June 2023. Again, the law was approved by a majority of the voters (61.9%).

Conclusion

The COVID-19 pandemic forced governments worldwide to take restrictive measures to contain the spread of the virus. Democracies were faced with the additional dilemma of having to weigh different fundamental rights: the protection of life and health on the one hand, and the protection of individual freedoms on the other. Quick action was also required—which put democratic procedures under (time) pressure. Different democracies reacted very differently to the acute crisis situation. In the first wave of the pandemic, strong democracies had difficulties taking drastic measures, while weaker democracies tended to react with above-average severity. Whether a high quality of democracy thus hindered the fight against the COVID-19 pandemic is, however, not yet clear. This question can probably only be answered in retrospect—when the pandemic is over. Nevertheless, based on the available evidence, it can already be stated that the violation of democratic standards is not a prerequisite for effectively combating the pandemic. A democratic approach is therefore not inferior to an autocratic approach.

As the Swiss example after the first pandemic wave shows, effective measures can also be taken within the existing democratic-legal framework. Of course, this framework is put under tension by the crisis situation. Switzerland is the only democratic country in the world where the electorate was able to vote on the COVID-19 legislation. It did so even three times. The clear results of the three votes on the matter impressively showed the broad support of citizens for the previous Corona measures—despite the drastic restrictions on individual freedoms that they entailed.

So far, democracy has passed the COVID-19 stress test. Democracies have demonstrated that they can act appropriately in a crisis. This is an important insight in view of the currently increasingly intense system competition between autocracies and democracies. And it also puts into perspective the increasingly louder calls for an autocratic approach in other crises—such as climate change (Mittiga, 2021). The experience of the COVID crisis suggests that such calls are unwarranted.

Acknowledgements The author would like to thank the organisers and participants of the conference "Politics and COVID-19 in a comparative perspective" held at the *Maison des sciences de l'homme* in Grenoble in September 2022 for helpful comments on an earlier draft of this chapter.

References

Bühlmann, M., Merkel, W., Müller, L., & Wessels, B. (2012). The Democracy Barometer: A new instrument to measure the quality of democracy and its potential for comparative research. *European Political Science, 11,* 519–536.

Cheibub, J. A., Hong, J. Y., & Przeworski, A. (2020). *Rights and deaths: Government reactions to the pandemic.* SSRN 3645410.

Coppedge, M., et al. (2022). *V-dem dataset v12.* Edited by Varieties of Democracy Project.

Edgell, A. B., Lachapelle, J., Lührmann, A., & Maerz, S. F. (2021). Pandemic backsliding: Violations of democratic standards during COVID-19. *Social Science & Medicine, 285*, 114244.

Engler, S., Brunner, P., Loviat, R., Abou-Chadi, T., Leemann, L., Glaser, A., & Kübler, D. (2021). Democracy in times of the pandemic: Explaining the variation of COVID-19 policies across European democracies. *West European Politics, 44*(5–6), 1077–1102.

Hale, T., Webster, S., Petherick, A., Phillips, T., & Kira, B. (2020). *Oxford COVID-19 government response tracker (OxCGRT)*. Last updated 8:30.

Heidelberger, A., & Bühlmann, M. (2021). APS- Zeitungs- und Inserateanalyse zu den Abstimmungen vom 28. November 2021. Zwischenstand vom 18.11.2021. In *Année Politique Suisse*. Institut für Politikwissenschaft.

Kriesi, H., & Wisler, D. (1996). Social movements and direct democracy in Switzerland. *European Journal of Political Research, 30*(July), 19–40.

Mittiga, R. (2021). Political legitimacy, authoritarianism, and climate change. *American Political Science Review*, 1–14.

CHAPTER 6

Territorial Countervailing Powers Under the Pandemic

Raul Magni-Berton

INTRODUCTION

It has become commonplace to say that among the vices and virtues of federalism, the ability to respond to emergencies falls under the first category. A look at emergency laws is enough to show that they tend to centralise power. In principle, federalism or decentralisation are expected to suffer from severe coordination problems, such as disorganised initiatives, conflicting messages and the need to constantly adjust policies. The COVID-19 crisis saw this idea largely spread among commentators. For example, Huberfeld et al. (2020) suggest that federalism complicated the U.S. response to the pandemic and attempts to provide insights to mitigate the harmful side effects of federalism.

However, when this assumption is put to empirical test in a comparative way, it is no longer so obvious. During the 2007 financial crisis, many studies analysed whether centralised states were more able to react quickly

R. Magni-Berton (✉)
European School of Political and Social Sciences,
ESPOL-LAB Université Catholique de Lille, Lille, France
e-mail: raul.magniberton@univ-catholille.fr

© The Author(s) 2024   97
C. Egger et al. (eds.), *Covid-19 Containment Policies in Europe*,
International Series on Public Policy,
https://doi.org/10.1007/978-3-031-52096-9_6

to the crisis than federal and decentralised states. Braun and Trein (2014) report no significant difference while Del Pino and Pavolini (2015) explain that regionalised states (Spain and Italy) stopped their decentralisation process during the crisis, without much positive impact on the management of the crisis.

Similar studies were conducted during the COVID-19 crisis. Hegele and Schnabel (2021) compare European federal states—such as Austria, Germany and Switzerland—and do not find same responses. While Austria and Switzerland had a centralised approach, Germany opted for a coordinated decentralised decision making. Nevertheless, Germany was one of the most effective countries in containing the pandemic (Greer et al., 2023). Similarly, Aubrecht et al. (2020) find that in developed countries, centralised systems were no more effective than decentralised ones. Also, Kuhn and Morlino (2022) show that the German decentralised management was more effective than the Italian centralised one. These articles argue that while decentralised systems reduce coordination, they improve the ability to reduce uncertainty because decentralised policies allow incumbents to gather information about which policies work better.

This chapter uses the EXCEPTIUS data to analyse the extent to which European countries change their territorial structure during the pandemic. The data show that there is no homogeneity in territorial responses, but most countries centralised decision making during the first wave and decentralised it during the second and third waves. Also, a simple comparison between territorial strategies and excess lethality during the crisis suggests that decentralisation is a better strategy, although after controlling for income levels, neither the territorial organisation nor the level of decentralisation of the responses seem to be relevant to explain cross-country differences in the level of lethality of the pandemic. As a result, the idea that extraordinary events cannot be managed with ordinary institutions does not seem to be confirmed.

THE TERRITORIAL ORGANISING OF POWERS IN EUROPE

Regarding the territorial structure of European states, there is no consensus on categorization. Formally, four federal states can be identified: Austria, Belgium, Germany and Switzerland. In practice, however, these states have very different systems. Switzerland is an example of competitive federalism, where subnational units (cantons) are constitutionally sovereign. In fact, while this sovereignty is mainly symbolic, the cantons are politically autonomous and their own revenues are substantial. Germany, an example of cooperative federalism, is also highly decentralised. The subnational entities (*Länder*) also have political autonomy and large revenues to exercise it. In contrast to these two countries, federalism in Belgium and Austria does not directly translate into strong subnational power. In Belgium, where federalism has been introduced since the 1970s, the different communities and provinces have a weak influence on the central power, although they benefit from a large autonomy. Also, according to the European Committee of the Regions, the relative share of total subnational spending compared to total government spending is much lower than in Germany (40% versus 75%). Austria is even less decentralised. Formally a federation, Austria has gradually got closer to a centralised country (Erk, 2004). According to the decentralisation index of the European Committee of the Regions, Austria ranks 18th in the European Union, while Germany ranks 1st and Belgium 7th. Despite these notable differences, we consider federal states to be an appropriate umbrella category for these countries because, constitutionally speaking, federal entities have more power over the system, and this could favour them in case of conflicts arising from crises.

As the other European countries are unitary, they are grouped here according to the share of consolidated local expenditure in total expenditure. The data is based on the Organisation of Economic Co-operation and Development and the European Committee of the Regions. Although these data are not identical, they are highly correlated ($r = 0.92$). The OECD data cover non-EU countries (including Switzerland, Norway and the United Kingdom), while their data are not available for some EU countries (Bulgaria, Croatia, Cyprus, Malta, Romania). Taken together, they cover all countries included in the EXCEPTIUS database.

These data allow identifying highly decentralised unitary states. Among them, in the Nordics (Denmark, Finland, Norway and Sweden), more than one-third of current expenditures are controlled by the subnational level. This is particularly true in Denmark, where about two-thirds of the expenditures are delegated to the subnational level. In addition, Spain and Italy are often considered as regionalised states, where the central state has devolved legislative powers to all or some of its regions. In Spain, the regions (*Comunidades Autónomas*) have great fiscal autonomy, and two of them can even raise taxes. In Italy, on the other hand, regionalisation is much less developed, an observation is confirmed by the level of fiscal expenditure, which is lower than in the countries of this group. However,

Italy has devolved health policy to the regions, which is particularly relevant for the pandemic. Given its traditional decentralisation, Italy is the last country in this category.

Lowly decentralised unitary states also form heterogeneous category. Some countries, such as the Czech Republic, the Netherlands and Poland, are almost as decentralised as Italy. Large states such as France or the United Kingdom are still much more centralised, as are some Balkan states (Croatia, Slovenia and Romania) and the Baltic states (Estonia, Latvia and Lithuania). Among them, Latvia certainly is the most decentralised state but is not covered by the version 2.0 of the EXCEPTIUS dataset.

Finally, many small states can be described as centralised. They have a negligible rate of local spending and sometimes no territorial organisation at all. This category includes Bulgaria, Cyprus, Greece, Hungary, Ireland, Luxembourg, Malta, Portugal and Slovakia. Figure 6.1 shows the types of regimes in the EXCEPTIUS database.

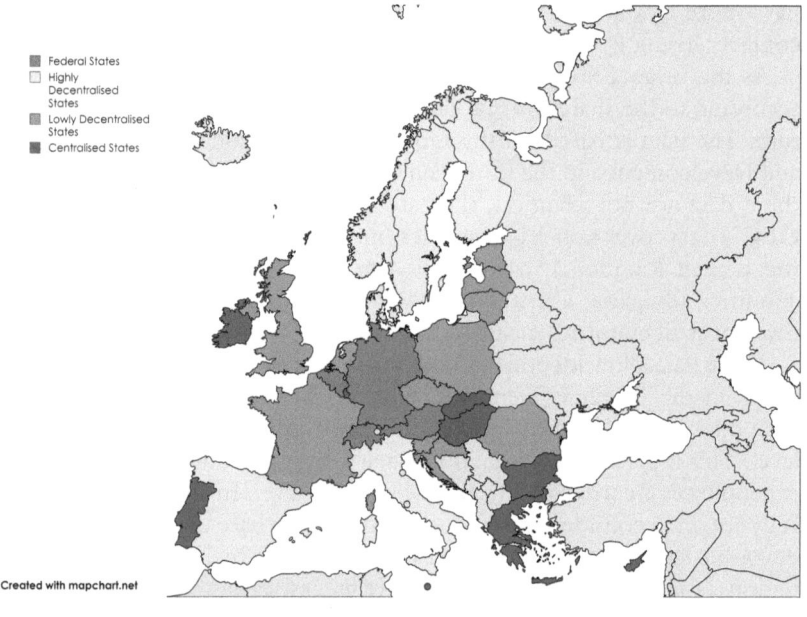

Fig. 6.1 Territorial systems in Europe. *Source*: OCDE and the European Committee of the Regions data, own rendering

SUBNATIONAL AND NATIONAL POLICIES UNDER THE COVID-19 CRISIS

There are two main ways of capturing the decentralisation of policymaking with the EXCEPTIUS database. The first way is to identify the authority that promulgates a legal text, be it national or local. This measure suffers from two potential problems. On the one hand, it only captures the number of political decisions, irrelative of their importance. In some cases, promulgating more legal texts does not mean being more powerful. However, it helps to identify the cases where local policies played a role in the pandemic. On the other hand, it is not so easy to collect decisions at the subnational level in every country. So, we cannot distinguish between the absence and the unavailability of policy data. While this problem is not secondary, the ability to find subnational is also a sign of their importance.

The second way is to identify transfers of authority during the pandemic. This approach focuses only on those regulatory texts that change the responsibility for future policy. Again, only their number is considered, not their importance. However, the most interesting aspect of this measure is to know in which cases states tend to centralise or decentralise during the first three waves of the pandemic. Moreover, this measure is consistently different from the previous one, so that when they provide consistent results, they reinforce each other.

Subnational versus National Authority

In the first wave, the percentage of decisions taken at the subnational level does not clearly depend on the degree of centralisation, but rather on the size of the country. While Germany is the country in which almost all policies were initiated at the subnational level (97%), the United Kingdom (79%), Italy (66%) and France (60%) follow. Surprisingly, only 13% of the Spanish policies were decided upon at the subnational level. In contrast to these large countries, the territorial system (federal versus unitary) is more relevant in smaller countries. In fact, in all these countries, almost all decisions were taken at national level, apart from the federal systems of Switzerland and Belgium, where subnational decisions accounted for 42% and 38%, respectively. The only exception was Austria, where crisis management policy was 100% centralised, despite its (weak) federal system. Faced with an emergency, large and federal countries, therefore, tend to make some decisions at subnational level, which is not the case for countries that do not have either of these characteristics.

During the second wave, the overall trend is similar, with some interesting changes. Compared to the first wave, some countries have become more centralised. This process of centralisation is particularly pronounced in Italy, where the central state controlled all decisions, and in the United Kingdom, where only 31% of decisions were made by the local power. Similarly, while Germany remained largely decentralised, only 64% of decisions in the second wave came from the *Länder*. In contrast, some countries significantly increased the percentage of decisions taken at the subnational level. In Spain, 95% of legislative texts were of subnational origin in the second wave. To a lesser extent, France increased its share of local decisions (72%). Finally, Finland, which, like most of the sparsely populated countries, reacted in an exclusively centralised way, greatly increased its local decision-making in the second wave (60%). The other countries did not significantly change their territorial decision-making, including Belgium (35%) and Switzerland (37%).

Finally, the third wave is the least reliable in terms of data collection, but also the least rich in terms of political decisions. The data show that compared to the previous waves, pandemic management has become more decentralised in Belgium, Finland, Portugal and the United Kingdom, and more centralised in Switzerland and Germany. Figure 6.2 summarizes the average level of decentralization of pandemic management and its evolution over the three first waves.

Overall, three lessons can be drawn. First, pandemic management was not always centralised. As expected, federal states are more likely to devolve authority to subnational entities. Large states also tend to manage the pandemic largely at subnational level. Second, centralisation does not increase over time. On the contrary, this is only the case for some federal states, notably Germany and, to a lesser extent, Switzerland. Unitary states tend to decentralise pandemic management over time, with the sole exception of Italy. This suggests that systems with different balances of territorial powers tend to converge during the pandemic, but the equilibrium is not centralisation. Third, the trajectories of centralisation/decentralisation are very different over time. The most extreme cases were Germany, where subnational decisions went from 97% in the first wave to 0% in the third wave, and Finland, which started with 0% and counted 93% of local decisions in the third wave. These different adjustments across waves mitigate

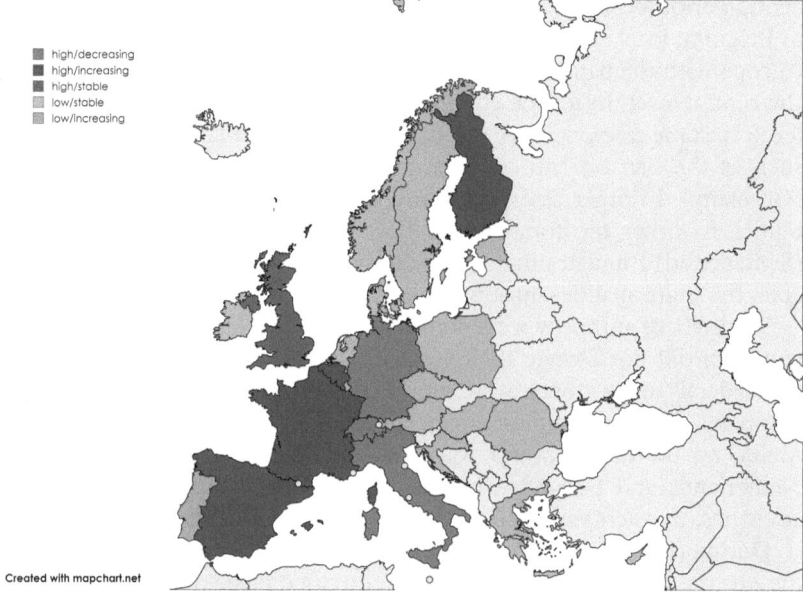

Fig. 6.2 Level of policies leaded by the subnational authority and evolution over the three first waves. *Source*: EXCEPTIUS database, own rendering

the tendency for convergence. Each country follows, at least in part, a specific evolution.

Transfers of Competencies

During a state of emergency, many countervailing institutions lose their powers to the benefit of the national government (see Poyet, Kuebler and Egger in this volume). Subnational powers are not exception: in the face of the pandemic, states are expected to centralise certain powers. This pattern does exist, but the opposite transfers have also been observed. On November 28, 2020, the Belgian government published a decree to "grant special powers to the Walloon government to deal with the second wave of the COVID-19 health crisis for matters governed by Article 138 of the Constitution". This is an example of the transfer of powers from the central to the subnational governments. In some cases, these transfers do not increase decentralisation, since they only contribute to revert the centralisation process initiated during the first wave. In other cases, such as Belgium, local governments benefit from unusual devolution of powers to cope with the pandemic. These transfers are not necessarily decided at the central level. In federal countries, many transfers come from the local level. In some cases, national standards are incorporated into local policies, such as the ban on anti-constitutional symbols on masks in Thuringia (Germany). In other cases, local governments have transferred responsibilities to other territorial levels. For example, the canton of Schwyz (Switzerland) stipulates that if the closure of a daycare centre is unavoidable, the municipalities must provide a suitable replacement.

Transfers of authority were common during the pandemic. Only a few countries did not change their territorial organisation of power. Among the federal states, there were no consistent transfers of authority in Germany. In four centralised states, Cyprus, Greece, Luxembourg and Malta, no transfer of power was observed. This is also the case in the Netherlands and Croatia, which are more decentralised. In the other countries, transfers varied considerably from one wave to the next.

During the first wave, almost all European countries centralised authority. Austria, Belgium and Switzerland centralised many regulations to fight the spread of the virus. This was also the case for all highly decentralised states (Nordic countries, Italy and Spain) and for almost all centralised states. The only country in which some decentralisation occurred in the first wave is the Czech Republic, where the government resolution of March 15 significantly centralised powers. At the end of March and beginning of April, three resolutions relaxed some of the decisions taken two weeks earlier. All in all, the expected centralisation of power in the face of the emergency is observed, especially in decentralised countries. The only exception is Germany, which has not changed its institutional structure.

During the second wave, this trend changed significantly. Centralisation only continued in the most decentralised systems. Such centralisation is reported in Belgium, Spain, Norway and Poland. In six countries, centralisation stopped in the second wave after increasing in the first wave. These countries are the Czech Republic, Estonia, France, Hungary, Italy and Romania. This does not mean that these countries were more decentralised than those in the first group. Rather, these countries adopted particularly stringent policies (see Chazel's contribution to this volume). It is plausible that the concentration of power in the first wave was already high and did not require adjustment in the second wave. More surprisingly, eight countries developed decentralised policies during the second wave after adopting centralised ones in the first wave. These are Austria, Denmark, Finland, Ireland, Portugal, Sweden, Switzerland and the United Kingdom.

The process of decentralisation observed during the second wave got even more accentuated during the third wave. At that time, no country centralised any powers. On the other hand, seven countries decentralised powers, be they originally exercised them at the subnational level or they did new devolutions. These countries are Belgium, Denmark, Poland, Portugal, Switzerland, Sweden and the United Kingdom. Most of them were already decentralised before the pandemic, and they decided to manage the pandemic in a more decentralised way. Figure 6.3 summarises the map of different pandemic response strategies.

Considering these data, I suggest that the COVID-19 pandemic has challenged the conventional wisdom that centralisation is an asset in the face of crises This is consistent with existing reports that suggest that

Fig. 6.3 Transfers of competencies between the central and the local level. *Source*: EXCEPTIUS database

decentralisation might be more effective (Kuhn & Morlino, 2022; Kuhlmann et al., 2021). As noted in the introduction, this is not really new, and the debate on the effectiveness of decentralised pandemic management policies is still open. What is new, however, is that this conventional wisdom has been challenged by policymakers themselves. While most of them opted for centralising powers at the beginning of the pandemic, they chose a more decentralised management afterwards. This may be due to the special case of Germany which served as a role model. While decentralised management has been discussed and criticised in the domestic arena (see Färber, 2021), the exceptionally low number of infections and deaths in this country may have presumably influenced management in other countries.

SOME EVIDENCE OF TERRITORIAL EFFECTIVENESS IN CRISIS MANAGEMENT

So far, I have analysed different territorial policies in various European countries with different territorial structures. Some of them centralised powers, others did not alter their territorial organisation and another group opted for a mixed strategy, increasing their centralisation in the first wave and then reducing it.

The most important takeaway would be to know which strategy is the most effective. Unfortunately, it is also the most difficult information to find. To rigorously assess the effects of territorial management, one would have to account for many confounding factors, such as the level of income of a country, its healthcare capacities, culture, trust and so on. These cannot be considered when the analyses are estimated at the national level, with only 25 countries. However, it is possible to provide some descriptive clues to initially assess territorial effectiveness for crisis management.

The first aspect to consider is how to measure an effective policy. Today, it is certainly simplistic to consider only the direct health consequences of COVID-19, since every policy also has economic, social and psychological consequences. However, the direct health consequences are a good starting point and give some indication of the best short-term health strategy. Health consequences have been measured in terms of either infections or (excess) deaths. In both cases, these measures are self-reported and can be influenced by COVID-19 testing strategies as well as by the way data is collected by each national authority. Deaths are certainly more reliable and more relevant than infections for measuring effectiveness because the main goal of any government is to avoid deaths, not to avoid infections. I, therefore, collected the number of deaths per 100,000 population, provided by Johns Hopkins University. Today, these data are considered to be close to reality because they roughly correspond to the excess mortality during the pandemic (Sanmarchi et al., 2021).

Table 6.1 shows the mean number of deaths according to the type of regime (federal, highly and lowly decentralised, centralised) and the type of territorial management chosen (no change, mixed, centralised). The last column displays the countries included in each category. In two of them, only one country appears, in others only two.

The first information provided by the table is that federal and highly decentralised countries experienced much lower mortality rates than centralised and lowly decentralised countries. However, this could be explained by other factors. The most important is income. GDP per capita is the main factor explaining why some countries have fewer deaths (Sorci et al., 2020). Wealth improves the technical capacity to contain the pandemic and provide the best quality health care. In each category, the richer the country, the fewer the deaths. Countries with low levels of decentralisation have the lowest average GDP per capita, while countries with high levels of decentralisation or federal systems have the highest GDP per

Table 6.1 Deaths according to the territorial organisation

Regime	Management	Mean deaths	Countries
Federal		213	
	No change	178	GER
	Mixed	162	SWI
	Centralised	257	AUT; BEL
Highly decentralised		172	
	Mixed	141	DEN; FIN; SWE
	Centralised	202	ITA, NOR, SPA
Lowly decentralised		278	
	No change	272	NED; CRO
	Mixed	308	CZE; FRA; UK
	Centralised	255	EST; POL
Centralised		252	
	No change	193	CYP; CRO; GRE; LUX; MAL
	Mixed	202	EIR; POR
	Centralised	419	HUN; ROM

Source: EXCEPTIUS and John Hopkins University data

capita. For example, in the first group, Denmark, Finland, Sweden and Norway have high GDP per capita and very low numbers of deaths. In contrast, Italy and Spain have more deaths than France and the Netherlands, which are less decentralised. Other factors, such as geography or trust, seem to play an important role. However, what the table can say at this stage is that decentralisation does not seem to create major problems in facing a pandemic.

The second relevant descriptive evidence concerns how the pandemic was managed. I used the data provided in this chapter to distinguish three strategies for each type of regime. The first decision is not to change the current territorial organisation. Germany is the only example for federal states, the Netherlands and Croatia for lowly decentralised states, and five centralised countries followed this strategy. No highly decentralised state fits in this group, confirming that decentralisation is fragile in unitary states. The second strategy is to mix centralisation in the first wave and decentralisation in the following. The relative majority of countries followed this strategy. Finally, the last strategy is to centralise power at the national level, which is the classical strategy. This does not mean that power is concentrated. In Belgium, for example, a large number of decisions are made at the subnational level during each wave. However, compared to the usual number of subnational decisions, Belgium centralised the governance of the pandemic except in the third wave, which is, in my view, too late to be considered as a truly mixed strategy. Only two countries further centralised their decisions while they were already largely centralised: Hungary and Romania.

In almost all political systems, mixed strategies are associated with lower mortality, except in countries with low decentralisation. Note, again, that the richer countries preferred a mixed strategy compared to the poorer ones. So, it is difficult to disentangle these different causes.

The most reliable result is probably the relative success of the COVID-19 containment that did not change the territorial organisation. Whether federal, centralised or decentralised, countries that managed the pandemic with the same territorial organisation as before the pandemic fared relatively better than others, even after controlling for economic and geographic factors. The only exception is Croatia, where the pandemic was particularly deadly despite the unchanged territorial organisation. Like the previous result, this one must be treated with caution. However, the descriptive data contradict two basic intuitions in crisis management. The first is that the normal organisation of power is inadequate to deal with exceptional events. The second is that territorial centralisation is more effective in times of crisis. These ancestral ideas do not appear at all in the actual policies of European countries.

CONCLUSION

It is not easy to compare territorial adaptation during the pandemic. Even in European countries, the territorial bases of political systems are very diverse, and their categorisation is not obvious. However, some preliminary insights can be drawn from the available data.

First of all, the expected centralisation of power during the pandemic did not occur. Most European countries centralised decision-making during the first wave, but in the following waves a more decentralised management was largely adopted. This can be seen either in the number of policy decisions made at the subnational level or in the laws that transferred powers from the subnational to the national level and vice versa. Also, in a not insignificant minority of countries, the territorial organisation has not changed.

As far as I know, this pandemic is the first crisis in which decentralisation has been documented as a common solution. Decentralised management could have the merit of better adapting policies to specific situations, which would also allow for faster responses. It also helps to compare different policies to assess the most effective one. These advantages may outweigh the disadvantages, which are mainly due to a lack of coordination. In developed countries, the quality of intergovernmental relations produces collaborative policies that enable effective pandemic response (Greer et al., 2023). All in all, decentralised crisis management is gradually being taken seriously and implemented, at least in developed countries (Vampa, 2021).

It is difficult to prove that such management is actually more effective than centralised management. The data show that, on average, decentralised countries experienced fewer deaths during the pandemic than centralised countries. The data also show that countries with decentralised pandemic management experienced fewer deaths. However, there is not a clear correlation between the level of decentralisation and GDP per capita. On average, richer countries are more decentralised and have managed the pandemic in a more decentralised way. Such a correlation is an example of how complicated it is to capture the net effect of decentralisation. Thus, this chapter cannot prove the superiority of decentralisation in crisis management, but it does provide initial evidence that centralisation is not always the best way to deal with an emergency.

REFERENCES

Aubrecht, P., Essink, J., Kovac, M., & Vandenberghe, A. S. (2020). *Centralized and decentralized responses to COVID-19 in federal systems: US and EU comparisons.* Available at SSRN 3584182.

Braun, D., & Trein, P. (2014). Federal dynamics in times of economic and financial crisis. *European Journal of Political Research, 53*(4), 803–821.

Del Pino, E., & Pavolini, E. (2015). Decentralisation at a time of harsh austerity: Multilevel governance and the welfare state in Spain and Italy facing the crisis. *European Journal of Social Security, 17*(2), 246–270.

Erk, J. (2004). Austria: A federation without federalism. *Publius: The Journal of Federalism, 34*(1), 1–20.

Färber, G. (2021). Germany's fight against COVID-19: The tension between central regulation and decentralised management. In *Comparative federalism and COVID-19* (pp. 51–69). Routledge.

Greer, S. L., Dubin, K. A., Falkenbach, M., Jarman, H., & Trump, B. D. (2023). Alignment and authority: Federalism, social policy, and COVID-19 response. *Health Policy, 127*, 12–18.

Hegele, Y., & Schnabel, J. (2021). Federalism and the management of the COVID-19 crisis: Centralisation, decentralisation and (non-)coordination. *West European Politics, 44*(5–6), 1052–1076.

Huberfeld, N., Gordon, S. H., & Jones, D. K. (2020). Federalism complicates the response to the COVID-19 health and economic crisis: What can be done? *Journal of Health Politics, Policy and Law, 45*(6), 951–965.

Kuhlmann, S., Bouckaert, G., Galli, D., Reiter, R., & Hecke, S. V. (2021). Opportunity management of the COVID-19 pandemic: Testing the crisis from a global perspective. *International Review of Administrative Sciences, 87*(3), 497–517.

Kuhn, K., & Morlino, I. (2022). Decentralisation in times of crisis: Asset or liability? The case of Germany and Italy during COVID-19. *Swiss Political Science Review, 28*(1), 105–115.

Sanmarchi, F., Golinelli, D., Lenzi, J., Esposito, F., Capodici, A., Reno, C., & Gibertoni, D. (2021). Exploring the gap between excess mortality and COVID-19 deaths in 67 countries. *JAMA Network Open, 4*(7), e2117359.

Sorci, G., Faivre, B., & Morand, S. (2020). Explaining among-country variation in COVID-19 case fatality rate. *Scientific Reports, 10*(1), 1–11.

Vampa, D. (2021). COVID-19 and territorial policy dynamics in Western Europe: Comparing France, Spain, Italy, Germany, and the United Kingdom. *Publius: The Journal of Federalism, 51*(4), 601–626.

PART II

Human Rights Protection in Crisis Times

CHAPTER 7

Limits and Lessons of COVID-19 Apps

Malcolm Campbell-Verduyn and Oskar J. Gstrein

INTRODUCTION

Technology giveth and technology taketh. This is one of the many paradoxes of human relationships with non-human objects. It applies both in good and in bad times, and the beginning of the COVID-19 pandemic was no exception to this techno-paradox. Modern technology—for example, in the form of airplanes facilitating international travel—enabled the SARS-CoV-2 virus to spread much more rapidly across the world when compared to plagues in past centuries.[1] Modern technologies also came to the foreground in responses to the COVID-19 pandemic, most notably in the rapid development of novel vaccines. Equally prominent in pandemic

---

[1] Such as the spread of the plague in seventeenth-century Florence, see, for instance, Henderson (2019).

M. Campbell-Verduyn (✉)
International Relations and International Organization, University of Groningen, Groningen, The Netherlands
e-mail: m.a.campbell-verduyn@rug.nl

O. J. Gstrein
Governance and Innovation, Campus Fryslan, University of Groningen, Groningen, The Netherlands

© The Author(s) 2024
C. Egger et al. (eds.), *Covid-19 Containment Policies in Europe*,
International Series on Public Policy,
https://doi.org/10.1007/978-3-031-52096-9_7

115

responses were the waves of information communication technologies (ICTs) rolled out to mitigate the spread of SARS-CoV-2 through personal location data collected via mobile phone networks, Bluetooth technologies, and satellite navigation systems (e.g., GPS, Galileo). The use of these technologies led to several waves of smartphone applications ('apps') bringing together these and various other existing technologies, such as mobile network signals.

Initially, smartphone apps were rolled out to locate, track and alert individuals to the spread of SARS-CoV-2. Subsequently, apps sought to facilitate the retrieval, processing and presentation to authorities of certificates of a negative test, recovery from COVID-19, or immunisation through vaccination. In between waves of infections, apps were used for quarantine enforcement. Particularly in East Asia—for example, China, Hong Kong, Taiwan and Singapore—global positioning systems signals were used in addition to networking data and Bluetooth to trace the precise geographical positions of individuals. In European countries, such as the Netherlands, intense discussions were held about whether such mobile network data could and should be used to track everyday movements of people using public transport or work from home. While not all implemented, use-cases for COVID-19 app data that were contemplated included: flow modelling to identify how many people passed through certain locations and how quickly, social graph making to identify which people meet frequently, self-evaluation of symptoms to assess if individuals have COVID-19 symptoms, as well as to distribute financial aid and serve as communication platforms (Blauth & Gstrein, 2021, 19).

This chapter investigates what happened, how and what is likely to emerge from what we argue was a timid turn to COVID apps in Europe during the initial outbreak of the pandemic. The first section highlights the wide variation in COVID-19 app (non-)deployment across Europe, providing a high-level overview of the various ways in which apps were deployed and used, as well as set aside. A second section lays out an initial explanation of the paths (not) taken in app deployment during the early days of the COVID-19 emergency. The third section links the European COVID-19 app experience to what we see as a troubling expansion of a permanent preparedness infrastructure both within the European Union (EU) and more widely beyond the continent.

Our central argument is that COVID-19 app reliance re-turned to and extended a long-standing emphasis on digital technologies as quick fixes to complex socio-ecological problems, a tendency known more widely as 'techno-solutionism'. Identified more widely in responses to crises ranging from climate change and migration to financial meltdowns (Morozov, 2013, 2020; Campbell-Verduyn & Lenglet, 2022; Coeckelbergh, 2021; Vavoula, 2021), techno-solutionism in the context of COVID-19 informed immediate attempts to address a complex and fast-evolving socio-political and ecological problem through a reduction to statistical calculations, electric signals, and automated algorithmic decision-making (see e.g. Helbing et al., 2021, 2; Campbell-Verduyn, 2021; Mann et al., 2022; Marelli et al., 2022; Martins et al., 2021; Milan, 2020).

Our analysis builds on and expands the growing literature on COVID-19 era techno-solutionism in two ways. First, we explain how smartphone apps showed anxious citizens and consumers the rapid responsiveness of both governments and companies to the emergency in ways that navigated tensions between privacy and surveillance. Second, we elaborate how app-based responses have solidified an increasingly permanently 'datafied' emergency management infrastructure that threatens the very solution governments and technology firms have sought between desires for privacy and surveillance. The technological fix COVID-19 apps provided in the short-term pandemic emergency period undermine the precarious balance of personal data protection and omnipresent monitoring in the medium and longer terms.[2] Enhancing opportunities for data collection and aggregation in exceptional times expands an emergency preparedness infrastructure with growing costs to citizens not only in exceptional times, but also for 'normal' times especially those living 'at the margins' (Milan et al., 2021b). It is this extension of the exceptional into less exceptional times that we find the most troubling lesson from an otherwise unexceptional fall back on smartphone apps in the initial outbreak of the COVID-19 pandemic. Our chapter concludes by pointing to further lessons to explore from this case of techno-solutionism in troubled times.

What Happened? Timid and Varied Turns to Tech

EXCEPTIUS data illustrates how, in the first 18 months of the COVID-19 pandemic, governments across Europe set out general parameters for digital contact tracing technology to be developed, tested and rolled-out in

---

[2] For related but later developed 'vaccine passports', see Gstrein et al. (2021).

smartphone apps on a rolling basis at subnational and national levels.[3] Varying forms of formal engagement with COVID-19 apps were undertaken in the emergency environment of the initial months of the pandemic, from January 2020 to April 2021, our main temporal focus in this section.

Table 7.1 shows that digital contact tracing apps were officially made voluntary in seven European jurisdictions: Austria, Estonia, Finland, Hungary, Portugal, Scotland and Switzerland. They were rendered obligatory at the national level in only two countries, Czech Republic and Denmark, as well as six regions of Italy. In five countries (Austria, Belgium, Denmark, France and Norway) as well as two regions of Spain (Madrid and Basque Country) "soft disadvantages" were rolled out for citizens to not use COVID-19 apps. Formal incentives to use the apps, meanwhile, were also legislated national in Denmark and Italy, as well as in seven Italian regions and the Swiss capital of Bern.

Most European countries relied on a privacy-preserving approach to decentralised data processing and storage of contact data, as well as Bluetooth-based tracing to inform measures that sought to prevent viral spread. This was the result of a gradually harmonised approach through networks associated with the European Union (EU). It took some time to develop this approach in response to national initiatives, and the development did not come without political tensions (European Commission, 2020). Still some countries maintained a more individualistic approach, emphasising their sovereignty and particular societal characteristics. For

Table 7.1 Official uses of COVID-19 apps in Europe

	National level	Sub-national level
Voluntary	6	1
Obligatory	2	6
Soft incentives	2	8
Soft disincentives	5	2

Source: EXCEPTIUS data

---

[3] And eventually for the regional level, with the European Commission not only initially tracking contact tracing apps, but promoting interoperability across national borders, see https://commission.europa.eu/strategy-and-policy/coronavirus-response/travel-during-coronavirus-pandemic/how-tracing-and-warning-apps-can-help-during-pandemic_en

instance, Norway made a notable and controversial exception by also using the global positioning system (GPS) for more accuracy to detect individuals. This led to an investigation of the Norwegian data protection supervisory authority, and the use of the app had to be changed several times before it was officially stopped (Lintvedt, 2021). Norway and later, in April 2021, Italy's cessation of its COVID-19 app were the earliest cases of apps being discontinued, many more of which occurred following the first 18 months of the pandemic. At the time of writing, COVID-19 tracing apps were discontinued in Austria, Belgium, Cyprus, Croatia, Czech Republic, Denmark, Finland, Hungary, Lithuania, Malta, the Netherlands, Poland, Portugal and Spain.[4]

Beyond the few cases in which COVID-19 app usage was mandated, the European turn to tech was a rather timid one. Governments largely took a 'hands-off' approach to the development and maintenance of apps after tendering their creation. Draconian impositions of the apps from governments were the exceptions rather than the rule in European countries. Though not wholly absent from the continent, only a few countries and regions imposed their use. A key question stemming from this brief overview of 'what happened' is how such timidity in the turn to smartphone apps as leading pandemic tech can be understood? The next section elaborates a necessarily preliminary answer to this 'how' question, building on the small but growing interdisciplinary literature on COVID-19 apps. We situate our understanding of these emergency responses in long-standing techno-solutionist impulses to locate quick technical fixes to complex, fast-evolving socio-political and ecological emergency.

How to Understand Timid Turns to Tech? Techno-Solutionism and Its Limits

Technical 'silver bullet' solutions formed prominent responses to a wide range of crises in the lead-up to the COVID-19 pandemic. To put this into context, regulatory technologies ('RegTechs') were developed in the wake of the global financial crisis of 2007–2008 and Eurozone crisis that followed in 2010 (Campbell-Verduyn & Lenglet, 2022). Sustainability technologies ('SusTechs') emerged as key solutions to a wide variety of environment and labour abuses around the world (Bernards et al., 2022;

---

[4] https://commission.europa.eu/strategy-and-policy/coronavirus-response/travel-during-coronavirus-pandemic/mobile-contact-tracing-apps-eu-member-states_en

Sætra, 2023), most notably to climate change. Notably, however, technological fixes in no way resolved any of what remain ongoing crises as the emissions of greenhouse gases has risen every year beyond 2020 and the banking system in particularly remains in a highly volatile state as illustrated by the panic of early 2023 in which Silicon Valley Bank was bailed out and Credit Suisse was taken-over by its rival UBS. Nevertheless, despite declines due to social media controversies, digital tech has consistently been amongst the most trusted economic sectors as measured by Edelman's Trust Barometer (Edelman, 2022).

This persistent yet exaggerated trust in technologies informed the timid turn to COVID-19 apps to track and trace the spread of a virus by governments across Europe. The response was both unexceptional and exceptional at the same time. On the one hand, smartphone apps seemingly provided quick solutions that concretely showed citizens that their governments were doing something. Apps formed responses that citizens could literally see on their smartphones, in a time where they were often staring at their screens. The largely voluntary and soft incentives to 'nudge' citizens towards adopting the apps also navigated privacy rights in exceptional times. Despite some exceptions, the main COVID-19 contact-tracing apps were developed within privacy and data protection principles set out in the expansive yet flexible General Data Protection Regulation (GDPR) (Bradford et al., 2020). This 'being seen to act' performative dynamic was accompanied by a flurry of various other forms of 'immunity theatre', 'border theatre', 'behavioural theatre' and 'equality theatre' in which actors on various different stages sought to demonstrate doing something, often without actually addressing the fundamental issues at stake (Milan et al., 2021a).

In contrast, the low number of total cases of officially sanctioned COVID-19 apps combined with the fairly rapid discontinuing of apps, including in the Italian and Norwegian cases during the first 18 months of the emergency, highlight the limits of this techno-solutionist dynamic. The rapid turn away from simple app-based contact tracing along with timidity in the turn to tech across Europe were also exceptional responses given the wider context of techno-solutionism. Nevertheless, as we will argue in the next section, the timid turn to tech have laid the socio-legal groundwork for a growing datafied permanent emergency response infrastructure. To provide the basis for our wider argument, however, this section first traces the congruence of app-based responses with four features of techno-solutionism (Morozov, 2013), drawing on studies of technological fixes in other areas of activity. The short-term technological fix that COVID-19 apps provide, however, overlooked deeper problems.

A Focus on Solutions Rather Than on Problems

By foregrounding solutions, techno-solutionism assumes and naturalises problems. As Morozov (2013, 6) writes, "solutionism presumes rather than investigates the problems that it is trying to solve". Key assumptions underlying the European COVID-19 smartphone app roll-out were that (a) the virus would spread without digital means to track and trace its spread and that these means were (b) superior to traditional human-centred forms of contact tracing that relied less on apps, while (c) creating new challenges stemming from the increasing collection of potentially highly sensitive personal data.

On their own, smartphone apps do little to investigate the first assumption above. They simply facilitate narrow functions, such as recording viral spread in near real-time. While there is some evidence that the use of digital contact-tracing apps could efficiently slow viral spread, it remains difficult to demonstrate this clearly with scientific evidence (see, e.g. Cencetti et al., 2021). Apps also do not investigate the second assumption above—namely, that older, less app-centric forms of contact tracing are somehow unfit or unsuitable to tracing the SARS-CoV-2 virus spread. This becomes particularly visible when considering how users should react to notifications of the app that they might have been in contact with an infected person, or which concrete actions should be taken. That a digital approach was prima facie better remained largely assumed rather than proven that digital solutions were superior to non-app-based contact tracing of the sort long used to tackle other pandemics. At the same time, the increased digital collection of data came with challenges for data management as evidenced in countries such as the Netherlands, where large-scale data leaks of potentially infected persons have re-occurred.[5]

---

[5] https://algorithmwatch.org/en/tracers/major-data-leak-affects-dutch-COVID-19-testing-system-and-app/

https://www.reuters.com/article/us-health-coronavirus-netherlands-datapridUSKBN29Y1H3

A Solidification of Existing at the Expense of New Paradigms

The timid turns to tech solutions across Europe in the context of emergency management post-2020 solidified existing pre-2020 fetishisation that there is 'an app for every problem' (Taylor, 2021). COVID-19 apps extended two existing processes in their "failure to 'problematize the norm' " (Williams, 2013: 556).

First were key roles of American Big Tech firms in app development and maintenance. These pre-COVID dominance of smartphone software by Apple and Google was simply extended into exceptional pandemic times. Nominally competitors, these two firms teamed up to harmonise requirements and capabilities of COVID-19-tracing apps whose successful implementation ultimately depended on both the support of their Android and iOS operating systems, as well as distribution through the app stores controlled by the companies. Fear of harming the reputation of their highly valuable app stores led to a privacy and security preserving approach by the two companies who did not want to be seen by their users as offering unsafe, badly functioning, and privacy-invasive apps. What this action effectively meant, however, was that two American companies were deciding on the framework for app-based COVID-19 tracing in Europe (Hoepman, 2022). Although some countries such as France tried to challenge this positioning based on concerns around sovereignty (Pohle & Theil, 2021), they ultimately remained unsuccessful (Hern, 2021).

In other periods of turbulence and exception, such as the 2008 global financial crisis, European governments had stepped far more forcefully into market processes, re-regulating and at times even nationalising key firms. In 2020–2021, by contract, such public steering of tech-based responses was timid. Standards for the design and maintenance of COVID-19 apps were largely left for Apple and Google. These two US-based Big Tech firms cooperated to make the market-based race to innovate a highly constrained and uneven affair, one metaphorically confined to an existing motor track, with little in the way of 'off-roading'. COVID-19 app development thereby remained on the existing, pre-pandemic route dominated by Apple and Google, who effectively set the key standards for digital contact-tracing apps, in part to protect the reputation of their mobile app stores. Reliance on Big Tech firms thereby stayed within—rather than outside—the pre-pandemic paradigm. Although there were attempts to undertake more 'out of the box' actions, for example, with more decentralised standards discussed further below, the main way in which existing trends were solidified in the European COVID-19 apps roll-out was the centralisation of activity around two American Big Tech firms.

Second, COVID-19 apps solidified digital dataveillance (Clarke, 1988; Csernatoni, 2020). Edward Snowden's disclosures in 2013 revealed just how pervasive surveillance had become via the spread into daily activities of digital technologies, including smartphone apps. The revelations instigated what amounted to a slow-burning 'tech-lash' prior to the pandemic outbreak in 2020 (Foroohar, 2019). Overlaps between American security agencies and Big Tech firms in the surveillance of even the most powerful European leaders, such as Angela Merkel, were especially decried. Yet, beyond vague invocations of 'digital sovereignty', little change had occurred to counter widespread dataveillance and the "disciplinary and control practice of monitoring, aggregating, and sorting data" (Raley, 2013, p. 124). The initial spread of SARS-CoV-2 had offered a historic opportunity to put grandiose declarations of digital and data sovereignty into action and push back on America's "surveillance valley" (Levine, 2018). As noted, however, the wholly unexceptional reliance on foreign tech firms—Apple and Google in particular—to standardise apps development solidified the privacy-surveillance imbalance in the generation, collection, and storage of COVID app data. Smaller start-up firms in consortia with academics in Europe did turn to 'distributed ledger technology' in attempts to better preserve privacy in generating different standards (Campbell-Verduyn, 2021; Zwitter & Gstrein, 2020). However, the leading pan-European consortium developing Decentralised Privacy Preserving Proximity Tracing (DP-3T) called Pan European Privacy-Preserving Proximity Tracing (PEPP-PT) collapsed as "the tech giants entered the scene" and it became clear that "[a]ll state-sponsored COVID-19 apps are de facto public–private partnerships between a government, Apple, and Google" (Veale, 2020). More privacy-preserving apps, based on blockchain or other more distributed technologies, were left to fringe projects as COVID-19 apps that came to be in-use across Europe were developed and maintained by Big Tech firms based in the United States. Even so-called 'privacy-preserving' apps, such as SafeTrace, ultimately relied on the proprietary IBM Cloud.[6]

---

[6] https://blog.enigma.co/safetrace-privacy-preserving-contact-tracing-for-COVID-19-c5ae8e1afa93

"Twisting" the Perception of Problems and Obscuring the Meaning of Success

In a focus on solutions, "the problem becomes something else entirely" (Morozov, 2013, 8). The need—especially of politicians—to be seen to be concretely 'doing something' while ensuring some degree of privacy in app-balance surveillance morphed measures of success for app-based techno-fixes. Success came to entail whether apps preserved (or at least did not significantly worsen) dataveillance by American Big Tech firms. While important, a focus on the means of maintaining some degrees of individual privacy in generating, storing as well as analysing data in accordance with the GDPR obscured the ends of app-based contact tracing responses: their very purpose as methods of limiting the actual spread of the SARS-CoV-2 virus. The 'innovation' here involved a rather dramatic silencing of potential alternatives (Sharon, 2021). In addition to the more decentralised technologies noted above, further notable alternatives included devoting resources to simpler non-, or less, app-based contact-tracing solutions. Giving limited resources of money and time that are very valuable in an emergency to tried and tested forms of contact tracing might have provided more accurate data to inform policy-makers in ways that would preserved health rather than just privacy. Evidence instead suggested a lack of actual success of digital apps in holding back the spread of the virus as possible contagion alerts became either too infrequent or too frequent and ignored. Nevertheless, success was re-framed away from preventing viral spread to preserving privacy to varying degrees. Yet, by their very stress on quantification (Milan, 2020), COVID-19 apps tended to obscure more than reveal to citizens how the spread of SARS-CoV-2 affected them, particularly in populations afflicted by the various digital divides with less or no access to smartphones (such as the elderly and the young) or mobile network coverage (rural populations). Success in limiting or taming spread even in better-resourced and well-connected adult populations twisted the ultimate policy goal of fighting the wider pandemic, which strikes at all populations, to one of preserving privacy in doing so. COVID-19 app techsolutionism, in short, betrayed a "predisposition to seek out quantitative and linear casual explanations that have little respect for the complexity of the actual human world" (Morozov, 2013, 260–261).

Universalising of Solutions as Always Applicable, Everywhere

Techno-solutions are "seen as eternal", as "timeless and never expire" (Morozov, 2013, 260). The universality of app-based contact tracing techno-solutions across both time and space is reflected in both the continent-wide turn to smartphone apps as well as the persistence of this turn in the face of critiques of their ineffectiveness in turning the tide against the spread of SARS-CoV-2. In almost every European country, a contact-tracing app was deployed, with the exceptions of Bulgaria, Luxembourg and Sweden, or contemplated even if not ultimately deployed as in Greece and Romania, leading to scarce resources being devoted to such responses in times of emergency.[7] While, as noted, mandates on the usage of these apps were confined to the few jurisdictions mentioned above—mandates that were ultimately struck down—the voluntary prompts towards app use persisted well beyond the first year of the pandemic. Though they were slowly set aside by the time of writing in February 2023, with just over a half dozen national apps remaining in use,[8] the initial turns across Europe towards app-based contact tracing has solidified a far wider infrastructural legacy. The limits of app uses were largely set aside in favour of a "hard-wiring" (de Goede, 2021) into both formal legislation and informal socio-technical relations between big tech firms, governments expert developers and citizen expectations that digital tools are to form important, if unexceptional, responses to exceptional times to come.

What Comes Next? A Datafied Europe and Beyond

On 22 December 2022, the European Commission published a report on the EU Digital COVID Certificate (EUDCC) to establish a standardised framework to coordinate the digital infrastructures of EU Member States pursuant to Article 16(3) of Regulation (EU) 2021/953. This report reflects the paths taken forward to catalyse regional sharing and action on health data in exceptional times. The initial drafts of the legal frameworks were criticised, however, for prioritising the continued free movement of capital, goods, and services in the bloc's single market while—once again—failing to address broader societal implications and concerns over

---

[7] https://commission.europa.eu/strategy-and-policy/coronavirus-response/travel-during-coronavirus-pandemic/mobile-contact-tracing-apps-eu-member-states_en
[8] ibid.

privacy safeguards (Gstrein, 2021, pp. 374–380). The legislation thus illustrated how economic circulation was set to remain enabled by digital circulations of data in order "to cancel out the effects of the illegitimate circulation of the virus through exactly replicating the pattern of the virus's mobility" (Langenohl & Westermeier, 2022).

Little indication was provided by the Commission of whether, or how, the emergency infrastructure under construction was ever to be rolled-back in less exceptional times. The report mentions that EUDCC ceased to apply at the end of June 2023.[9] Yet, in an attempt to avoid criticism for being unprepared to protect European unity in times of crisis (Alemanno, 2020), a proposal was presented for a Regulation to establish a 'Single Market Emergency Instrument' on 19 September 2022. This instrument was "put in place a flexible and transparent mechanism to respond quickly to emergencies and crises, threatening the functioning of the single market" (report, p. 24). At the time of writing, however, it remains unclear whether such a legal framework will be adopted by the legislators of the EU. Nevertheless, what is suggested by these activities is a state of "permanent emergency" (Wolff & Ladi, 2020) wherein technical fixes initiated at the beginning of the pandemic form the 'installed base' (Star, 1999) of a growing regional health and economic data infrastructure.

The remit and rapid growth, both real and potential, of this data infrastructure in governing everyday life is striking. According to the Commission (report, pp. 1–2), more than 2 billion certificates were issued in the 27 member states to certify either testing, recovery or vaccination between the inception of the EUDCC on 14 June 2021 and 31 October 2022. Member States mostly used the EUDCC to regulate access to events and cultural activities, as well as restaurants, bars, and nightclubs. Additionally, the EUDCC was used to monitor access to hospitals, nursing homes and other health-care facilities, wellness facilities, hotels, the workplace, universities and public transportation (report, p. 12).

Not only is it Europe that is affected by this infrastructural expansion. The Commission has high hopes that the EUDCC will become an international benchmark and amongst the leading manifestations of the 'Brussels effect' in which European regional standards come to form

---

[9] The EUDCC is still being celebrated as a success by the European Commission and the WHO is interested in developing it further, https://commission.europa.eu/strategy-and-policy/coronavirus-response/safe-covid-19-vaccines-europeans/eu-digital-covid-certificate_en.

global standards (Bradfords, 2020). Within Europe, but also beyond the continent, movements of people are increasingly reliant on the data infrastructures being carved out of standards initiated and catalysed during the first years of the COVID-19 pandemic, when the roll-out of contact-tracing apps formed what scholars increasingly understand as a major standard setting exercise (Kokoulina, 2023). The EC reported that 49 non-EU countries and territories facilitate international travel based on these standards, including large countries such as Indonesia, Malaysia and Vietnam (report, p. 19). The Commission is actively trying to build on the 'international success' (report, p. 25) of the EUDCC in coordinating with countries around the world to establish, reuse and extend the techno-fix established at the beginning of the COVID-19 pandemic to generate, collect and analyse information without (further) eroding privacy rights.

In sum, the European Commission and EU Member States are setting up 'Single Market Emergency' (report, pp. 24–25) infrastructures that are expanding across both space and time. This is a medium- to longer-term agenda emerging out of the short-term solutionist fix to the regional experience of emergency pandemic management in 2020–2021. Blanket permissions to extend techno-solutions are being developed to respond to whatever the next emergency might be. Digital technologies are being enshrined as means for extending the status quo of privacy surveillance (in)balance in (hopefully distant) future emergencies. They are also being hard-wired into daily activities during less exceptional times, with important implications that future research needs to remain attuned to.

Conclusion

This chapter has provided an overview of what happened with COVID-19 apps developed in Europe and how we can understand the timid turn to technology as an emergency solution with major implications for the future. We first argued that European COVID-19 apps formed largely unexceptional techno-solutionist responses to exceptional emergency times. Although the returns to tech were largely timid and varied greatly across the continent, they were largely successful in demonstrating to anxious citizens that governments and big firms were 'doing something' while maintaining a balance between individual autonomy and state monitoring of digital traces. Second and what we argued is more troubling, however, is that this timid return to tech has laid the basis for a permanent emergency infrastructure that threatens to skew the precarious balance between privacy and datafied surveillance in Europe and beyond in the medium- to long term.

In this concluding section, we identify two paths for research and policy practice going forward. First is a need for critical consideration of how (un)exceptional paths emerge out of and structure responses to exceptional events like pandemics. Scrutinising claims that 'everything will change' or that the spread of a novel virus bifurcated stimulates novel policy responses, scholarly analysis needs to navigate between policy-makers' tendency to simply fall back on existing modalities or to develop new, untried ones (Campbell-Verduyn et al., 2021). As the present case illustrated, long-standing techno-solutionist impulses led to familiar fixes in the short-term responses to a pandemic while encoding actions taken in exceptional times to less exceptional times. Change in other words emerged out of continuity, an outcome that complicates simple dichotomised diagnoses that 'everything stays' and 'everything changes'. There are also lessons here to be learned from similar tendencies in other exceptional periods, like financial crises, where the 'flight to safety' supports the international status of American dollar even when the likes of the 2007–2008 'global' financial crisis centred on the United States. This leads us to a related take-away.

Second, the European experience needs to be considered as not only informing but also informed by unexceptional techno-solutionism to exceptional times elsewhere in the world. As noted, the idiosyncrasies of the far grander European socio-political and technological infrastructure emerging out of timid tech-solutionism in 2020–2001 are being exported worldwide. Yet, given the transboundary nature of modern technological diffusion, there are both overlaps and important divergences between the European experiences with COVID-19 apps and those of democratic and non-democratic countries. For instance, East Asian democracies like South Korea were "presented as a model" for democracies elsewhere through their use of "fine-grained locational data and social network analysis to track and target individuals for containment and treatment" early in the COVID-19 pandemic (French & Monahan, 2020). Parallels can productively be drawn out in the differing forms of "algorithmic vulnerability" that app-based responses posed for citizens in Europe, China and beyond (Xue, 2021). COVID-19 tech, including apps, are part of a growing surveillance infrastructure that is spreading, if unevenly, across democratic and non-democratic alike that scholars need to understand by focusing on legislation, citizen trust and the work of police organisations (Pathi et al.,

2022). In short, there are many lessons to draw on and draw out of the limits of the COVID-19 app experience in Europe's initial approach to exceptional times.

REFERENCES

Alemanno, A. (2020). The European response to COVID-19: From regulatory emulation to regulatory coordination? *European Journal of Risk Regulation, 11*(2), 307–316.

Bernards, N., Campbell-Verduyn, M., & Rodima-Taylor, D. (2022). The veil of transparency: Blockchain and sustainability governance in global supply chains. *Environment and Planning C: Politics and Spaces.* firstView.

Blauth, T. F., & Gstrein, O. J. (2021). Data-driven measures to mitigate the impact of COVID-19 in South America: How do regional programmes compare to best practice? *International Data Privacy Law, 11*(1), 18–31.

Bradford, A. (2020). *The Brussels effect: How the European Union rules the world.* Oxford University Press.

Bradford, A., Aboy, M., & Liddell, K. (2020). COVID-19 contact tracing apps: A stress test for privacy, the GDPR, and data protection regimes. *Journal of Law and the Biosciences, 7*(1).

Campbell-Verduyn, M. (2021). The pandemic techno-solutionist dilemma. *Global Perspectives, 2*(1).

Campbell-Verduyn, M., & Lenglet, M. (2022). Imaginary failure: RegTech in finance. *New Political Economy,* 1–15.

Campbell-Verduyn, M., Linsi, L., Metinsoy, S., & van Roozendaal, G. (2021). COVID-19 and the global political economy: Same as it never was? *Global Perspectives, 2*(1), 27212.

Cencetti, et al. (2021). "Digital proximity tracing on empirical contact networks for pandemic control." Nature Communications 12: 1655. https://doi.org/10.1038/s41467-021-21809-w

Clarke, R. (1988). Information technology and dataveillance. *Communications of the ACM, 31*(5), 498–512.

Coeckelbergh, M. (2021). *Green leviathan or the poetics of political liberty: Navigating freedom in the age of climate change and artificial intelligence.* Routledge.

Csernatoni, R. (2020). New states of emergency: Normalizing techno-surveillance in the time of COVID-19. *Global Affairs, 6*(3), 301–310.

De Goede, M. (2021). Finance/Security Infrastructures. *Review of International Political Economy 28*(2), 351–68.

Edelman. (2022). *Trust barometer special report: Trust in technology.* https://www.edelman.com/sites/g/files/aatuss191/files/2022-10/2022%20

Trust%20Barometer%20Special%20Report_Trust%20in%20Technology%20 Final_10-19.pdf

European Commission. (2020). *Coronavirus: Commission adopts recommendation to support exit strategies through mobile data and apps*. Accessed February 8, 2023, from https://ec.europa.eu/commission/presscorner/detail/ en/IP_20_626

Foroohar, R. (2019). Don't be evil: How big tech betrayed its founding principles – And all of us. *Currency*.

French, M., & Monahan, R. (2020). Dis-ease surveillance: How might surveillance studies address COVID-19? *Surveillance and Society, 18*(1), 1–11.

Gstrein, O. J. (2021). The EU digital COVID certificate: A preliminary data protection impact assessment. *European Journal of Risk Regulation, 12*(2), 370–381.

Gstrein, O. J., Kochenov D., & Zwitter, A. (2021). *A terrible great idea? COVID-19 'vaccination passports' in the spotlight*.

Helbing, D., et al. (2021). Triage 4.0: On death algorithms and technological selection. Is today's data-driven medical system still compatible with the constitution? *Journal of European CME, 10*, 1. https://doi.org/10.1080/2161408 3.2021.1989243

Henderson, J. (2019). *Florence under siege: Surviving plague in an early modern city*. Yale University Press.

Hern, A. (2021, April 21). France urges Apple and Google to ease privacy rules on contact tracing. *The Guardian*.

Hoepman, J.-H. (2022). A critique of the google apple exposure notification (GAEN) framework. In *Privacy symposium 2022: Data protection law international convergence and compliance with innovative technologies (DPLICIT)* (pp. 41–58). Springer International Publishing.

Kokoulina, O. (2023). Tell me who your contacts are, or what can we learn from standard setting in the context of COVID-19 tracing apps. *Computer Law and Security Review, 48*, 105802.

Langenohl, A., & Westermeier, C. (2022). Safe assemblages: Thinking infrastructures beyond circulation in the times of SARS-CoV2. *Journal of International Relations and Development, 1*–21.

Levine, Y. (2018). Surveillance valley: The secret military history of the Internet. *PublicAffairs*.

Lintvedt, M. N. (2021). COVID-19 tracing apps as a legal problem: An investigation of the Norwegian 'Smittestopp' app. *Oslo Law Review*, (2), 69–87.

Mann, M., Mitchell, P., & Foth, M. (2022). Between surveillance and technological solutionism: A critique of privacy-preserving apps for COVID-19 contact-tracing. *New Media & Society*, 14614448221109800.

Marelli, L., Kieslich, K., & Geiger, S. (2022). COVID-19 and techno-solutionism: Responsibilization without contextualization? *Critical Public Health, 32*(1), 1–4.

Martins, B. O., Lavallée, C., & Silkoset, A. (2021). Drone use for COVID-19 related problems: Techno-solutionism and its societal implications. *Global Policy, 12*(5), 603–612.

Milan. (2020). Techno-solutionism and the standard human in the making of the COVID-19 pandemic. *Big Data & Society, 7*(2).

Milan, S., Veale, M., Taylor, L., & Gürses, S. (2021a). Promises made to be broken: Performance and performativity in digital vaccine and immunity certification. *European Journal of Risk Regulation, 12*(2), 382–392.

Milan, S., Treré, T., & Masiero, S. (2021b). COVID-19 from the margins: Pandemic invisibilities, policies and resistance in the datafied society. *Theory on Demand, 40.*

Morozov, E. (2013). To save everything, click here: The folly of technological solutionism. *Public Affairs.*

Morozov, E. (2020). Dat Big Tech een Pandemie Moet Oplossen is Het Politieke Probleem van Deze Tijd. *De Correspondent.* https://decorrespondent. nl/11146/dat-big-tech-een-pandemie-moet-oplossen-is-het-politieke-probleem-van-deze-tijd/16670845468068-b82823e2

Pathi, K., Wu, H., & Burke, G. (2022, December 21). *Police seize on COVID-19 tech to expand global surveillance.* Associated Press.

Pohle, J., & Thiel, T. (2021). Digital sovereignty. *Practicing Sovereignty: Digital Involvement in Times of Crises, 13*(7), 47–67.

Raley, R. (2013). Dataveillance and counterveillance. In L. Gitelman (Ed.), *Raw data is an oxymoron* (pp. 121–145). MIT Press.

Sætra, H. S. (2023). *Technology and sustainable development: The promise and pitfalls of techno-solutionism.* Routledge.

Sharon, T. (2021). Blind-sided by privacy? Digital contact tracing, the Apple/Google API and big tech's newfound role as global health policy makers. *Ethics and Information Technology, 23*(Suppl 1), 45–57.

Star, S. L. (1999). The ethnography of infrastructure. *The American Behavioral Scientist, 43*(3), 377–391.

Taylor. (2021). There is an App for that: Technological solutionism as COVID-19 policy in the Global North. In *The new common: How the COVID-19 pandemic is transforming society* (pp. 209–215).

Vavoula, N. (2021). Artificial intelligence (AI) at Schengen borders: Automated processing, algorithmic profiling and facial recognition in the era of techno-solutionism. *European Journal of Migration and Law, 23*(4), 457–484.

Veale, M. (2020). Sovereignty, privacy, and contact tracing protocols. In L. Taylor, G. Sharma, A. K. Martin, & S. M. Jameson (Eds.), *Data justice and COVID-19: Global perspectives* (pp. 34–39). Meatspace Press.

Williams, J. W. (2013). Regulatory technologies, risky subjects, and financial boundaries: Governing 'fraud' in the financial markets. *Accounting, Organizations and Society, 38*(6–7), 544–558.

Wolff, S., & Ladi, S. (2020). European Union responses to the COVID-19 pandemic: Adaptability in times of permanent emergency. *Journal of European Integration, 42*(8), 1025–1040.

Xue, J. (2021). Algorithmic vulnerability in deploying vaccination certificates in the European Union and China. *European Journal of Risk Regulation, 12*(2), 332–342.

Zwitter, A., & Gstrein, O. J. (2020). Big data, privacy and COVID-19 – Learning from humanitarian expertise in data protection. *Journal of International Humanitarian Action, 5*(1), 1–7.

CHAPTER 8

The Impact of Measures Against COVID-19 on Freedom of Press and Expression

Catarina Neves, Roberto Merrill, Ricardo Miguel, and Rui Forte

INTRODUCTION

COVID-19 has proved to be a fertile ground for the spread of disinformation. Clear examples are the references to COVID-19 as a bioweapon created by China or the United States, the denial that the virus even existed (idea of it being a hoax), or that it was a plot from the pharma industry to profit from a health crisis. The rise of so-called fake news as 'social media rumors, online political disinformation or state-sponsored internet propaganda' (International Press Institute, 2020) coincided with the emergence of social and political movements COVID-19 containment measures. These included protests against quarantine periods or the use of masks or social distancing (Wolff & Ladi, 2020, see De Saint Phalle contribution). These movements further fuelled the spread of misinformation, by consuming such content online, but also by helping to promote it and by sharing it within their networks. Government officials from

C. Neves (✉) • R. Merrill • R. Miguel • R. Forte
Centre for Ethics, Politics and Society, University of Minho, Braga, Portugal
e-mail: roberto.merrill@elach.uminho.pt

© The Author(s) 2024
C. Egger et al. (eds.), *Covid-19 Containment Policies in Europe*,
International Series on Public Policy,
https://doi.org/10.1007/978-3-031-52096-9_8

several countries, most notably the former president of the United States of America, Donald Trump, also contributed to downplay the role of the pandemic but also shared many of the claims based on misinformation, namely the statement that people could try injecting bleach or disinfectant to fight COVID-19.[1]

Such statements, whether made by government officials or people from civil society, became controversial because of their role in challenging public action that could prevent the spread of the disease. But they also resonated strongly with claims about the extent to which an existential threat and its consequences, namely the distrust and fear that fake news generates, can legitimise political action against freedom of expression or press freedom (Daemen, 2022; Goh et al., 2022; Palmer, 2022; Committee to Protect Journalists, n.d.), a topic to which we will now turn.

Restricting Freedom in the Name of Public Health

COVID-19 placed strains and difficult challenges on national governments and international cooperation. In a globalised world, where economies are highly interdependent and there is a significant daily movement of goods and people, the pandemic highlighted the need for international cooperation to close borders and pool resources to find the pandemic, but also for political and scientific cooperation to produce treatments and a vaccine that could halt the global spread of the disease. But these challenges were accompanied by equally difficult ones, namely the legitimacy of governments to implement measures to contain the development of COVID-19, but also the willingness of citizens to accept and comply with such measures. On the one hand, governments were faced with what became obvious trade-offs between public health and the spread of the disease, and avoiding economic disaster, but also mitigating social challenges, such as ensuring children's education, avoiding exacerbation of domestic abuse and violence, and monitoring mental health indicators, among others, until a vaccine was in circulation and a certain segment of the population (nationally and globally) was inoculated. On the other hand, governments were faced with the need to justify such measures—legally and politically to other representatives and heads of state, but also

---

[1] See, for example, the BBC coverage of the general outcry created after Donald Trump suggested injecting disinfectant to fight COVID-19: https://www.bbc.com/news/world-us-canada-52407177, accessed December 27, 2022.

to their constituents. What emerged from these challenges has been discussed as a set of issues that have implications for discussions of the legitimacy of governments, the effectiveness of international cooperation, or the interplay between scientific knowledge and political agency.

But it has also led to discussions about freedom, especially freedom of expression. It is noteworthy that the movements that have emerged against national and global measures to combat the pandemic—whether the vaccination mandates or the vaccine imposed by the state (see Egger and Magni-Berton in this volume)—have often used concerns and freedom-based arguments to make their case. A case in point is the Portuguese 'Médicos Pela Verdade', a movement founded by health professionals against the measures taken by the Portuguese government, namely the quarantines imposed or the mandates for the use of masks. Since its creation, the right to express their demands, on social media, but also to their patients or in the media, has been an integral part of their action. Their manifesto, in which they claim to be moving away from public eyes (but hint at going 'underground'), illustrates the extent to which freedom is part of the legitimisation of their actions:

> Our will and determination to spread awareness of science and present alternatives is alive and will continue, despite the centralised, reactionary and repressive environment in which we currently live, and which has been growing since we were founded as an organisation. We will suspend our online page and website until we are all free again.
>
> This is for everyone, even those who do not want to be free or do not know how to be free. Because freedom is like air, you breathe it; because thought is free, and the verb is the most important weapon you have.

Freedom of expression can be defined as a fundamental right "that contain both a personal and a social dimension. They are considered "indispensable conditions for the full development of the person", "essential for any society" (...) Without free speech, the enjoyment of other rights is not possible." (Howie, 2018, pp. 12–13).

It is, therefore, worth looking at how restrictions on freedom have been the result of measures taken to mitigate the effects of the COVID-19 pandemic, before analysing empirical data to identify any trend in this respect, and concluding whether the pandemic legitimises restrictions on freedom of expression and whether this can hinder liberal democracies.

We can distinguish between 'direct and indirect measures' that affect freedom of expression.

Direct action is linked to what became the COVID-19 messaging campaign. In many ways, governments were faced with the task of communicating the strict measures they wanted to enforce, which meant convincing citizens of the public health risks of not adopting such measures. It was an effort to balance scientific evidence and messaging with rhetoric and emotional communication. Particularly in the early stages of the pandemic, this meant communicating the threat of COVID-19 in a way that avoided panic, but also either instilling a degree of fear (or related emotions) or appealing to scientific rationality to contribute to public acceptance of the measures being taken. However, as noted above, the emergence of the pandemic was accompanied by a simultaneous rise in misinformation campaigns, fuelled by social groups, individuals on the Internet and even government officials. This led to calls for action to curb the spread of misinformation, with health authorities calling on governments and social media companies to limit the opportunities for fake news. These measures are what Engler and her co-authors call 'public sphere restrictions', namely by 'weakening the media' through the 'introduction of so-called fake news laws, restricting media coverage of COVID-19 and government responses to it' (Engler et al., 2021, pp. 1080–81). For example, a study by the International Press Institute (IPI) in 2020 found that at least 17 states have enacted regulations to control disinformation during the pandemic. While these may include small measures, such as imposing fines on those who spread unsourced and potentially dangerous information, in some countries, governments have passed significantly restrictive legislation on the issue.

It is worth noting that efforts to combat misinformation have also been taken up by other actors. The European Union, through the European External Action Service (EEAS), has begun to combat the various disinformation campaigns. Social media companies such as Facebook, Instagram and Twitter are also adjusting their apps and services, highlighting warnings and blocking the promotion of misinformation. In many ways, a triangulation between public, private and supranational spheres helped to mitigate the impact of misinformation during the COVID-19 waves (Amadio Viceré & Tercovich, 2020; Council of Europe, 2021).

In addition to what we have termed 'direct measures', that is, those relating to the management of pandemic-related information, there were also 'indirect measures' that affected freedom of expression. These included the quarantine measures, especially the social distancing measures, which made protests and rallies illegal for a period of time, or even the closure of parliaments, which reduced opportunities for scrutiny of government action (see Poyet in this volume). Such measures effectively shrank the public arena, limiting opportunities for debate and the expression of dissent. As such, they largely contributed to the fact that much of the debate took place either in private forums (i.e. among friends, families) or on social media.

In what follows, we will analyse the data from the EXCEPTIUS codebook, which examined the impact of COVID-19 measures on several variables, namely freedom of expression (through freedom of speech and the press), before discussing the significance of such results for the discussion of freedom and democracy.

Insights from EXCEPTIUS Data on Freedoms of Expression and Press

The present comparative analysis is based on EXCEPTIUS data focusing on the first, initial wave of the pandemic, from January to June 2020.[2] The analysis of this data is complemented with additional documentation on the 22 countries studied.

From the 22 European countries included, the results show that Romania is the only country that enforced restrictions on freedom of speech through 'Decret no. 195' in article 54, which states that public and private actors must contribute to the spread of information about protective measures against COVID-19, whilst containing the spread of fake news. To achieve that, public authorities should act and inform people with the correct information. Hosting service providers and content providers are obliged to immediately interrupt the transmission of information to their users if the respective content promotes false information regarding COVID-19 and jeopardizes the application of preventive measures. Moreover, the 'ORDONANȚĂ DE URGENȚĂ no. 28', foresees, in its article 326, sanctions for those who spread false information, resulting in 'imprisonment from 6 months to 2 years or with a fine'.

---

[2] Twenty-one countries include: Austria, Belgium, Croatia, Cyprus, Czechia, Denmark, France, Germany, Hungary, Ireland, Italy, Latvia, Lithuania, Netherlands, Norway, Poland, Portugal, Slovenia, Sweden, Switzerland, United Kingdom.

It is worth pointing out that while EXEPTIUS only mentions one country that has taken direct measures to restrict freedom of expression, media coverage and international reports have exposed policies that appear to have had the same effect in countries other than Romania.

In Hungary, since March 2020, the government of Prime Minister Viktor Orbán has adopted measures that criminalise the dissemination of fake news. In addition, journalists faced fines and even prison sentences of up to five years and were targeted for coercion through unlawful denial of access to medical personnel (testimonial sources) and places (in this case, hospitals). Poland supported pro-government media outlets and restricted organisations as foreign media, while at the same time the government and state-owned companies brought cases against journalists. In addition, the Bulgarian government implemented a measure stating that any 'fake news' related to the pandemic would be punishable by imprisonment (Council on Foreign Relations, 2021).

In addition, efforts to combat misinformation have also been taken up by other actors. Although this was not the focus of the EXCEPTIUS study, including them allows us to better understand the scope of restrictions that have been implemented so far. The European Union, through the European External Action Service (EEAS), took steps to fight the various disinformation campaigns. Social media companies such as Facebook, Instagram and Twitter have also adjusted their apps and services to highlight warnings and block the promotion of misinformation. In many ways, a triangulation between public, private and supranational spheres helped to mitigate the impact of misinformation during the COVID-19 waves (Amadio Viceré & Tercovich, 2020; Council of Europe, 2021).

In summary, there is evidence that at least Romania introduced restrictions on freedom of speech and the press in the early stages of the pandemic, while other countries, such as Poland and Hungary, also appear to have introduced such restrictions at the beginning of the pandemic, although these were not systematically recorded by the EXCEPTIUS study. This small set of countries justify the claim that governments were cautious in implementing restrictions on freedom of expression during the early stages of the pandemic. Before moving on to debating the legitimacy of such measures, it is worth considering possible explanations for these findings.

One possible reason for these results stem from the difficulties most European countries face when it comes to restricting freedom of the press and freedom of speech. Since the entry into force of the Lisbon Treaty, which incorporated the Charter of Fundamental Rights of the European Union into European law, every EU state is legally obliged to respect freedom of expression in its laws and in the exercise of its powers and competences. Alongside national constitutions, which in themselves often oblige states to protect freedom of expression, EU law has made such an obligation more binding, with sanctions for states that choose not to comply. Thus, constitutional and EU protection of freedom of expression may explain why, at the onset of the pandemic, 21 of the 22 countries analysed in the study appear not to have adopted any restrictions on freedom of expression, despite the surge in misinformation, notably through fake news.

However, there may be a second reason, which also helps to explain why such results appear to have been observed at the start of the pandemic. Degerman and his co-authors (2020) discuss the ways in which the COVID-19 pandemic illustrates the role of fear in the juggling of scientific and political authority and decision-making. Countering Nussbaum's assertion that fear is an irrational emotion, they instead discuss how, in the early stages of the pandemic, a lack of fear on the part of government officials was detrimental in enabling governments to make decisions that would benefit the public, but also promote greater citizen engagement with the measures that the government might need to implement. They highlight the cases of Sweden and the UK to argue that the lack of fear characterising such governments led to a delayed response to the virus in March 2020, but also 'contributed to public complacency about the outbreak'. Thus, they argue, "the apparent issue was not that government and citizens acted in fear instead of waiting for scientific evidence; it was that they did not experience sufficient fear in the face of the available evidence" (Degerman et al., 2020, p. 6).

We can certainly remember the early stages of COVID-19, when most governments urged against panic and often downplayed the potential consequences of the pandemic, not only as a response to public fear (expressed in forms of panic buying), but also as a way of trying to outweigh the potential economic consequences of closing borders, schools or businesses. To the extent that this is true, it may also help explain the results we discussed above: the health threat of COVID-19 took some time to sink in, and consequently the phenomenon of misinformation, or at least the potential threat of misinformation, and the political debate about whether or not fake news should be restricted in some way.

However, while the data do not suggest massive legal restrictions directly targeting freedom of speech or the press, it is possible to consider other measures that have had an indirect impact on these freedoms, namely legal restrictions implemented since the onset of the pandemic that have reduced the size of the public arena and thus reduced the opportunities for public speech and debate, which we have termed 'indirect measures'. The shrinking of the public arena helped to further increase the relevance of social media. Combined with the absence of restrictions on freedom of speech and the press, namely the lack of a regulatory framework to monitor and/or restrict information online, fake news has flourished. Moreover, early evidence suggests that while such direct measures were not implemented in the early stages of the pandemic, they became more prevalent as the second and third waves emerged, and misinformation was also more damaging to governments' efforts at social distancing and masking mandates, as well as the implementation of vaccination plans.

In conclusion, this movement cannot be understood as a constant or fixed event, because since July 2020, most European countries have applied restrictions on the press and speech or referred to fake news as 'infodemics' (Borrell, 2020). In what follows, we will discuss whether we can look at such direct and indirect measures and assess their legitimacy.

COVID-19 Misinformation, Freedom of Speech and Democracy

In what follows, we will discuss some normative arguments connecting the observed restrictions with conceptions about freedom of speech and press, and in general, liberal democracies. We start with the main insights provided by EXCEPTIUS but also consider, March 2020, countries implemented indirect measures, which impacted freedom of expression.

Let's start by considering the position that freedom of expression should be limited or restricted to limit misinformation about COVID-19.

Such a position can be justified on several grounds. One can argue that not restricting instances of misinformation can contribute to instances that can promote harm. If one considers the former president of the United States, Donald Trump, and his claims that people should try drinking bleach to cure COVID-19, it is not difficult to conclude that such a statement, on a major media outlet, by someone with political authority may lead many people to drink bleach and risk their lives. If this were the case, then even a negative conception of freedom, such as John Stuart Mill's one, based on non-interference and respect for basic liberties (2001), could accept such a restriction on such speech and conduct, and even could condemn the author of such discourse. Mill's harm principle would be applied, and restrictions on freedom of speech would be deemed legitimate in these cases.

However, it is unclear whether such an exception based on the harm principle would be sufficient to maintain restrictions on misinformation in the context of COVID-19. In fact, the harm principle might be too limited and leave a lot of misinformation unchecked. Take, for example, all the conspiracy theories surrounding COVID-19. There has been a lot of misinformation about the source and origin of the virus. Particularly in the early stages of the pandemic, many argued that COVID-19 was the 'Chinese' or 'Wuhan' virus, which helped to fuel prejudice and hatred against Asian minorities, especially in places where anti-Asian racism was already entrenched, such as the United States (Degerman et al., 2020, p. 11). Such narratives do not necessarily lead to physical harm in Mill's sense, but they can contribute to increased hatred and fear of certain minorities, even to violence, or certainly to social condemnation and exclusion of these groups.

Justifying restrictions on freedom of expression on the basis of a thin rule, such as the harm principle, can also leave unaddressed cases of misinformation that could have dire consequences for public health but were unlikely to be easy to appeal to the harm principle. Let's take the mask mandates that have been implemented around the world since March 2020. Misinformation has often targeted such mandates, arguing that masks are not effective, or that they may even endanger lung health and be more harmful than beneficial. Not using masks is mostly a collective issue: you may be sick, and by not covering your face you may be contributing to the spread of the virus. While it might protect us individually, it is above all a protection for other people. But not all COVID-19 was fatal or caused significant physical harm, and it would be difficult to say with certainty that those who chose not to wear masks on one occasion caused direct physical harm to others. Therefore, if one chooses to use the harm principle only to limit misinformation, such narratives are likely to be accepted.

We could take a different reading of freedom. John Stuart Mill's view of freedom of speech is based on a negative conception of freedom. Isaiah Berlin's essay on freedom famously distinguished between positive and negative freedom: the latter is "simply the area within which a man can act unobstructed by others" (Berlin, 1969, p. 16). Negative freedom is, therefore, about avoiding interference. Positive freedom, on the other hand, is about autonomy: "I wish to be a subject, not an object; to be moved by reasons, by conscious purposes, which are my own, not by causes which affect me, as it were, from outside" (Berlin, 2014 [original publication 1969], p. 231). Positive freedom is, therefore, associated with the notion of freedom to do what we want, what is best for us, that is, self-fulfilment and development, while negative freedom is about freedom from coercion and interference. Mill's conception is based on a notion of basic liberties, namely a defence of individual freedom of conscience, expression, association and occupation as something that should not be interfered with by anyone or by the state, except where the harm principle could be applied. But one could consider other readings of freedom that might help to justify restrictions on basic liberties, namely freedom of expression. Daemen discusses how a republican reading of freedom as non-domination might justify restrictions on freedom of expression that, while restricting people's choices, do not necessarily constitute unlawful interference. Indeed, she argues that if such measures are implemented against a background where "checks on state power are in place and policies are the product of democratic decision-making, they do not entail domination" (Daemen, 2022, p. 11), then one could legitimise such restrictions even through a negative conception of freedom. However, it would be necessary to ensure that restrictions on fake news or public speech that spreads misinformation are debated and subjected to a rigorous democratic decision-making process to be deemed acceptable. In many cases where such measures have been adopted, these processes have not taken place, either because parliaments have been constrained in their activities, or because governments have seen the pandemic as an opportunity to implement these restrictions—on speech or on the press—an issue we will discuss below. Regardless, it is worth pointing out that while it is not easy to justify restricting freedom of expression, there are ways of doing so, even when appealing to a negative conception of freedom.

This leads us to our second position, which argues that freedom of expression should not be limited or restricted, despite misinformation about COVID-19.

Let's start by considering one of the more familiar arguments used by those who want to restrict fake news. They have often said that the problem with such misinformation is that it is 'fake'. The reason why we should restrict it is because it spreads information that is factually untrue, thus justifying its restriction. However, such a justification seems less robust to us, and can become an argument in favour of no restrictions. Similar to John Stuart Mill, Thomas Scanlon in "Theory of Freedom of Expression" (2000) argues for a "Millian Principle" based firmly on respect for the autonomy of the individual. Thus, the fact that a particular message conveys falsehoods that lead others to believe them to be true could not be a justification for imposing legal restrictions on it. To do so would be to restrict our freedom to make judgements about what we believe and want to do.

For Mill, the same is true, because being able to form an independent judgement is essential for self-development and flourishing. Individuality can only be realised through the nurturing of the capacities for reasoning, and the pursuit of truth. If doing so demands open debate in order for truth to be able to make "such head as to withstand all subsequent attempts to suppress it" (Mill, 2001, p. 29), one needs open debate and deliberation, where all conceptions, including those considered false or absurd, in order for truth to shine light to their falsehood or illogical nature.

Another argument in favour of unrestricted freedom of expression is based on appeals to the health of democracy. It is not only the pursuit of truth that can benefit from unfettered debate, but also the health of democracy's deliberative process. Henry Voigt, for example, has argued that political demonstrations and impassioned debates on social media about government decisions may "actually enlarge the scope of politics in these societies. Such incidences make the breadth of democratic alternatives evident, however weird or non-scientific the protest opinions may occasionally be" (Voigt, 2021, p. 552; Daemen, 2022, p. 10).[3]

Finally, a further justification for non-intervention is the possibility of democratic backsliding or the promotion of an 'authoritarian slip'. Degerman et al. discuss Hannah Arendt's conception of fear as an "'anti-political' principle that destroys the possibility of political action by citizens, which for Arendt was synonymous with freedom" (2020, p. 13). Implementing restrictions on fundamental freedoms based on fear of an

---

[3] Daemen argues for a similar position, when discussing whether infringement of basic liberties should or not be justified: "Although the general public indeed sometimes wants issues to be securitised, the process is not without dangers: it may 'for example, result in the systematic infringement of key rights, the loss of civil liberties, an increase in police powers, "othering"/alienation of suspect individuals and groups, the use of lethal force, and because the issue itself is removed from democratic decision making, a reduction of the democratic process' (ibid.)." (2022, p. 10).

existential threat, such as COVID-19, could demobilise citizens and promote the opposite of political action, thus paving the way for totalitarian state solutions *(idem)*. Furthermore, the securitisation of COVID-19 and the tight grip of governments like China, whose authoritarian nature has allowed them to impose tight restrictions on social distancing or mask mandates, has also been portrayed as successful—considering the metric of security—and as such may further lead to the legitimisation of more stringent measures, many of them illiberal in nature, by presenting and arguing for a trade-off between freedom and security. As Voigt points out: "This could also lead us to believe that the narrative of the efficiency with which authoritarian societies have been able to control the pandemic—and not just the pandemic, but many other problems as well—is the right and desirable one" (2021, p. 552), thus contributing to the legitimisation of authoritarian government solutions.

And while such a threat exists in liberal democracies, it is even more prevalent in contexts where democracy is already 'backsliding'. While countries like Bangladesh, China and Egypt have laws that initially only targeted fake news, their broad application can be manipulated to develop a unique censorship of critical reporting. For illiberal leaders, such crises as health threats or 'infodemics' present a golden opportunity to apply laws without scrutiny and expand their arsenal of political tools. A Human Rights Watch study (2021) of 83 countries that used COVID-19 to justify controlling the exercise of freedom of expression showed that authorities used such manipulation to prosecute and criminalise journalists, activists and protesters. The authorities also closed media outlets and, as noted above, introduced vague laws to criminalise speech that could threaten public health. The survey highlighted, for example, the role of Bangladesh, China and Egypt, where people were imprisoned simply for criticising the government's actions against COVID-19. Furthermore, 24 countries "have enacted vague laws and measures that criminalize spreading alleged misinformation or other coverage of COVID-19", while 51 countries 'have used laws to prevent COVID-19, as well as counterterrorism "to arrest, detain, and prosecute critics of government response to the coronavirus" (Human Rights Watch, 2021). Finally, the study also highlighted how measures to restrict freedom of expression were common, but only 44 of the 83 countries surveyed declared a state of emergency, which usually includes restrictions on the spread of the virus (i.e. social distancing). Thus, creating a sense of constant emergency and threat from the pandemic or misinformation can become a "permanent mechanism of freedom-curtailing domination" and thus a threat to democracies.

The above arguments highlight how limiting restrictions on freedom of expression can be a necessary condition for uncovering the trust and ensuring democracy's deliberative process (let's consider them argument 1.1 and 1.2), but also to avoid democratic backsliding (argument 2). In what follows, we will consider a range of objections to all three.

Let's consider arguments 1.1 and 1.2: While Mill's point about the importance of uncovering truth through open debate is worth considering, the unrestrained nature of misinformation does not seem to have contributed to a more salutary democratic debate or the uncovering of truth. Instead, fake news has often been found to have nothing to do with an intention to pursue or uncover a particular truth. As Brown points out: "In some cases, originators of fake news diffuse articles which contain claims they know to be false or misleading. In other cases, they simply diffuse claims they have no good reason to believe are accurate because such claims are not the product of a process that reliably leads to truth" (Brown, 2023, p. 4).

Thus, it is not a commitment to truth that tends to be behind the spread of misinformation. Moreover, beyond the motivation of those who spread misinformation, fake news seems to undermine trust in the media. Brown summarises a recent Pew Research Centre survey, which shows that "68% of Americans get their news from social media (primarily on Facebook), but over half of them (57%) expect this news to be inaccurate given the spread of misinformation. Moreover, the percentage of Americans who reported reducing the amount of news they get overall in response to made-up news varies between 31% (for highly politically aware respondents) and 50% (for less politically aware respondents)" (Brown, 2023). Thus, fake news undermines individuals' trust in the media, contributes to a reduction in the amount of news consumed, and thus reduces the amount of information individuals use to make independent judgements. Therefore, not only does it undermine trust in the press, but more fundamentally, an open debate in which fake news is common does not lead to more information being consumed and used for decision-making, but quite the opposite.

Second, fake news may also jeopardise our ability to make accurate, independent judgements. Fake news not only leads us to mistake falsehoods for truths, but also truths for falsehoods. Our picture or reality can thus be manipulated by misinformation, making it difficult to make decisions and judgements (Brown, 2023), thus violating autonomy and undermining the argument for unrestricted information based on Scanlon's 'Millian principle'. For example, we might receive information based on a candidate's values or past record, which is not true, and be led to vote for them in a local election. After winning, we might realise that we have supported a candidate who does not reflect our political preferences or political values.

Finally, let's consider argument 2 about the possibility of restrictions leading to democratic backsliding. As noted above, it seems to be true that some governments have used COVID-19 as an opportunity to introduce restrictions, particularly on freedom of speech and the press, which have helped to strengthen their discretionary power. But while this has been the case, the political responses of 'democratic systems' have been extremely varied. As Engler et al. point out, "political institutions constrain policy choices in times of crisis: previous decisions on the design of political institutions create legacy effects by decreasing the decision space for political actors. Countries that are more dedicated to individual liberties continue to do so even in moments of emergency" (Engler et al., 2021, p. 1095). Their findings, therefore, provide a compelling case for considering the extent to which political responses were not so much a direct result of the fear and demands of the pandemic, but rather a response constrained by political institutions. As such, the case for the role of restrictions during COVID-19 in leading to democratic backsliding may be too hasty. While restrictions may have opened this possibility in countries with authoritarian tendencies, less robust democratic political institutions and that had already experienced democratic backsliding, the opposite is true in other cases. In fact, what the EXCEPTIUS results seem to indicate is that constitutional principles seem to have worked in most European countries, at least in the early stages of the pandemic. Not only "executive overreach has generally been avoided" but "mechanisms of legal oversight have, by and large, proved sufficiently strong" (Voigt, 2021, p. 552).

CONCLUSION

This chapter aims to contribute to existing debates on COVID-19 restrictions on freedom of speech and expression and their impact on democracy. Using EXCEPTIUS data for the first pandemic wave as well as other relevant sources, we found that, with three exceptions, European countries have not introduced laws directly restricting freedom of speech and the press. We argued that this may be a result of constitutional principles protecting basic liberties, namely freedom of expression, or simply a reflection of the time frame of the study. If the latter is the case, new waves of EXCEPTIUS data may lead us to different conclusions.

Given these results, but also the likelihood that later waves of data would show more common cases of restrictions on freedom of expression in several countries, we wondered in what way these could be considered legitimate. Furthermore, we considered not only laws that directly restrict freedom of expression, namely the press (i.e. laws restricting fake news), but also those that indirectly contribute to shrinking the space for debate (i.e. laws on social distancing).

Overall, the case for not restricting freedom of expression, especially through direct measures, seems strong. Open debate not only promotes individual deliberative capacity, but also protects autonomy by ensuring that individuals are able to form independent judgements about the pandemic and the government's measures to contain the spread of the virus. This is Scanlon's 'Millian principle', inspired by the work of John Stuart Mill. It also contributes to democratic decision-making and deliberation, and, as Mill pointed out, it is essential to ensure that trust is not only exposed but also seen as robust, withstanding open confrontation with falsehoods.

However, we would like to conclude by asserting that, while one should be sensitive to the arguments about the relevance of an open debate, for the most part the COVID-19 pandemic and the tandem restrictions on freedom of expression, namely those restricting fake news, seem to be justified to some extent, particularly in contexts where strong constitutional principles still protect press freedom and limit what laws can be applied and to whom. For one thing, in such contexts it does not appear that governments have used the pandemic to increase their executive power. Concerns about democratic backsliding do not seem to apply in such cases. Moreover, arguments about the importance of not limiting misinformation for the integrity and preservation of deliberative decision-making seem to be unfounded. As fake news undermines trust in the media, thereby reducing news consumption, but also distorts our perception of reality by turning truth into falsehood and falsehood into truth, it becomes difficult to make independent judgements. Finally, we should consider whether private companies, namely those in charge of social media, should be in charge of deciding who sees what and when. While we consider whether governments should restrict fake news and misinformation, private companies already significantly restrict the information we receive, often contributing to the spread of tailored misinformation and the omission of counterfactuals. Therefore, while not all restrictions need to be justified, and in certain contexts any restriction may prove to be another step towards authoritarian government solutions, it is worth considering some mechanisms that could be the outcome of a democratic decision-making process and contribute to limiting the spread of fake news and misinformation.

REFERENCES

Amadio Viceré, M. G., & Tercovich, G. (2020). The high representative and the COVID-19 crisis: A preliminary assessment. *Global Affairs, 6*(3), 287–299.

Berlin, I. (2014). "Two Concepts of Liberty". *Reading Political Philosophy*, 231–237. Routledge. (originalpublication 1969).

Borrell. (2020). Response to disinformation around COVID-19: Remarks by High Representative/Vice-President Josep Borrell at the Read-out of the College meeting. https://www.eeas.europa.eu/eeas/response-disinformation-around-COVID-19-remarks-high-representativevice-president-josep_en

Brown, Étienne. (2023). Free speech and the legal prohibition of fake news. *Social Theory and Practice*.

Committee to Protect Journalists. (n.d.). COVID-19 and Press Freedom. https://cpj.org/COVID-19/

Council of Europe. (2021). Journalism and COVID-19: Press freedom is essential in times of crisis. https://www.coe.int/en/web/portal/-/journalism-and-COVID-19-press-freedom-is-essential-in-times-of-crisis

Council on Foreign Relations. (2021). COVID-19 and the threat to Press Freedom in Central and Eastern Europe. https://www.cfr.org/in-brief/COVID-19-and-threat-press-freedom-central-and-eastern-europe

Daemen, J. A. M. (2022). Freedom, security, and the COVID-19 pandemic. *Critical Review of International Social and Political Philosophy*, 1–21. https://doi.org/10.1080/13698230.2022.2100961

Degerman, D., Flinders, M., & Johnson, M. T. (2020). In defence of fear: COVID-19, crises and democracy. *Critical Review of International Social and Political Philosophy*, 1–22. https://doi.org/10.1080/13698230.2020.1834744

Engler, S., et al. (2021). Democracy in times of the pandemic: Explaining the variation of COVID-19 policies across European democracies. *West European Politics, 44*(5–6), 1077–1102. https://doi.org/10.1080/0140238 2.2021.1900669

Goh, Z. H., Tandoc, E. C., Jr., Salmon, C. T., Kim, H. K., & Shi, J. (2022). Can press freedom enhance the effect of news exposure on COVID-19 health beliefs? A health belief model perspective. *Health Communication, 37*(5), 1–9.

Howie, E. (2018). Protecting the human right to freedom of expression in international law. *International Journal of Speech-Language Pathology, 20*(1), 12–15. https://doi.org/10.1080/17549507.2018.1392612

Human Rights Watch. (2021). COVID-19 triggers wave of free speech abuse. https://www.hrw.org/news/2021/02/11/COVID-19-triggers-wave-free-speech-abuse

IPI. (2020). Rush to pass 'fake news' laws during COVID 19 intensifying global media freedom challenges. https://ipi.media/rush-to-pass-fake-news-laws-during-COVID-19-intensifying-global-media-freedom-challenges/

Mill, J. S. (2001). *On liberty*. Batoche Books.

Palmer, L. (2022). Press freedom during COVID-19: The digital discourses of the International Press Institute, Reporters Sans Frontières, and the Committee to Protect Journalists. *Digital Journalism, 10*(6), 1079–1097.

Scanlon, T. (2000). *A theory of freedom of expression*. Routledge.

Voigt, H. (2021). COVID-19 and freedom. *Social sciences information. Information sur les sciences sociales, 60*(4), 548–559. https://doi.org/10.1177/05390184211050850

Wolff, S., & Ladi, S. (2020). European Union responses to the COVID-19 pandemic: Adaptability in times of permanent emergency. *Journal of European Integration, 42*(8), 1025–1040.

CHAPTER 9

Restrictions on Religious Worship

Wojciech Brzozowski, Maksymilian Hau,
and Oliwia Rybczyńska

INTRODUCTION

Life can be truly surprising. As recently as a few years ago, we might have thought that the debates on the future developments concerning freedom of religion or belief in Europe would focus on issues such as the relationship between populism and religion, the ever-growing scope of conscientious objection, or the accommodation of Islam in the European legal space. No one could have foreseen that in 2020, the main challenge to religious freedom would be governmental restrictions to collective worship, and that European churches would only be able to welcome a handful of those who were lucky enough to join the service before the maximum number of participants was reached.

At the onset of the COVID-19 pandemic, the need to curve the spread of the novel coronavirus became everyone's overriding focus, and the measures which cut people off from their social life did not spare religious freedom. In fact, this freedom became one of their first collateral victim of

W. Brzozowski (✉) • M. Hau • O. Rybczyńska
University of Warsaw, Warsaw, Poland
e-mail: w.brzozowski@wpia.uw.edu.pl; m.hau@uw.edu.pl;
o.rybczynska@uw.edu.pl

C. Egger et al. (eds.), *Covid-19 Containment Policies in Europe*,
International Series on Public Policy,
https://doi.org/10.1007/978-3-031-52096-9_9

151

the pandemic, since churches were commonly identified as hotbeds for infection. The outbreak of the pandemic brought a radical change to the exercise of religious worship and suddenly made a scarce commodity out of what had long been taken for granted.

The chapter addresses restrictions on religious worship. It is rooted in the database collected under the EXCEPTIUS project, but not limited to it, for raw data do not give a full picture of the situation. Freedom of religion or belief is indeed a very special case: any of the imposed restrictions face barriers and challenges of their own kind, and the effectiveness of the law enforcement measures depends on a number of highly specific factors.

In this respect, we believe that the message from the times of the pandemic, although it has received considerable scholarly attention in recent times, has still not been sufficiently understood and processed in academic terms. Many studies on the response to COVID-19 simply reflect the experiences of specific countries. The generalisability of this research is often problematic. Some authors address more general questions and offer considerations as to whether giving priority to public health over freedom of religion or belief is always correct. If detached from the actual numbers, such findings may be difficult to implement. And this is where the EXCEPTIUS dataset can be useful. In this chapter, we aspire to contribute to the extant literature by generalising examples from a number of jurisdictions, thus making it possible to discover patterns in the legal response to COVID-19 within the area under study. This broader picture also allows us to offer policy recommendations based on both pre-existing theoretical considerations and the actual experience of European countries.

The first section of this chapter presents the taxonomy of measures defined within the EXCEPTIUS project, whereas the second section addresses the level of policy responses across Europe, using this taxonomy. This will be followed by a preliminary assessment of the design of restrictions in the light of the requirements established by the European Convention of Human Rights (ECHR). In the next section, the implementation of measures is discussed, with the use of comparative data compiled in the project's database. The penultimate section will outline the lessons learnt from the response of European countries to the pandemic and explore the potential for comparative research in this field. The final part will briefly conclude the chapter with key policy recommendations.

Taxonomy of Measures

In EXCEPTIUS data, restrictions on religious freedom are classified as a specific restriction of fundamental rights and civil liberties. If the legal act refers to freedom of religion or belief, its content is coded in five categories, which represents the level of burden of restrictions of this freedom. The first category includes situations in which all restrictions are lifted (0). The following categories concern: (1) light restrictions on religious practice, (2) heavy restrictions on religious practice, (3) light restrictions on specific religions, (4) heavy restrictions on specific religions, and (5) light restrictions on religious practice combined with heavy restrictions on specific religions.

The restrictions are identified as heavy if they entirely suspend religious activity or limit the number of people allowed to gather to a maximum of 15. In turn, limitations are considered light if at least 15 persons are allowed to participate in religious activities at the same time, if an obligation to wear masks or keep social distance are imposed, if time or the use of certain objects of worship during religious events are limited or if certain elements of religious ceremonies or worship are affected in certain ways.

Restrictions on religious freedom are identified in 22 out of 25 countries for which the data was collected. Of the European countries under study, Hungary, Ireland, and Luxembourg did not pass legislation that directly restricted freedom of religion. However, this does not mean that such restrictions did not actually affect the believers in these countries. Some constraints imposed on freedom of movement and freedom of assembly, in particular stay-at-home requirements or restrictions on public gatherings (see Chazel's contribution in this volume), had a direct impact on exercising the collective dimension of religious freedom. Also, face mask requirements, social distancing or similar rules governing social behaviour placed a significant burden on the performance of religious rituals and ceremonies.

With the above in mind, the restrictions on religious freedom discussed in this chapter will encompass both those which specifically target this freedom and those which introduce restrictions on funeral attendance—coded under a specific category in EXCEPTIUS. This approach will make it possible to focus on the characteristics of the restrictions directly related to the exercise of religious worship. Moreover, data collected for the first three waves of the pandemic do not allow the full picture of the shape and effectiveness of the restrictions with respect to freedom of religion or belief to be grasped. This concerns mainly the lack of information regarding sanctions imposed in case of non-compliance with the restrictions and the duration for which the restrictions were established. While it is fair to assume that most penalties took the form of fines (as in the case of the funeral attendance ban, where sufficient data is available) and the potential overstepping of the State's powers in this area did not affect fundamental rights so much, the period for which the restrictions were adopted should be investigated in greater detail, since the arbitrary extension of this period was one of the major threats to human rights resulting from the legal response to COVID-19.

Restrictions on Religious Freedom in Numbers

Turning now to the conclusions emerging from the data analysed, the most important observation is that light restrictions on religious freedom dominated during the first three waves of the COVID-19 pandemic. As Table 9.1 shows, they were imposed twice as often as heavy restrictions on religious practice. Heavy restrictions were introduced in Belgium, Croatia, Cyprus, Estonia, Finland, France, some German federal states (*Länder*), Greece, Italy, Poland, Portugal, Romania, Spain, Switzerland, and the United Kingdom. Furthermore, there was no single case of restrictions, light or heavy, aimed at specific religions.[1] This might give grounds for optimism: it appears that the European governments did not shape these restrictions in a way that discriminated against any particular religion, especially religious minorities.

As for country-by-country data, it follows that particularly intense law-making in the subject area has been observed in Germany, Spain, Cyprus and, in a lower degree, in Greece, Switzerland, Italy, and Belgium. In the remaining countries, the legislative activity in this area was marginal. The high intensity of legal response in Germany and Spain corresponds with the data concerning the legal form and spatial coverage of restrictions

---

[1] In certain jurisdictions, the law identified elements of religious worship that objectively posed an increased risk of virus transmission. Technically, one could argue that specific religions might have been singled out in this way. We do not think that this would be a correct conclusion. Neither do we believe that an individual application of a general norm which is by its nature and design applicable to many subjects of law (e.g. the cancellation of a religious festival of a particular denomination on the basis of laws allowing for the suspension of mass events) should be considered as targeting a specific religion.

Table 9.1 An overview of the light and heavy restrictions on religious practice in analysed countries

Country	Restrictions on religious practice		
	Light	Heavy	Total
Austria	1	N/A	1
Belgium	12	8	20
Croatia	N/A	4	4
Cyprus	41	39	80
Czech Republic	14	N/A	14
Denmark	12	N/A	12
Estonia	6	2	8
Finland	5	1	6
France	2	1	3
Germany	70	24	94
Greece	6	44	50
Italy	5	14	19
Malta	1	N/A	1
Netherlands	1	N/A	1
Norway	1	N/A	1
Poland	10	4	14
Portugal	4	4	8
Romania	3	3	6
Spain	140	4	144
Sweden	2	N/A	2
Switzerland	23	3	26
United Kingdom	5	5	10
Total	364	160	524

Source: EXCEPTIUS, own rendering

introduced, as indicated in Table 9.2. Regarding Germany, all acts imposing restrictions of religious freedom were implemented at the subnational level by the state (*Länder*) authorities (see Magni-Berton's chapter for an analysis of decentralised patterns of pandemic management). The case of Spain is similar, as the restrictions introduced by the State authorities concerned the regional level of autonomous communities (*comunidades autónomas*). Considering the remaining countries, the limitations were generally enforced by national executive bodies, and they covered uniformly entire jurisdictions.

There is also a difference between unitary and non-unitary countries in terms of the frequency with which restrictions were adopted. In

Table 9.2   An overview of restrictions of religious practice in terms of territorial coverage

Country	Territorial level		
	National	Subnational	Regional/local
Austria	0	2	0
Belgium	16	4	0
Croatia	3	0	1
Cyprus	3	77	0
Czech Republic	14	0	0
Denmark	13	0	0
Estonia	11	1	0
Finland	0	4	2
France	2	0	1
Germany	0	98	0
Greece	13	0	37
Italy	10	10	1
Malta	2	0	0
Netherlands	1	0	0
Norway	1	0	0
Poland	15	1	0
Portugal	7	0	1
Romania	7	0	0
Spain	9	114	25
Sweden	2	0	0
Switzerland	21	6	0
United Kingdom	2	10	1
Total	152	327	69

Source: EXCEPTIUS dataset

Note: Value of 0 means no data were reported

federalised and quasi-federalised countries (with the exceptions of Greece and Cyprus), the number of legal acts adopted was significantly higher. These countries, most likely due to their decentralised organisation, adopted new regulations more frequently, which allowed them to be more flexible and modify the legal response in accordance with the pandemic situation. This adaptative approach contributed to safeguarding freedom of religion or belief, as it allowed the State to react in a proportional manner, especially during the first periods of the pandemic, when little was known about the routes via which the virus was transmitted.

What is also characteristic of the first three waves of the pandemic is the almost complete lack of legal review of the restrictions. The relatively highest intensity in this respect is observed in Spain, where nine acts were subject to judicial review and one act to constitutional review. In Malta, one act was scrutinised by administrative bodies, while in Romania and Italy two acts were subject to parliamentary approval. Given the almost complete absence of ad-hoc legislation it is plausible to assume that this deficit of legal review is best explained by the common social readiness for tolerating even far-reaching restrictions during the first periods of the pandemic.

Restrictions that specifically targeted funeral ceremonies were introduced in 22 out of the 25 countries analysed to the notable exception of Estonia, Norway or Sweden. As illustrated in Table 9.3, restrictions were

Table 9.3 An overview of restrictions on funeral attendance in terms of authority

Country	Authority				
	National legislative	National executive	Subnational executive	National administrative	Subnational administrative
Austria	0	16	2	0	0
Belgium	0	20	8	0	0
Croatia	0	2	0	0	0
Cyprus	0	31	0	0	0
Czech Republic	0	4	0	0	0
Denmark	0	13	0	0	0
Finland	0	0	0	0	1
France	1	2	1	0	0
Germany	0	0	57	0	0
Greece	0	17	0	0	0
Hungary	0	3	0	0	0
Ireland	0	33	0	0	0
Italy	0	6	2	0	0
Luxembourg	0	1	0	0	0
Malta	0	1	0	1	0
Netherlands	0	1	0	0	0
Poland	0	6	0	0	0
Portugal	0	41	0	0	0
Romania	0	2	0	0	0
Spain	1	4	11	92	34
Switzerland	0	37	12	0	0
United Kingdom	0	67	9	0	0
Total	2	307	102	93	35

Source: EXCEPTIUS dataset

Note: Values 2 (subnational executive), 5 (national judiciary) and 6 (subnational judiciary) have been omitted due to the fact that no data were collected in this respect mostly introduced by national executive authorities. It was only in France and Spain that two national acts were adopted by the legislative authority. Any breach of the ban on funeral attendance would have resulted in fines (Belgium, Denmark, France, Germany, Hungary, Ireland, Netherlands, Switzerland, UK) or, alternatively, a fine and imprisonment (France, Denmark). Considering the scale of the funeral attendance ban, in most cases (353 out of 539 legal acts), the number of people who could attend the funerals was fixed at approximately 10–50. Less burdensome restrictions were introduced in Austria, Belgium, Denmark, Germany, and Spain, where the number of people allowed to participate in funeral ceremonies ranged from 60 to 250. To a small extent, governments chose to impose restrictions that limited the number of participants to a maximum of nine. While very strict restrictions remained in place throughout the three waves of the pandemic, acts introducing medium restrictions (10–50 people) were more numerous during the first and second waves of the pandemic.

Assessing the Design of Restrictions Through a Human Rights Lens

The greater and more direct the threat, the more likely people appear to be tolerant of restrictions on human rights in general, especially restrictions on religious freedom (Hill, 2021, p. 94). This does not mean, however, that the pandemic offered a *carte blanche* to policy makers. According to Article 9 para. 2 ECHR, "[f]reedom to manifest one's religion or beliefs shall be subject only to such limitations as are prescribed by law and are necessary in a democratic society in the interests of public safety, for the protection of public order, health or morals, or for the protection of the rights and freedoms of others." It follows from this provision that in order to be permissible, restrictions of this freedom must not only be prescribed by law, but they also must pursue a legitimate aim, at least one of those listed above. In the case of the COVID-19 pandemic, the commonly invoked aim was the protection of public health. The restrictions must also be necessary, which presupposes effectiveness. There is no doubt that religious practices, especially rituals performed in the presence of other people, could directly contribute to an increase in coronavirus cases, so technically speaking, the curtailment of religious freedom could work. However, it is highly questionable whether even a serious and imminent health threat justified such broad restrictions through executive acts. And, more importantly, everything depends on the design of a restriction. Most of the measures which were aimed at preventing the spread of the coronavirus restricted access to religious gatherings by limiting the number of people allowed to gather or by suspending religious events entirely. The most popular tendency was to make the number of people allowed to participate in a religious event dependent on the size of the religious premises. There are several arguments against this kind of measures due to their lack of proportionality. First and foremost, restrictions which focus on the capacity of religious premises place a very high burden on the enjoyment of freedom of religion or belief, while their effectiveness in preventing the spread of coronavirus appears to be low (for a further discussion see Hau, 2022, p. 37). Second, the governments did not provide an explanation as to why the limit was set at the given size. Third, the restrictions based on limiting number of participants were not responsive to the rapidly changing pandemic situations and the growing body of knowledge on how the virus is transmitted. Additional objections may be raised with respect to the ban on attending funerals: since many funeral ceremonies take place outdoors, where the exposure to infection is considered to be much lower, there was little justification for setting the same restrictions as for indoor events.

The collected data also provide examples of other approaches to restrictions. In Bavaria, religious gatherings could not last longer than 60 minutes. This type of measure represents a different approach, but its proportionality is just as questionable as in the case of restrictions dependent on the size of the premises: it places a significant burden on the enjoyment of religious freedom while its effectiveness is doubtful.[2]

In Cyprus, participation in ceremonies, such as weddings, baptisms, and funerals, was conditional on proof of degree of kinship: only first- and second-degree relatives, but no more than ten people, were allowed to participate. Similar restrictions were also introduced in Greece, where funeral attendance was allowed only with the participation of an immediate circle of relatives.

According to other Greek restrictions, participation in religious ceremonies was only allowed for the clergy, without the presence of the

---

[2] Nevertheless, it should be taken into account that this particular measure was agreed between the local church units and the Bavarian state government, see Berkmann (2020, pp. 194–195)

faithful and only with a limited number of participants keeping their distance from one another and complying with sanitary measures. In addition, it was mandatory that the entrance and exit doors to the place of worship be locked, and the clergyman in charge of the religious ritual was responsible for taking all reasonable steps to ensure that no person entered the place of worship while the service was being conducted.

On the other hand, in Spain certain restrictions took a more tailored form as they involved the prohibition of choir services, a ban on the use of blessed water, and the performing of ritual ablution outdoors only. Similarly, in Italy, a law was passed which differentiated the types of restrictions depending on the specific traits and needs of a particular religion (Protocolli per le celebrazioni delle confessioni religiose diverse dalla Cattolica, 2020). Such a tailored model of restrictions, which, based on scientific knowledge, focuses on elements of worship activities which pose an increased risk of transmission, deserves approval. This approach allows the regular operation of the religious ceremonies while protecting public health at the same time. The main objection regarding tailored restrictions is that they can interfere with the freedom of religion or belief, especially by arbitrarily prohibiting certain (potentially crucial) elements of worship. Therefore, the implementation of such measures must be subject to prior approval of religious groups and should involve cooperation with religious leaders at the stage of drafting the measures.

But the key issue remains the proportionality of the restrictions. In a recent Strasbourg decision, the European Court of Human Rights (ECtHR) identified the timespan for which restrictions had been established and the size of the target group as essential factors to be considered when assessing the proportionality of the COVID-19 restrictions. The ECtHR initially found that the restrictions imposed by the Swiss government had violated Article 11 ECHR in both its procedural and substantive aspects (ECtHR, 2022).[3] The procedural violation resulted from the lack of judicial review of the restrictions, whereas the substantive infringement concerned, among other things, the general character of the restrictions and the long duration of the ban (ibid., para. 91; Smet [2022]). The decision concerned freedom of assembly and not freedom of religion or belief, but it perhaps illustrated the emerging attitude of the ECtHR towards COVID-19 restrictions: those established for a shorter period of time and

---

[3] In September 2022, the case was referred to the Grand Chamber of the Court, which declared the application inadmissible on formal grounds (ECtHR, 2023).

addressed to specific groups rather than to the entire population were more likely to pass the proportionality test.

THE IMPLEMENTATION OF MEASURES

The urgency of the epidemiological situation forced the public authorities to immediately impose a wide range of restrictions, from the obligation to wear face masks to stay-at-home orders. The growing fear of the virus and the accompanying social anxiety fostered an expectation that governments would come up with quick solutions. This, however, all too often resulted in ordinary legislation being bypassed with the issuance of executive acts. Soon enough, controversy arose as to the extent to which executive acts can impose restrictions on fundamental rights, including freedom of religion or belief.

As explained in the previous section, the introduction of restrictions on religious freedom through executive acts deserves criticism, especially when such extraordinary measures were imposed in breach of statutory laws. On the other hand, it needs to be admitted that there was a reason for the sudden spate of executive acts: it would be going too far to say that parliaments had no opportunities to convene during the pandemic, but it is true that their functioning was hindered. More importantly, it takes time for a parliament to pass new legislation. Against this background, it is easy to understand why executive acts became a convenient tool for making and enforcing rapid decisions during the pandemic. But there was a price to pay for this initial efficiency: the use of executive acts for the purpose of limiting fundamental rights, including freedom of religion or belief, had an impact on the States' ability to enforce compliance and uphold administrative penalties before the courts.

Based on EXCEPTIUS data, it can be confirmed that the restrictions on freedom of religion were implemented for the most part through executive acts (a total of 529 out of 548 acts), both at the national (355 acts) and the subnational levels (174 acts). This is inconsistent with the principle that legislative acts be established by the legislature.

Also, it is worth mentioning that in some countries (Malta, the United Kingdom) restrictions on religious freedom were implemented through advisory acts that had no legal force but simply offered guidelines. In the UK, the government issued non-binding guidelines on the safe use of places of worship during the pandemic. The document included general recommendations on the use of measures such as staggering entry, providing multiple entrances and one-way routes to enter and exit the premises, providing hand sanitizers, and so forth. More importantly, the guidelines encouraged religious leaders to consider changes that could be introduced to religious rituals that typically involve close contact between individuals, and gave examples such as preventing worshippers from touching or kissing religious objects that are handled together, removing books and shared resources such as prayer mats, worship sheets or devotional items from use, avoiding chanting and/or playing instruments, ensuring that any initial washing/ablution rituals be conducted outside the place of worship, and closing off common washing areas. The recommendations might not have been binding, but they provided important guidance for religious associations and worshippers. And besides, this way of crafting the government response ensured transparency, which is best achieved when all segments of the population, including minorities, are involved in decision-making (Ó Cathaoir, 2021, pp. 47–48).

Restrictions on religious freedom were mostly introduced for a limited period. Only in 107 cases they were introduced for an unlimited period. In 100 cases, the restrictions were imposed for less than 30 days. Restrictions on funerals were also mainly introduced for a limited period. In 108 cases (out of 539), they were imposed for an unlimited time. In 94 cases, the restrictions were introduced for less than 30 days. In most cases, the duration of the restrictions was intended to be as short as possible, in order not to suppress the freedom of religion or belief, while also sufficient to ensure safety for a period of time. It seems that the introduction of severe restrictions on religious freedom for a period longer than 30 days is likely to have constituted an unjustified interference with the rights of believers, especially in the light of the dynamically changing pandemic situation.

The Reality Behind the Numbers

As illustrated by the collected data, the views of European States on the need to restrict religious worship during the COVID-19 pandemic were remarkably similar. Collective forms of worship were seen as a threat to public health since they require many people to be present at the same time in confined settings, and involve activities that facilitate the spread of the virus, such as loud singing or reciting prayers in unison. The review of the measures taken to slow down the rate of new infections—or to *flatten the curve*, as the popular saying went—reveals that the public authorities used a legal toolbox similar to that which ultimately proved useful when dealing with freedom of assembly. Consequently, gatherings were banned or suspended, the number of people allowed to attend services was reduced, strict hygiene rules were required, and social distance policies were enacted. Much less of a threat were individual forms of worship in designated public places, such as individual prayer in a temple. These too, however, were restricted as a consequence of reduced access to church premises. By contrast, the restrictions did not extend to individual forms of worship taking place in private places, as these did not pose any threat to public health.

Yet, to draw complete parallels between freedom of worship and freedom of assembly can be deceptive. In the case of freedom of assembly, mass attendance is, or might be, a value in itself. The more the merrier: a large number of attendees sends a message that the cause for which people have chosen to leave their homes and stand together enjoys broad public support. By contrast, with religious worship, the essence lies in a collective spiritual experience whose value does not depend on its social impact. Moreover, the use of legal measures similar to those that might have been appropriate with regard to freedom of assembly did not really have the same effect when restricting religious worship. It should be borne in mind that the first restrictions were introduced in March 2020, at a time when churches belonging to the Christian tradition, still dominant in the European religious landscape, were preparing to celebrate Easter. Restricting access to religious worship during this period had a particularly severe impact on religious life in Europe (see e.g. Papazoglou et al., 2021, pp. 3219–3220).

Another important difference is that in some cases physical presence at a specific time and place can be a condition *sine qua non* for the validity of a ritual: not just part of a religious protocol, but the essence of the ritual. While the purpose of a political assembly can sometimes be partially achieved online, or with a slight delay, there are certain religious practices which simply cannot be postponed to another day, moved to the digital sphere, or performed over the phone. One obvious example is the Sacrament of Eucharist in the Roman Catholic Church, which is a consequence of the theological doctrine of transubstantiation and the corresponding belief that, at consecration, the substance of the bread and wine is truly being transformed into Jesus Christ's body and blood (Martínez-Torrón, 2021, p. 57). Another example is the Sacrament of Penance (confession), as it requires face-to-face contact between the penitent and the confessor. Also, in the Jewish tradition, the recitation of Kaddish is expected to involve the physical presence of those performing the ritual. Interestingly, the prolonged duration of the pandemic prompted religious communities to seek ways to adapt religious beliefs to the new situation (see e.g. Macaraan, 2021, p. 531; McElwee, 2020; Cooper, 2021).[4]

And it is precisely cooperation with religious communities, as many believe, that should be the starting point for the design and implementation of restrictions intended to mitigate the spread of the virus.[5] There is at least one but powerful argument for this: the need to respect the autonomy of religious groups—an essential component of freedom of religion or belief in its collective dimension (see e.g. ECtHR [GC] 2000: para. 91; ECtHR [GC] 2014: para. 127). The religious groups know best which elements of their rituals are easy to replace and which belong to the core of their religious identity. Any top-down interference in this field is always questionable. It is also unnecessary in practice. It is no coincidence that the initiative to introduce certain liturgical changes, such as distributing the Holy Communion in the hand rather than on the tongue in regions where this was not commonly accepted (Budaev, 2021, pp. 2342–2344), came from the churches themselves.

The data collected for the EXCEPTIUS project do not reveal disparities in the treatment of different religions, that is, legislation adopted in response to COVID-19 did not target particular religious denominations. On the face of it, this offers grounds for optimism. The pandemic might easily have become a pretext for adopting openly discriminatory measures against specific religions, especially minority ones. This would have been particularly likely in countries that provide a differentiated legal framework for the functioning of religious groups—this is actually what most European countries do (Uitz, 2007, p. 87)—especially if there are separate acts that define the relationship between the State and the respective church, such as in Italy or Poland. It is well known that such a model significantly hinders the principle of equal rights for religious groups. Had the anti-COVID measures been introduced individually for each

---

[4] It is hard to ignore the great potential for the study of religion which lies in exploring the COVID-induced developments in the field; c.f. Baker et al. (2020).

[5] Javier Martínez-Torrón is right to observe that 'in a number of countries of Europe and America, governments have approached limitations on religious freedom … with an attitude that is characterized by unilateralism, imposition, and improvisation, instead of turning to consultation, cooperation and reflection'; Martínez-Torrón (2021, p. 58).

denomination at the time, the risk of unequal treatment would have greatly increased, and in the atmosphere of panic about the new threat, such abuses of power were likely to have gone unnoticed. Luckily, the pressure of time prevented the public authorities from yielding to this particular temptation, for the restrictions on religious worship were mostly enacted in general anti-COVID acts rather than through meticulous amendment of the laws on the exercise of religion.

But quantitative data do not tell the whole story. The measures may have been the same, but the effects they triggered varied from one jurisdiction to another. The absence of discriminatory criteria in the body of the regulation does not necessarily mean that various religions were affected to the same extent by the restrictions (Madera, 2021, pp. 3–4). The true picture of the impact of the pandemic on collective worship only becomes apparent when the religious diversity of European countries is considered.

It is no secret that the various religions, even if they respond to the same deepest human needs, differ profoundly in their doctrine, habits, and attitude towards any earthly power. Activities that pose different epidemiological risks are present in varying degrees of intensity: for some communities, singing, eating together, and kissing objects of religious veneration may be central to the ritual, whereas for others such activities may be merely complementary or even unnecessary. Also, there are variations in the degree of *juridisation* of churches, a factor which apparently had an impact on their resilience in times of pandemic (Valenzi, 2021). Even more importantly, there are religious groups that, for various reasons—whether due to doctrinal motives or because of negative past experiences in a particular country or region, or both—may be distrustful of public institutions,[6] which obviously makes cooperation in responding to pandemics much more difficult. To make matters even more complicated, a religious group which dominates in one country and enjoys the support of the government may be a minority in another jurisdiction.

For all these reasons, when trying to summarise and compare the impact that the COVID-19 pandemic had on religious worship, it is necessary to consider this less obvious aspect: not just the measures taken but also their varying effects on different religious communities. From this perspective, the experience of a Roman Catholic in Germany and a Roman Catholic in Portugal may have had more in common than the experience

---

[6] Jehova's Witnesses can be a good case in point; see e.g. Brace (2021).

of a Roman Catholic and a Jehovah's Witness living in the same country or even city. This peculiarity should be taken into account in any future comparative research.

CONCLUSION

The outbreak of the COVID-19 pandemic profoundly affected the conditions in which religious worship was practised. While individual expressions of devotion at home were possible throughout any lockdown, religious life in a communal setting was affected by severe restrictions. But difficult times are there to draw lessons from. If the experience of recent years is not to go to waste, it may be appropriate to draw up three main policy recommendations for the future. These recommendations are based on the EXCEPTIUS dataset, but they also find inspiration in the rapidly growing scholarship on the subject matter and the relevant views of the Strasbourg Court.

First, public health may take priority over spiritual well-being, yet the latter ought not to be completely disregarded. The data collected show that this simple truth was not acknowledged in all jurisdictions. In some cases, religious worship was heavily suppressed, which suggests that not all States showed understanding for the needs of believers.

Second, it does not appear to be necessary to achieve uniformity in public policies on the access to places and practices of worship during pandemics. The existing tools, including the principle of proportionality, provide sufficient consideration for freedom of religion or belief. But proportionality is to be taken seriously: there is no justification for applying different maximum occupancy rates to churches and beauty parlours if the level of risk is similar. Nor is there any justification for extending restrictions beyond the necessary period.

Third, tailored restrictions, that is, those which focus on high-risk elements of religious worship instead of banning worship in general, may or may not be discriminatory and they may or may not interfere with religious autonomy. We believe that if the policy makers wish to avoid discrimination and interference while keeping the restrictions effective, it is crucial for them to act in consultation with religious communities and their leaders. Continuous dialogue and the willingness on the part of the authorities to explain the purposes of the restrictions increases the likelihood of their actual—and not just apparent or superficial—implementation, since they benefit from the authority of a person who enjoys the trust and obedience of the faithful. Such a consensual approach also reduces the level of suspicion of those who might otherwise think that the restrictions imposed are in fact motivated by hostility to religion or a particular church.

REFERENCES

Baker, J. O., Martí, G., Braunstein, R., Whitehead, A. L., & Yukich, G. (2020). Religion in the age of social distancing: How COVID-19 presents new directions for research. *Sociology of Religion, 81*(4), 357–370. https://doi.org/10.1093/socrel/sraa039

Berkmann, B. J. (2020). The COVID-19 crisis and religious freedom: The interaction between State and Church norms in Germany, especially in Bavaria. *Journal of Law, Religion and State, 8*(2–3), 179–200. https://doi.org/10.1163/22124810-2020013

Brace, T. (2021). Jehovah's witnesses and the law: 'Caesar's things to Caesar, but God's things to God. In E. Barker & J. T. Richardson (Eds.), *Reactions to the law by minority religions* (pp. 37–57). Routledge.

Budaev, S. (2021). Safety and reverence: How Roman Catholic Liturgy can respond to the COVID 19 pandemic. *Journal of Religion and Health, 60*(4), 2331–2352. https://doi.org/10.1007/s10943-021-01282-x

Cooper, L. (2021). Kaddish during COVID: Mourning rituals during a pandemic. *Contemporary Jewry, 41*(1), 39–69. https://doi.org/10.1007/s12397-021-09395-x

ECtHR (GC). (2000). Hassan and Chaoush v. Bulgaria. App no. 30985/96. October 26.

ECtHR (GC). (2014). Fernández Martínez v. Spain. App no. 56030/07. June 12.

ECtHR (GC). (2023). Communauté genevoise d'action syndicale (CGAS) v. Switzerland. App no. 21881/20. November 27.

ECtHR. (2022). Communauté genevoise d'action syndicale (CGAS) v. Switzerland. App no. 21881/20. March 15.

Hau, M. (2022). COVID-19 restrictions on religious worship: How to ensure effectiveness while respecting religious autonomy? *Stato, Chiese e pluralismo confessionale, 16*, 37–53. https://doi.org/10.54103/1971-8543/18820

Hill, M., QC (2021). Coronavirus and the curtailment of religious liberty. In A. Madera (Ed.), *The crisis of religious freedom in the age of COVID-19 pandemic* (pp. 77–95). MDPI. https://doi.org/10.3390/books978-3-0365-2280-7

Macaraan, W. E. R. (2021). The sacrament of confession during COVID-19 pandemic. *Journal of Public Health, 43*(3), e531–e532. https://doi.org/10.1093/pubmed/fdab193

Madera, A. (2021). The implications of the COVID-19 pandemic on religious exercise: Preliminary remarks. In A. Madera (Ed.), *The crisis of religious freedom in the age of COVID-19 pandemic* (pp. 1–10). MDPI. https://doi.org/10.3390/books978-3-0365-2280-7

Martínez-Torrón, J. (2021). COVID-19 and religious freedom: Some comparative perspectives. In A. Madera (Ed.), *The crisis of religious freedom in the age of COVID-19 pandemic* (pp. 51–66). MDPI. https://doi.org/10.3390/boo ks978-3-0365-2280-7

McElwee, J. J. (2020). *Vatican makes clear: General absolution allowed during Coronavirus contagion.* National Catholic Reporter. March 20. Retrieved March 9, 2022, from https://www.ncronline.org/news/vatican/vatican-makes-clear-general-absolution-allowed-during-coronavirus-contagion

Ó Cathaoir, K. (2021). Human rights in times of pandemics: Necessity and proportionality. In M. Kjaerum, M. F. Davis, & A. Lyons (Eds.), *COVID-19 and human rights* (pp. 35–51). Routledge.

Papazoglou, A. S., Moysidis, D. V., Tsagkaris, C., Dorosh, M., Karagiannidis, E., & Mazin, R. (2021). Spiritual health and the COVID-19 pandemic: Impacts on Orthodox Christianity devotion practices, rituals, and religious pilgrimages. *Journal of Religion and Health, 60*(5), 3217–3229. https://doi.org/10.1007/s10943-021-01347-x

Protocolli per le celebrazioni delle confessioni religiose diverse dalla cattolica. (2020). DIRESOM. Retrieved September 16, 2022, from https://diresom.net/2020/05/15/protocolli-per-le-celebrazioni-delle-confessioni-religiose-diverse-dalla-cattolica

Smet, S. (2022). First violations in a COVID-19 case: Communauté genevoise d'action syndicale (CGAS) v. Switzerland. *Strasbourg Observers,* May 9. Retrieved July 24, 2022, from https://strasbourgobservers.com/2022/05/09/first-violations-in-a-COVID-19-case-communaute-genevoise-daction-syndicale-cgas-v-switzerland/#more-8278

Uitz, R. (2007). *Freedom of religion in European constitutional and international law.* Council of Europe Publishing.

Valenzi, I. (2021). L'impatto del COVID-19 sugli ordinamenti giuridici delle Chiese cristiane protestanti. Prime note. *Quaderni di Diritto e Politica Ecclesiastica, 24*(speciale), 305–320. https://doi.org/10.1440/102139

CHAPTER 10

Freedom of Movement

José Enrique Conde Belmonte,
Ana María Huesca González,
and Paloma Villacián Goncer

INTRODUCTION

Practically all the European Union's and the Schengen area's members decided to enact unilateral movement restriction measures for both citizens and residents in the Member States in response to the COVID-19 pandemic. The development of the European economy, which is based on the continuous movement of goods, people and, specially, workers, as well

J. E. Conde Belmonte (✉)
Department of International Law and International Relations, University of Comillas, Madrid, Spain
e-mail: jeconde@comillas.edu

A. M. Huesca González
Department of Sociology and Social Work, University of Comillas, Madrid, Spain
e-mail: ahuesca@comillas.edu

P. Villacián Goncer
Faculty of Humanities and Social Sciences and Department of Sociology and Social Work, University of Comillas, Madrid, Spain
e-mail: paloma.villacian@alu.comillas.edu

© The Author(s) 2024   171
C. Egger et al. (eds.), *Covid-19 Containment Policies in Europe,*
International Series on Public Policy,
https://Doi.org/10.1007/978-3-031-52096-9_10

as citizen fundamental rights were both hampered by this situation. Such restrictions to the free movement of people have been unprecedented since the start of the regional integration process based on the single market idea.

This chapter uses a variety of bibliographic sources, including the primary sources of European Union Law, scholarly classics, and the database of the European project EXCEPTIUS. The literature on freedom of movement during the COVID-19 pandemic in the European region has focused on the various restrictions and measures implemented by governments to slow down the spread of the virus. These measures have included border closures, quarantine requirements for travellers, and mandatory testing for COVID-19 upon arrival.

The restrictions have had a significant impact on the free movement of people within the EU, with many individuals and businesses facing economic and personal disruption as a result. The literature has also shown that these measures have disproportionately affected certain groups, such as low-income workers and individuals from marginalized communities. Many studies have pointed out that the restrictions have also led to a decline in cross-border travel and trade, which has had a negative impact on the economy.

This chapter aims to analyse the different implementation of measures carried out by countries in the European region; the diversity of measures, as well as the different degree of restrictions taken by the states, shows us that the response to this problem, regarding the free movement of people, has not only been inconsistent but most of the time, ineffective.

Freedom of Movement in the EU Member States

Legal Development

The historical and legal development of free movement of people at the European level originate from the very beginning of the European Coal and Steel Community (the precursor of the current European Union). This regional organization developed around the liberalization of tariffs of these two raw materials and only recognized free movement for workers; however, the evolution of the concept and rights associated with this freedom would evolve around a concept that bridged the gap between national borders and international borders.

Today, it is governed by Article 21 of the Treaty on the Functioning of the European Union, which states that "Every citizen of the Union shall have the right to move and reside freely in the territory of the Member States, subject to the limitations and conditions provided for in the Treaties and in the provisions adopted for their application," as well as Article 3 of the Treaty on European Union, concerning the goals of the Union itself (Schade, 2021).

Moreover, the worldwide recognition of the right to freedom of movement is encapsulated in Article 13 of the 1948 Universal Declaration of Human Rights. The definition is completed by Articles 12 and 13 of the International Covenant on Civil and Political Rights; however, General Comment No. 27 of the United Nations Human Rights Committee provides a more in-depth explanation of the content of this human right. The Human Rights Committee develops and comments on the rights enshrined in Articles 12 and 13 of the ICCPR in this General Observation, establishing, among other things, that free movement of people is an essential condition for the free development of the person and that every person who is legally within the territory of a State has the right to move freely within it. This right, inextricably linked to the concept of human mobility, includes not only the aforementioned freedom of movement within a country but also the option of choosing residence within a State, freely leaving or returning to it (United Nations, 1967).

In the European Union, however, the concept of freedom of movement encompasses the economic expansion of the Schengen area. Despite this, the significance of European social ideals has increased as a result of the European Union's progress toward a more connected structure (Jiménez Garcia, 2014), therefore, freedom of movement now also has a social significance.

As a result, while it is a human right with great prodigality and breadth, it is not, like the vast majority—if not all—of the rights enshrined in the Universal Declaration of Human Rights, a right of absolute nature. This means that, while there is constant influence on the common characteristics that underpin Human Rights, such as their universality, indivisibility, and interdependence, their enjoyment in any circumstance free of State interference or limitations is only applicable to the prohibition of torture and inhuman or degrading treatment (Ramji-Nogales & Goldner, 2020).

The complete enjoyment of this right may be slightly restricted, as is common in international law and in regional European law, but such limitations or interference must be fair in light of the individual circumstances and in conformity with the terms and purposes of this right.

Most of the doctrine agrees that freedom of movement is the most well-known and respected benefit of EU citizenship. The mobility regime applicable to EU residents and their family members, which distinguishes them from citizens of third countries, is characterized by the ability to travel freely, problem-free, and without being burdened by paperwork, as well as the freedom to reside in another EU state (Guild, 2020b). EU residents do not need to meet any additional conditions in order to enter another EU country and stay there for the first three months. The sole requirement is a valid ID or passport. EU workers are entitled to the same treatment as national workers under EU law, and their employment in another EU state is not subject to work permits or quotas (Article 45 TFEU). The elimination of internal border controls within the Schengen area and the priority given to EU free movement legislation by the Schengen Borders Code, particularly while crossing borders, are further indications of the advantage enjoyed by EU nationals (Guild et al., 2019).

Due to the return of internal border controls and the imposition of outright travel bans or restrictions in response to the pandemic, EU members' freedom of movement has been severely restricted for the most of the year 2020. Reports of EU citizens being arrested at internal Schengen borders as a result of state border closure activities cast doubt on the utility of EU citizenship and the right to free movement in times of crisis. Similar concerns were voiced when the EU originally failed to respond swiftly enough to the rise of national law-based restrictions. In addition, the closure of internal EU borders has revealed how dependent the EU economy is on the labour of EU migrants, a situation made worse by the installation of an EU travel ban on its exterior borders.

National travel restrictions and prohibitions are permissible under EU law so long as they comply to the proportionality principle and do not discriminate against residents of other Member States residing in the host Member State. Transit restrictions for EU citizens and residents returning to their Member State, as well as exemptions to entry bans that apply only to nationals and not to EU citizens residing in other Member States, would therefore violate EU law.

Restrictions to Mobility

The free movement of people has a unique significance in the context of the European integration process, and it can also be restricted or limited, although the terminology used in European legislation (both in the Original Treaties and in derived law) is "proportionality" and not "reasonableness". A priori, it is vital to assess the activities of the various European states regarding containment measures for the population and the pandemic. This investigation reveals that two groups of states have decided to restrict this right.

Within the Schengen area, an initial set of 17 states implemented procedures to regulate their internal borders. These sorts of actions, which have not been seen since the founding of "a Europe without internal borders", not only brought back border controls with the Union's Member States but also strengthened their borders, if they ever had any, with third countries. This kind of measure would render the Schengen area ineffective a few weeks after the start of the pandemic. Furthermore, even though the "Schengen Borders Code" does not make any express mention of the possibility of reintroducing controls at internal borders, the European Commission, prior to the exceptional situation caused by the pandemic, decided to approve the restrictions imposed by the Member States by recognizing that a situation of uncontrollable contagious disease, such as the one caused by the pandemic (European Commission, 2020a).

The second group of states is comprised of those that have implemented restrictive measures for certain forms of transportation, including the suspension of travel by plane, train, or sea, as well as the prohibition of entry and exit from or to national territories. We have found ourselves with a vast catalogue of measures that are not only different from one another but are also frequently unconnected or contradictory, which is understandable given the disparate nature of the decisions that have been made by the various Member States of the Union. As a result, we can see that a large percentage of the prohibitions to enter and leave the national territory included exceptions for citizens of the country, people who had permanent residence, or foreigners who had passed a test; however, when applied to other states, these exceptions were limited to those that were justified by "valid reasons".

This legal "short circuit", which has been in effect in a community-based legislative area since the 1990s, is based on a criterion that is difficult to articulate, such as the notion of "public health". The Schengen Borders

Code, the Treaty of the Union in its wording from Lisbon, and other norms of derivative law of the European Union all make an exception for the internal borders of the Union, which have become detached and ethereal as a result of the European integration process and the entry into force of the Schengen agreement. This is because the internal borders of the Union are a consequence of the European integration process. In this sense, these principles clearly empower states to impose restrictions to the free movement of people for reasons of public health so long as they are administered in a manner that is non-discriminatory and appropriate to the issue at hand.

In this context, it is important to refer to Directive 2004/38/EC of the European Parliament and of the Council of April 29, 2004, which directly addresses this matter in its Chapter VI. This directive states that individual or collective restrictions on the right of free movement in Europe can only be invoked for reasons of serious risk to public health, as those terms are defined by the World Health Organization, and only under the condition that the disease in question is either infectious, parasitic, or of another type. In other words, the disease in question must meet all three.

On March 11, 2020, the WHO proclaimed COVID-19 a global pandemic. However, by February 2020, a number of EU states, notably Italy, were already reporting a dramatic increase in COVID-19 cases. Lombardy (among the wealthiest regions of the country) was hit the worst and had the most trouble providing medical care to victims. As COVID-19 took hold in February and March 2020, one of the first steps EU governments took was to close their international borders. There was a significant decrease in air traffic (Remuzzi & Remuzzi, 2020).

Ferry, bus, and train transportation soon followed. Despite the EU Heads of State or Government's March 10 announcement on the necessity for a coordinated EU action, these international border procedures began in a very disorganized manner (Zemskova, 2020). Extremely few states closed all international (or intra-EU) borders. However, the permitted motives for overseas travel varied considerably. Among the difficulties was getting agreement on permissible travel for essential and non-essential personnel (Paterlini, 2020). The European Commission was especially active in gaining Member State agreement that all EU (and Schengen-associated states) citizens and their family members must be excluded from temporary travel restrictions in order to return home. Schengen Member States have also begun to implement border controls on intra-Schengen travel. Here, both the Schengen Agreement and the Free

Movement Directive were involved (Davies, 2020). Schengen Borders Code does not permit Member States to prohibit entrance to EU nationals based on public health hazards, although the Free Movement Directive does (Eckardt et al., 2020).

As it can be seen in the Fig. 10.1, virtually all the members of the Union, as well as the rest of Europe, have taken measures to alleviate COVID-19. These measures have led to legitimate restrictions and prohibitions on the entry and exit of people from the country, as well as travel

Fig. 10.1 Travel restrictions between countries. (Source: EXCEPTIUS dataset, own rendering)

restrictions for citizens (Goldner Lang, 2021). Moreover, the kind of restrictions were not consistent or coordinated, especially during the first wave of the pandemic, which would lead to an array of different policies and positions regarding this topic.

By analysing the data collected by the EXCEPTIUS project one can see that—with slight differences—there were seven different policies regarding freedom of movement that range from no travel at all (including between countries and within the same country) to travel restrictions between certain countries.

Although in the past, and primarily for reasons of security, some European States have asserted exceptions to the general rule of free movement at the European level, the health crisis caused by COVID-19 has led to an unprecedented closure of the internal borders of the Union, or "soft borders", such as those of the community territories like Norway or Switzerland, which has ended up making a dent in the European systems of free movement and border management. COVID-19 has led to an unprecedented closure of the internal borders of the Union, because various states have chosen various solutions according to their priorities, which are often dictated by economic considerations. When confronted with such a disparity and taking into consideration the negative effects that the pandemic situation had on the European economy and markets, this would cause the European Union to try to give a more or less coordinated response in terms of mobility within and outside of the Union. This would be as a result of the pandemic situation (Montaldo, 2020).

When Europe became the epicentre of the pandemic in March 2020, politicians and public health agencies scrambled to identify acceptable and effective solutions. The EU obligation stipulated in Article 9 of the Treaty on the Functioning of the European Union (TFEU) compels the EU (including the Member States to achieve a common protection on human health, however, seems to have been missing from the responses). Instead, borders and their control became the subject of major political debate across Europe as a potential arena for implementing effective steps to prevent the pandemic's spread (Guild, 2020a).

While the more intrusive COVID-19 measures (lockdown, business closures, etc.) have been implemented within EU states (see Chazel's chapter), limitations on cross-border movement have been significant. In the European Union, this has relevant ramifications for EU law regarding border controls, particularly the free movement of individuals and the absence of border controls between Schengen states. It also entailed border restrictions with third countries, such as the European Free Trade Area (EFTA and Switzerland), the EU surrounding states, the United Kingdom (which left the EU on January 1, 2020), the Western Balkans, and Turkey. While EU law distinguishes between Schengen borders, where no controls are conducted on persons, non-Schengen EU borders, where controls are conducted but are limited to identity checks and border controls with third countries, and external borders with third countries (non-EFTA or Swiss), many Member States and EU institutions abandoned many of these distinctions in practice.

Indeed, the distinction between border controls between states (inside the Schengen area, the European Union, the European Free Trade Association, or outside) and internal limitations on travel grew increasingly muddled. Two approaches—public health and public policy—were implemented concurrently, although not necessarily in ways that were mutually consistent or consistent with the Article 9 TFEU commitment. While the public health approach to movement of persons is focused on guaranteeing identification of those in need of treatment or possibly carrying the disease, giving treatment as promptly as feasible, or quarantine, the public policy approach is based on refusing admission to persons who pose a risk, regardless of what that may mean in terms of the spread of the pandemic in surrounding or origin states.

The initial criticism of the European Union's response focused on its failure to match the recommendations for collective actions to the criteria of legality and proportionality under European Union law (Carrera & Chun Luk, 2020). Despite the preceding, an attempt was made to uphold the historic right to freedom of movement enjoyed by European citizens and their families. In relation to the shared borders of the Union, members were urged to implement travel and access limitations for "non-essential" employees from third countries between March and June 2020, with a progressive removal of restrictions dependent on the epidemiological status of the countries of origin (European Commission, 2020b).

This type of limits would be tied to the general requirement, based on international law, to readmit their nationals in any circumstance, as well as the obligation to respect this "right of return" not just for citizens but also for family members and other benefits of residence in union members. In this approach, not only would the fundamental rights of European residents be honoured, in terms of the right of return to the country of residence, but also the European law itself, under the rubric of the rights associated with European citizenship. In addition to diplomatic and consular protection, it includes this right to a safe return.

While European nationals continued to receive favoured or privileged treatment based on a probable departure—in some situations—and future return to their home country—in any case—intra-community mobility was not at the same level.

In the first few months of the pandemic, a small number of states would restrict, if not outright forbid, entry and leave, as seen in the Fig. 10.2. In the early days of the COVID-19 pandemic, many European countries implemented strict restrictions on freedom of movement to slow the spread of the virus and protect public health. Denmark, France, Italy, Malta, the Netherlands, Portugal, and Spain were among the countries that took such measures.

For example, all of these countries closed their borders to non-essential travel, and imposed a nationwide lockdown, which included requiring citizens to stay at home except for essential activities such as grocery shopping and exercise. Public gatherings were also banned, and businesses were forced to close or limit capacity. This was done in an attempt to slow

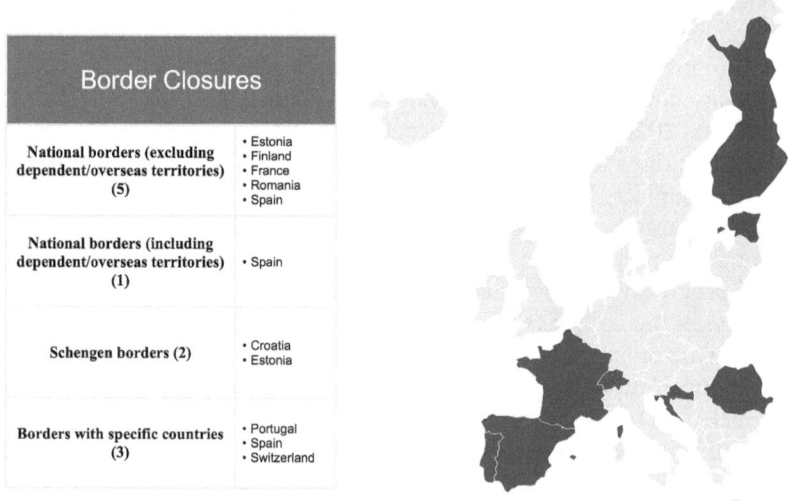

Fig. 10.2   Border closures. (Source: EXCEPTIUS dataset, own rendering)

the spread of the virus and protect public health. Additionally, some countries also introduced curfew and restricted the movement of people from certain areas.

As the situation progressed, these countries have adjusted their restrictions accordingly, based on their own unique situation. Some have lifted the restrictions, some have implemented targeted measures, and others have introduced a phased approach. While some have opened up their borders for travel and have lifted the curfew, others have continued to enforce strict measures. Each country has been closely monitoring the situation and taking decisions accordingly.

This would even prompt some nations to choose a complete closing of their borders, which has not occurred since the European unification project began. We can demonstrate that European nations have attempted numerous, frequently contradicting solutions to the problem of boundaries. Thus, certain countries would opt for strict border closures, which, in some cases like France, could include overseas territories, or the DOM-TOM (*départements d'outre-mer* and *territoires d'outre-mer*), while in other cases it would focus on specific bordering territories, such as the "hard closure" of the border between Spain and Morocco along the external border of the autonomous cities Ceuta and Melilla.

In the most extreme circumstances, we have a classification of countries that not only impose travel restrictions to and from their own country but also prohibit movement within the same state. This form of prohibition could range from a total closure of bordering national regions, provinces, or geographical divisions—such as autonomous communities in Spain or the *Länder* in Germany—to the prohibition of circulation between neighbouring municipalities in the case of Spain. In some instances, or in conjunction with the aforementioned, checkpoints, control points, or security controls between the various parts of the country would be included, as shown in Fig. 10.3 below.

Checkpoints are physical barriers set up to monitor and control the movement of people. During the pandemic, checkpoints have been used to prevent the spread of the virus by restricting travel between regions with high infection rates and those with lower infection rates. Checkpoints typically involve temperature checks, health screenings, and other measures to assess the risk of individuals carrying the virus.

Travel bans, on the other hand, are measures implemented by governments to completely ban non-essential travel to and from specific countries, regions or cities. These bans are put in place when a region is

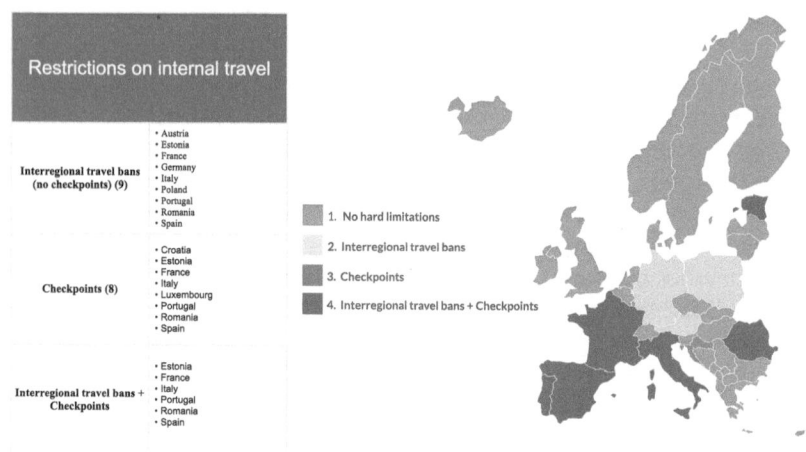

Fig. 10.3 Restrictions on internal travel. (Source: EXCEPTIUS dataset, own rendering)

experiencing a high rate of COVID-19 cases and the government wants to prevent the spread of the virus to other areas. Travel bans can also be imposed on individuals who have been in close contact with infected individuals or who have recently travelled to high-risk areas. The purpose of travel bans is to slow down or stop the spread of the virus by limiting the movement of potentially infected individuals.

The Lifting of Restrictions

Despite all these constraints, we discovered that many states would prefer to remove mobility or access restrictions for employees classified as "essential" by ESCO (European Skills, Competencies, Qualifications, and Occupations). This categorization encompasses a vast array of vocations at all levels of expertise, including health professionals, scientists working in health-related subjects, food manufacturers and food preparers, maintenance workers and transportation workers. This group of workers in crucial occupations is exceptional in that it transcends the legal distinctions between regular and unemployed workers. This includes regular mobile employees, frontier workers, posted workers, and, under certain circumstances, seasonal workers who perform vital jobs (Anderson et al., 2020).

In a number of EU nations, the agricultural and food industries have proven to be especially vulnerable. Therefore, seasonal agricultural workers who conduct essential harvesting, planting, or tending duties are regarded as performing essential labour (European Commission, 2020a). To enable border crossings with a consistent flow of border workers and posted workers, the Commission encouraged Member States to create specific procedures for seasonal workers. The proposed solution would include the construction of so-called special border corridors by some Member States for thousands of seasonal employees, a radical departure from the common view that the right to free movement of persons must be temporarily abandoned for the benefit of public health.

In addition, the way such mobility lanes were constructed and arranged, without taking public health precautions into account (Bejan, 2020), is inconsistent with existing measures against COVID-19, calling into question their adequacy. On the other hand, if it had been possible to organize such mobility corridors while adhering to all public health standards, one cannot help but wonder why it would not have been possible to do the same on a larger scale, thereby calling into question the need for mobility restrictions within and between European states.

In addition, there are divergent opinions regarding the reasonableness of travel restrictions and bans, taking into account other competing interests, that is, whether they justify the degree of interference with EU free movement. The answer to this question can vary depending on a society's level of wealth and its capacity to withstand the economic consequences of lockdowns. This explains why, in the summer of 2020, a number of EU Member States whose economies depend on tourism decided to loosen travel restrictions and bans, despite the fact that a number of them face a higher infection rate than in the winter or spring of 2020. In most cases, these are countries whose GDP depends to a large extent on tourism, such as Spain, where tourism represents approximately 13% of its GDP, or other countries such as Portugal, Italy, Greece, France or Italy with percentiles close to 10% (OECD, 2020).

Instead of evaluating national initiatives that promote mobility inside the EU to ensure compliance with EU legislation, the EU's approach was to protect economic interests and the integrity of the internal market. Restrictions on intra-EU mobility and a restriction on employee travel within the EU have highlighted the crucial role migrant workers will play in the economy, with some industries at risk of significant disruption in the case of labour shortages (Fasani & Mazza, 2020). The Commission considered a number of declarations specifying certain groups of individuals whose migration should not be restricted to vital occupations (European Commission, 2020b). EU citizens continued to hold a special status while performing crucial and necessary jobs.

CONCLUSION

The free movement of people has a unique significance in the context of the European integration process, and it can also be restricted or limited, although the terminology used in European legislation (both in the Original Treaties and in Derived Law) is "proportionality" and not "reasonableness". A priori, we can analyse the actions of the various European states in terms of population and pandemic containment measures, such that we can identify two groups of states that decided to implement restrictions on this right.

The application of the proportionality principle to COVID-19-alleviating policies that restrict the free movement of people creates particular challenges. Given the inherent scientific ambiguity underlying COVID-19, it can be difficult to determine if a given restrictive measure, such as the introduction of border restrictions or a travel ban, is proportional to the amount of human health protection it offers. Before the eventual emergence of another global sickness or pandemic.

It is far more difficult to evaluate if travel limits or bans and border controls meet rigorous requirements of need and proportionality, despite the fact that they are plainly adequate for protecting public health and aiding in the reduction of virus infections. Reduce the number of personal contacts and transmissions of the SARS-CoV-2 virus. The level of knowledge about COVID-19 at the time that the majority of EU Member States decided to impose strict travel restrictions and bans was insufficient and inconclusive to determine with certainty that any less restrictive alternative measures would protect the interests of public health with the same level of effectiveness, which calls into question whether the necessity criterion has been met, especially when we consider the disparity in decision-making among EU Member States.

REFERENCES

Anderson, M., Mckee, M., & Mossialos, E. (2020). COVID-19 exposes weaknesses in European response to outbreaks. *BMJ, 368*(1). https://doi.org/10.1136/bmj.m1075

Bejan, R. (2020). COVID-19 and disposable migrant workers. *Verfassungsblog*, April 16. Retrieved April 20, 2022, from https://verfassungsblog.de/COVID-19-and-disposable-migrant-workers

Carrera, S., & Chun Luk, N. (2020). *In the name of COVID-19: An assessment of the Schengen internal border controls and travel restrictions in the EU*. Policy Department for Citizens' Rights and Constitutional Affairs, Directorate-General for Internal Policies. Retrieved May 20, 2022, from https://www.europarl.europa.eu/RegData/etudes/STUD/2020/659506/IPOL_STU(2020)659506_EN.pdf

Davies, G. T. (2020). Does evidence-based EU law survive the COVID-19 pandemic? Considering the status in EU law of lockdown measures which affect Free Movement. *Frontiers in Human Dynamics, 2*(584486). https://doi.org/10.3389/fhumd.2020.584486

Eckardt, M., Kappner, K., & Wolf, N. (2020). *COVID-19 across European regions: The role of border controls*. Elsevier.

Egger, C., de Saint-Phalle, E., Magni-Berton, R., Aarts, K., & Roché, S. (2022). EXCEPTIUS Dataset v1.0. https://doi.org/10.34894/TTS0MF

European Commission. (2020a). Communication from the Commission to the European Parliament, the European Council and the Council COVID-19: Temporary restriction on non-essential travel to the EU. COM/2020/115. Retrieved June 7, 2022, from https://eur-lex.europa.eu/legal-content/EN/TXT/HTML/?uri=CELEX:52020DC0115&from=EN

European Commission. (2020b). *Communication from the Commission*. Guidelines Concerning the Exercise of the Free Movement of Workers During COVID-19 Outbreak. 2020/C 102 I/03. Retrieved June 7, 2022, from https://eur-lex.europa.eu/legal-content/EN/TXT/?uri=CELEX%3A52020XC0330%2803%29

Fasani, F., & Mazza, J. (2020). Immigrant key workers: Their contribution to Europe's COVID-19 response. *IZA Policy Paper*, No. 155. http://ftp.iza.org/pp155.pdf

Goldner Lang, I. (2021). *'Laws of fear' in the EU: The precautionary principle and public health restrictions to free movement of persons in the time of COVID-19*. Cambridge University Press.

Guild, E. (2020a). COVID-19 using border controls to fight a pandemic? Reflections from the European Union. *Frontiers in Human Dynamics, 2*(606299). https://doi.org/10.3389/fhumd.2020.606299

Guild, E. (2020b). Who wants to be an EU citizen? In S. Mantu, P. Minderhoud, & E. Guild (Eds.), *EU citizenship and free movement rights* (pp. 17–35). Brill Nijhoff.

Guild, E., Peers, S., & Tomkin, J. (2019). *The EU citizenship directive: A commentary*. Oxford University Press.

Jiménez Garcia, F. (2014). Tomarse en Serio el Derecho Internacional de los Derechos Humanos. Especial Referencia a los Derechos Sociales, el Derecho a la Vivienda y la Prohibición de los Desalojos Forzosos. *Revista Española de Derecho Constitucional, Centro de Estudios Políticos y Constitucionales, 101*(1), 79–124.

Koutrakos, P., Shuibhne, N. N., & Syrpis, P. (2016). *Exceptions from EU free movement law: Derogation, justification and proportionality*. Bloomsbury Publishing.

Montaldo, S. (2020). The COVID-19 emergency and the reintroduction of internal border controls in the Schengen area: Never let a serious crisis go to waste. *European Forum*, April 25. Retrieved March 11, 2022, from https://www.europeanpapers.eu/en/europeanforum/COVID-19-emergency-and-reintroduction-internal-border-controls-schengen-area

OECD. (2020). 'EC' policy responses to Coronavirus (COVID-19): Tourism policy responses to the Coronavirus (COVID-19). Retrieved June 7, 2022, from https://www.oecd.org/coronavirus/policy-responses/tourism-policy-responses-to-the-coronavirus-COVID-19-6466aa20/

Paterlini, M. (2020). Closing borders is ridiculous: The epidemiologist behind Sweden's controversial coronavirus strategy. *Nature, 580*, 574. https://doi.org/10.1038/d41586-020-01098

Ramji-Nogales, J., & Goldner Lang, I. (2020). Freedom of movement, migration, and borders. *Journal of Human Rights, 19*(5), 593–602. https://doi.org/10.1080/14754835.2020.1830045

Remuzzi, A., & Remuzzi, G. (2020). COVID-19 and Italy: What next? *Lancet, 395*, 1225–1228. https://doi.org/10.1016/S0140-6736(20)30627-9

Schade, D. (2021). Crisis-proof Schengen and freedom of movement: Lessons from the COVID-19 pandemic. *Hertie School, Jacques Delors Centre*, May 25. Retrieved November 31, 2022, from https://opus4.kobv.de/opus4-hsog/frontdoor/deliver/index/docId/3929/file/210525_Schengen_Schade_JDI-Paper.pdf

United Nations. (1967). Protocol relating to the status of refugees: 606 UNTS 267. https://www.refworld.org/docid/3ae6b3ae4.html

Zemskova, A. (2020). Guest note on the impact of the COVID-19 outbreak of EU law. *Nordic Journal of European Law, 3*(1), 3–9.

CHAPTER 11

COVID-19 and Asylum Rights

*Cristina Churruca-Muguruza, Anca Cretu,
and Gorka Urrutia-Asua*

INTRODUCTION

The COVID-19 pandemic had and continues to have multiple impacts in many areas (political, social, cultural, economic, etc.). Some of these were directly affected in the early stages of the pandemic, with governments responding to the pandemic in a variety of ways. In the case of the European Union (EU), the Member States adopted a wide range of measures, including, particularly in the early stages, punitive and coercive measures, which were closely scrutinised for their impact on the exercise of fundamental rights. Moreover, the measures developed dynamically during the different stages of the pandemic. At the beginning, the official

C. Churruca-Muguruza (✉) • G. Urrutia-Asua
Faculty of Social and Human Sciences, Human Rights Institute,
University of Deusto, Bilbao, Spain
e-mail: cristina.churruca@deusto.es; gorka.urrutia@deusto.es

A. Cretu
Hegoa, Institute for International Cooperation and Development Studies,
University of the Basque Country (UPV/EHU), Bilbao, Spain
e-mail: anca.cretu@ehu.eus

© The Author(s) 2024
C. Egger et al. (eds.), *Covid-19 Containment Policies in Europe*,
International Series on Public Policy,
https://doi.org/10.1007/978-3-031-52096-9_11

formalities were closer to a context of high insecurity than to a pandemic. During the second and third waves, the role of legal threats and police reports became more meaningful than before, clearly showing that their role was ancillary, not nuclear, and that we were facing a pandemic, not a security problem. Inequalities in general have been exacerbated, and they particularly impacted vulnerable groups.

The purpose of this chapter is to provide some insights into the situation of a specific vulnerable group that has received little attention—migrants and asylum seekers. The intersection of the COVID-19 pandemic and the ongoing challenges of asylum and migration along the EU's southern border has exacerbated the difficulties of an already complex issue. The pandemic has deepened existing challenges on a number of fronts, from legal and procedural ones to ensuring basic human rights and dignified living conditions. Amidst the urgent focus on public health, the measures taken have often led to a reduction in asylum applications and, in some cases, to an effective suspension of asylum procedures.

The chapter is divided into four parts. The first presents the context and the exceptional measures adopted with the emergence of the COVID-19 pandemic in the EU, highlighting the main issues. The second part analyses the impact of these measures on the right to asylum at EU level, highlighting the main approaches and measures taken by Member States and their impact on fundamental rights. The third part focuses on Europe's southern border. This particular region contains a high concentration of challenges related to asylum and migration in Europe, due to its geographical proximity to Africa and its status as the first point of entry for many migrants and asylum seekers. The fourth section provides an in-depth analysis of the unique situation of migrants and asylum seekers in Melilla, a specific but representative context within the Spanish southern border. It is here that the interplay between pandemic response, border control and the treatment of vulnerable populations can be most clearly observed.

Fundamental Rights in the Context of the Pandemic

Context and Main Challenges

The EXCEPTIUS dataset provides comprehensive data on the range of measures implemented across Europe in response to the pandemic. While existing strategies varied from one country to the next, they were generally centred on a shared set of themes that embodied the severity of the crisis. These measures encompassed: (1) the limitation of the freedom of movement (a vast majority of European nations enacted severe lockdowns, primarily confining their citizens to their homes); (2) the disruption of conventional education systems (many countries suspended in-person classes); (3) the restriction of non-essential commercial activities (businesses within the hospitality, entertainment, and leisure sectors); (4) contention of worship services and (5) the reinforcement of healthcare systems.

The COVID-19 pandemic's unprecedented challenges also precipitated numerous tensions and debates throughout the European Union, both at social and political levels, as well as legal. New mechanisms were introduced to facilitate governance during these testing times, shedding light on several key problematics that echoed across Member States:

- Prioritisation of security and detention measures. Many European countries prioritised security measures during the initial months of the pandemic. In addition to focusing on public health responses, countries implemented tough restrictions to maintain law and order, often accompanied by heightened police and military presence. The emphasis on enforcement and compliance, especially through penalties and fines, evoked a martial atmosphere, causing apprehension and resistance among populations.
- Debate over limitation or suspension of civil rights. Directly related to the security focus, the debate on the limitation or suspension of rights has been a key issue and a highly politicised one across the EU. Various national courts across the EU, among them the Spanish Constitutional Court (Tribunal Constitucional 2021), evaluated the constitutionality of the restrictive measures implemented. The discourse highlighted a critical dichotomy—the urgency to control the pandemic versus the potential erosion of civil liberties.
- Public confusion and legal insecurity. The sudden imposition of strict measures led to significant confusion among citizens due to insufficient communication from authorities about permissible activities during lockdowns. Regulations often appeared ambiguous, generating legal uncertainty and providing law enforcement authorities with extensive powers, which in turn led to accusations of discriminatory practices (Civic Space Watch, 2020). States generally did not consider the condition of the population with a non-regularised admin-

istrative situation that were affected by the immigration laws. Many of them were working on some of the so-called essential services (domestic work, agriculture) and were not able to prove the need to circulate.

While it may seem self-evident that the COVID-19 pandemic has irreversibly changed our global reality, the specific impact of this change is highly nuanced and varies significantly according to individual socioeconomic circumstances and living conditions. In recent years, there has been an outpouring of academic work examining the disproportionate impact of the pandemic, with a clear focus on the exacerbation of pre-existing inequalities (Bambra et al., 2020; World Bank, 2021). Certain measures—restrictions on movement, border closures, quarantine and isolation measures, closure of schools and universities—have had particularly harsh consequences for certain vulnerable populations and have generated controversy and criticism from a range of national and international organisations. In particular, a vulnerable group—migrants and asylum seekers—has been disproportionately affected by both the pandemic itself and the measures taken in response.

For many migrants and asylum seekers, border closures and restrictions resulted in limited access to international protection. In addition, those already in the EU faced increased health risks due to poor conditions in overcrowded reception centres. Since the beginning of the COVID-19 crisis, several international and human rights institutions have called for fundamental rights to be taken into account in the fight against the pandemic. Most of these institutions carried out initiatives to monitor the human rights situation in general and the situation of specific (vulnerable) groups.

One of these bodies, the EU Fundamental Rights Agency, has produced reports over the past 3 years monitoring the general human rights situation and the plight of specific vulnerable groups. A comprehensive report in 2021 draws attention to three main areas of concern: (1) states of emergency and other emergency situations; (2) the impact on key areas of daily life, such as social life, healthcare, education, work, business, justice, travel and privacy; and (3) the impact on specific groups in society, including the elderly, disabled, victims of domestic violence, ethnic minorities, Roma, LGBTQ+ people, homeless people, prisoners, migrants and asylum seekers (Fundamental Rights Agency, 2021). The report underlines that the challenge to fundamental rights posed by the pandemic has been particularly severe for the most vulnerable populations. The following section examines the impact of COVID-19 measures on the right to seek asylum in the European Union.

COVID-19 and the Right to Asylum in the European Union

Since the beginning of the so-called migration crisis that started in 2015, the European asylum system has been challenged by various crises and discrepancies between Member States. Reception centres were often overcrowded and under-resourced, and asylum procedures were long, confusing and full of administrative obstacles. The sudden onset of the pandemic exacerbated these already difficult conditions, affecting both the physical and procedural aspects of the asylum system. The impact of the COVID-19 pandemic on this already complex system was multifaceted and significant, resulting in changes that deserve to be studied.

The application of the Dublin Regulation, which determines which Member State is responsible for processing an asylum application, was significantly disrupted. Asylum procedures were effectively frozen in some states due to the border closures, leading to an administrative backlog and causing considerable delays in processing asylum claims (European Asylum Support Office, 2021). Nevertheless, there were notable differences in the specifics of the legislation adopted by each country, based on their legal frameworks, the evolution of the pandemic and the guidance of the health authorities.

Table 11.1 provides a clear picture of the trends in the number of asylum applications in the EU at the start of the pandemic. At EU level, there was a sharp decline in applications, dropping from 55,735 in February to a mere 7990 in April. This drastic reduction is reflective of the widespread limitations put in place by the Member States due to the health crisis. France, Germany, Spain, and Greece, four of the countries with the highest number of asylum applications in February, saw significant reductions in their numbers.

Germany, despite experiencing a sharp decrease, still led with the most significant number of applications in April. Germany's approach to asylum seekers during the COVID-19 pandemic was marked by a reduction in asylum-related activities but without complete suspension. The processing of asylum applications was delayed due to pandemic measures and asylum seekers were provided with temporary residence permits and were urged to stay within their initial reception centres to maintain control over social

Table 11.1   First-time asylum applicants—monthly data

Country	February 2020	March 2020	April 2020
Austria	960	755	320
Belgium	1625	895	170
Bulgaria	35	70	60
Croatia	145	80	30
Cyprus	1285	790	55
Czechia	90	40	15
Denmark	160	105	35
Estonia	10	0	0
Finland	205	130	50
France	9920	6015	175
Germany	11,030	7865	5620
Greece	8510	2320	0
Hungary	25	5	5
Ireland	240	175	30
Italy	3060	850	120
Latvia	5	25	5
Lithuania	25	5	0
Luxembourg	120	120	25
Malta	285	105	0
Netherlands	1500	1005	265
Poland	235	85	10
Portugal	130	120	5
Romania	320	335	60
Slovakia	15	10	10
Slovenia	130	150	15
Spain	14,210	7960	60
Sweden	1450	1475	845
European Union	55,735	31,475	7990

Source: Eurostat (2023a)

distancing and movement (Reches, 2022). Despite these measures, the right to seek asylum was still upheld, which could partly explain why Germany had a comparatively higher number of asylum applications even in April.

The situation in Spain was particularly notable for the severity of the fall in applications. The reduction from 7960 in March to just 60 in April is indicative of the extreme measures taken. Spain enforced strict border controls and declared a state of alert, resulting in a de facto suspension of asylum procedures. Furthermore, the general measures of detention and

social distancing, which affected face-to-face services in asylum procedures, led to the suspension of appointments for the formalisation of asylum applications and preliminary interviews (Pinyol-Jiménez et al., 2020).
Asylum seekers were unable to submit applications, which led to an almost
complete halt in registered applications.

Sweden presents a contrasting picture. There was a slight increase in
asylum applications from February to March, followed by a decrease in
April. However, the decrease was not as dramatic as in other countries.
One possible explanation is that Sweden took a more lenient approach to
COVID-19 restrictions in the early months of the pandemic than other
European countries. Although the country introduced some measures to
limit the spread of the virus, these were less stringent and may have allowed
more asylum procedures to continue.

Interestingly, some countries, like Bulgaria and Romania, saw an initial
increase in applications from February to March, only to follow the general descending trend in April. In contrast, other states, such as Estonia,
Lithuania and Malta, reduced the number of applications to zero by April,
indicating a complete halt in their asylum procedures during this period.

If we look at the evolution of first-time asylum applications in the EU
in annual terms (see Table 11.2), the figures further point to a considerable shift, underlining the substantial effect of the COVID-19 pandemic
on the right to seek asylum. Across the EU, there was a significant con-
traction in asylum applications, down from 631,285 in 2019 to 417,070 in
2020. Again, countries such as Germany, France, Spain, and Greece that
traditionally received most asylum seekers saw drastic reductions in applications in 2020. The stringent measures they adopted during the pandemic—such as border securitisation practices and suspension of asylum
procedures—have had a pronounced effect on individuals' ability to seek
protection.

Nonetheless, the data also display interesting anomalies. Both Bulgaria
and Romania experienced increases in asylum applications from 2019 to
2020, despite the pandemic. This could reflect a reorientation of migration routes caused by strengthened restrictions elsewhere, further displaying how these measures can lead to unintended shifts in asylum-seeking
patterns. Austria, too, experienced rise in application numbers during this
period, a trend running counter to most EU countries. Its adaptation of
asylum procedures in response to the pandemic was comparatively less
restrictive, enabling more individuals to exercise their right to seek asylum.
During the first months of the COVID-19 pandemic, Austria reduced

Table 11.2   Asylum and first-time asylum applicants—yearly data

Country	2019	2020
Austria	10,985	13,400
Belgium	23,105	12,905
Bulgaria	2075	3460
Croatia	1265	1540
Cyprus	12,695	7065
Czechia	1570	790
Denmark	2605	1420
Estonia	100	45
Finland	2445	1445
France	138,290	81,735
Germany	142,450	102,525
Greece	74,910	37,860
Hungary	465	90
Ireland	4740	1535
Italy	35,005	21,330
Latvia	180	145
Lithuania	625	260
Luxembourg	2200	1295
Malta	4015	2410
Netherlands	22,485	13,660
Poland	2765	1510
Portugal	1735	900
Romania	2455	6025
Slovakia	215	265
Slovenia	3615	3465
Spain	115,175	86,380
Sweden	23,125	13,595
European Union	631,285	417,070

Source: Eurostat (2023b)

asylum activities but did not suspend them. Nevertheless, the restrictions imposed in order to be allowed access to Austrian territory included the obligation to present a valid health certificate, thus undermining the right to asylum (AIDA, 2020a).

The case of Hungary is also noteworthy. Following the closure of borders, there was no access to the asylum procedure. Since the so-called migration crisis in 2015, a state of emergency due to mass migration was still in effect at the time of the pandemic. The police was authorised to pushback across the border fence irregularly staying migrants (including those who sought asylum) from any part of the country, without any legal procedure or opportunity to challenge this measure (AIDA, 2020b). This resulted in a low number of asylum applications (90 in 2020).

What the data reveals is how the fundamental right to seek asylum has been affected by COVID-19 in different ways across Europe. Whether through outright denial of access or the unintended consequences of restrictive measures, the right to seek asylum has been dramatically affected, with potential long-term consequences for both asylum seekers and EU countries. The situation across the European Union was largely influenced by each country's approach to the pandemic, its geographical location and its pre-existing asylum policies. The different outcomes underline the wide range of impacts of the pandemic on asylum seekers and the different responses of EU Member States. In the following section, we will take a closer look at the specific case of asylum seekers at Europe's southern border and provide a more detailed analysis of the challenges and implications in this particular context.

ASYLUM SEEKERS AND BORDER MANAGEMENT PRACTICES IN THE SOUTHERN EUROPEAN BORDER: THE CASE OF MELILLA

Asylum Seekers and the European Southern Border

The EU's southern border is a particular area where the challenges of migration and border control are most pronounced, compounded by the geographical realities of the Mediterranean. Regional strategies to manage this situation have evolved into a mixed approach of externalisation and securitisation, further complicated by the COVID-19 pandemic. Greece, Italy, Malta and Spain, with their proximity to Africa and the Middle East, have become the main entry points for those seeking refuge.

In the years leading up to the pandemic, the securitisation and externalisation of the EU's southern border became increasingly evident. This involved the extension of border controls and responsibilities beyond the geographical borders of the EU and the involvement of third countries in border control efforts. The pandemic reinforced these tendencies, with increased military presence and practices such as pushbacks and indirect refoulement raising serious human rights concerns.

In the case of Greece, the pandemic situation added to the challenges of an already undermined asylum system with the temporary closure of asylum offices and the suspension of administrative deadlines for asylum applications. In addition, the escalation in arrivals, coupled with the need to maintain public health measures, led to strained resources and critical conditions in migrant camps. Vulnerable groups, including women and minors, were detained without proper identification of their vulnerability or individual assessment prior to detention. Despite legal provisions on access to social assistance for beneficiaries of international protection, bureaucratic barriers meant that many were unable to access these rights and benefits. The Greek government used the virus as a pretext to extend the suspension of asylum, making asylum-seekers more vulnerable due to their stay in overcrowded reception centres and continued uncertainty about their refugee status (Reches, 2022).

In Italy, the government managed to maintain legal procedures for asylum applications throughout the pandemic. However, access to the system was complicated by delays and logistical challenges. Asylum seekers were often subjected to de facto detention in hotspots. Italian ports were declared unsafe between April and July 2020, and several cases of indirect refoulement to Libya were reported during this period, suggesting a precarious situation for refugees (AIDA, 2020c). Individuals arriving in Italy were quarantined for 10 days, after which they had access to reception facilities, but in hotspots there was de facto detention of asylum seekers.

Malta, one of the smallest but most important countries in this context, took a tough approach to the crisis. It closed its borders completely in March 2020 and refused to allow any migrants to disembark, including those rescued at sea by the Maltese authorities (Government of Malta, 2020), who were instead detained on private vessels outside territorial waters without any individual assessment, including vulnerable persons such as minors. The legal regime under which they were detained varied according to their nationality, with some detained under the Reception Conditions Directive without the possibility to challenge their detention, while others were detained under public health legislation or without any legal basis. These practices were found to be unlawful by the Maltese courts (AIDA, 2020d). Access to detention centres for NGOs and others was restricted during the COVID-19 pandemic, leaving detained migrants without information or legal representation.

Finally, Spain, as one of the principal gateways into Europe, experienced considerable pressures on its asylum system. At the start of the pandemic, a de facto suspension of the right to asylum was enacted as a result of the national state of alarm. This led to an abrupt 99% drop in asylum applications between March and April 2020 (see Table 11.1). This was especially notable in the autonomous cities of Ceuta and Melilla, where strengthened border controls significantly reduced the number of asylum applications. During the second half of the year 2020, the exceptional nature of the almost non-existent arrival of new applicants by air was maintained, but the number of people arriving by sea, especially to the Canary Islands doubled—from 20,103 in 2019 to 40,106 in 2020 (Lo Coco et al., 2021). The paralysation of the transfer of people from the Canary Islands, Ceuta and Melilla to the peninsula, overwhelmed an already undermined reception system and intensified the policy of blocking migrants in territories outside the Iberian Peninsula. This situation, characterised by bureaucratic hurdles, detentions and deportations, severely interrupted access to asylum procedures.

The geographical realities of the Mediterranean, coupled with the socio-political complexities of the region and the pandemic, highlight systemic challenges in the EU's approach to asylum, exacerbating existing problems (long waiting times, detention of vulnerable applicants without individual assessment, inadequate legal assistance, backlogs, etc.) and introducing new ones (temporary closure of asylum offices, suspension of administrative deadlines, etc.). The comparative analysis of the four countries reveals a common thread of increased securitisation and strained resources, further undermining the right to asylum. In the next section, we analyse the unique situation of Melilla and its role in the European migration and asylum system. A closer look at Melilla serves to illustrate the different layers of externalisation in action and to highlight the main aspects of the EU's approach to border management.

Melilla: A Case Study of Enforcement and Detention Practices at the EU's Southern Border

Melilla, the only European land border with Africa, a condition shared only by Ceuta, is located at a European migratory crossroads. Before the adoption of the exceptional measures of the COVID-19 pandemic, these two territories were already exceptional. The management of the southern border plays an important role in the externalisation of European border control, which has been accompanied by a steady erosion of the rights of migrants, refugees and asylum seekers to enter and settle in the European

Union (Castles, 2003; Rijpma & Cremona, 2007; Lemberg-Pedersen, 2012; Moreno-Lax & Lemberg-Pedersen, 2019; Churruca-Muguruza 2019). For this reason, over the last three decades, Melilla has become increasingly important as a gateway for migratory flows from Morocco, the sub-Saharan region and, more recently, the Middle East. This, in turn, has transformed Melilla into an exceptionally securitised city (Gabrielli, 2015; González-Páramo et al., 2019; Johnson & Jones, 2016).

The practice of various forms of pushback through the gates that mark the fences and in Melilla's territorial waters is constant, as are returns at the border with only formal guarantees, usually to implement the 1992 bilateral readmission agreement (Ministerio de Asuntos Exteriores, 1992). Administrative malpractice persists in the failure to process the documentation of foreign minors under administrative guardianship, leaving them in an irregular situation when they reach the age of majority. The slow pace of DNA testing and excessive administrative zeal condemn family members to separation when it comes to minors under the guardianship of the Autonomous City of Melilla. In addition, asylum seekers are not transferred until their case has been resolved, which can take months (Buades Fuster et al., 2020).

The city's geopolitical location explains why the management of this southern border has long been of particular interest to contain unwanted migration flows. A robust non-entry regime, 'Fortress Europe', was gradually built to protect European borders (Jüneman et al., 2019; Orchard, 2014; Zetter, 2014). With the entry into force of the Schengen Agreement in 1995, Spain developed a more elaborate border control policy, erecting increasingly high fences around the two enclaves of Melilla and Ceuta.

Spain was the first EU country to erect fences on its external borders to prevent migrants and refugees from entering European territory. In Melilla, those who manage to jump over the three fences without being immediately returned, the so-called rejection at the border, have the right under Spanish law to be temporarily housed in the Centre for the Temporary Stay of Immigrants (CETI). They can also move freely in Melilla while their expulsion procedure for administrative irregularity or their asylum application is being processed.

When the Spanish government declared the state of alarm on 14 March 2020, the CETI was overcrowded. Throughout 2020, the CETI, which has an initial capacity of 780 people, was inhabited by more than 1600 people. Two hundred of them were minors who had come with their families. On 21 March, in a state of alert and with the aim of limiting the spread of COVID-19, the authorities decided to temporarily close the land crossings authorised for entry into and exit from Spain via the cities of Ceuta and Melilla (Ministerio del Interior 2020). The number of irregular entries fell drastically when the border with Morocco was closed, but few entries still took place. In order to prevent the spread of the pandemic, Order No. 3221 of 25 August 2020 on coercive preventive health measures to be applied in the municipality of Melilla suspended the free entry and exit of persons in the CETI (Ciudad Autónoma de Melilla 2020).

The lack of suitable places for initial reception and detention meant that temporary facilities had to be improvised for this purpose. People were housed in tents in an improvised space in an area close to the border fence called V Pino, in extremely unhygienic conditions. Spaces such as the Melilla bullring and the mosque were also used, which also did not meet the conditions for housing people. The V Pino, which closed on 31 May 2020, housed over 200 people, including Moroccans trapped in Melilla, homeless Melillans and young migrants who have just come of age (Soto, 2020), on the outskirts of the autonomous city, in poorly waterproof tents that filtered rainwater, with overcrowded bunks and few blankets. Health care was a particular concern, as medical teams did not visit regularly. Conditions in the bullring were no better. The Geum Dodou Association reported that people in this area were living in very degrading and unsanitary conditions, with no place for new arrivals to be quarantined separately from the rest of the group.

During the periods in which the confinement was mitigated by allowing the population to go out during certain time slots according to age, people were not allowed to leave the CETI or the temporary facilities under any circumstances, not even to buy food. And although each shelter is allowed to adopt its own rules to guarantee the health of the people living there, these rules have never been published and are not covered by any specific legal framework within the state of emergency or approved by any court.

Of particular concern was the situation of school-age children and adolescents, who had no access to education. The blockade policy meant that there was no policy for the distribution of minors from the autonomous cities of Ceuta and Melilla to the rest of the autonomous communities, leading to the search for unsafe means of arrival on the peninsula. In addition, the blockade and the conditions in the Child Protection Centres in Melilla have led many minors to take to the streets, with all the health and emotional problems that this entails. Likewise, the lack of clear criteria for deciding on access to the CETI has left some on the streets waiting to travel to the peninsula.

During the months of the pandemic, the "La Purisima" Residential Educational Centre for Minors housed 900 minors, creating a situation of overcrowding in the context of the health emergency. From November 2020 to July 2021, successive measures restricting freedom of movement, "preventive health measures of a coercive nature," were applied to minors residing in "La Purísima" in view of the appearance of outbreaks of COVID 19. For the same reason, restrictive measures were also adopted in December 2020, suspending the free entry and exit of people staying in the Plaza de Toros at the Municipal Shelter for Transients and Disadvantaged People of the City of Melilla.

The situation in Melilla is a stark reminder of the human rights concerns and logistical challenges posed by the externalisation of European border control. These problems have been exacerbated by the pandemic, underlining the need for adequate facilities and fair asylum procedures at these key points of entry into Europe.

Conclusion

The COVID-19 pandemic has been an unprecedented situation that has brought many extraordinary measures not imposed before. These measures and their impacts have generated many tensions between authorities at different levels and between authorities and citizens. The confinements, limitations on the freedom of movement and border closures have exponentially aggravated the situation of an especially vulnerable group such as asylum seekers and have posed serious challenges in terms of access to the right to asylum. The closure of internal and external EU borders and the suspension of resettlement programmes not only reduced asylum seekers' chances of reaching safety but also increased the risks associated with irregular journeys to the EU, exacerbating the challenges faced by those fleeing persecution or conflict.

During the states of alarm and even after, migrants and asylum seekers have seen their rights limited beyond what is established in the regulations governing the state of alarm and have lived with deficient minimum services such as lack of food, water and healthcare, among others. In particular, in Melilla the already daunting reception conditions and coercive measures were intensified with the excuse of the pandemic. The Ministry of Interior minimised the transfer of migrants and applicants for international protections from Melilla to the mainland. This is a dissuasive strategy used by the authorities to prevent people from seeking asylum. It carries with it forms of restriction and deprivation of liberty without legal basis. And, it has placed people in a legal limbo if they did not have an identity card relating to their stay. Moreover, this policy has consequences for the public health of the entire population as it subjects the migrant population housed in temporary facilities to undignified living conditions.

In conclusion, while the pandemic has posed significant challenges to the European asylum system, it has also exposed structural weaknesses and highlighted the need for robust and flexible mechanisms that can adapt to unexpected situations and ensure that the rights of asylum seekers are protected in all circumstances. It is crucial that the strategies adopted do not further marginalise these vulnerable groups or undermine their fundamental rights. The experience of the COVID-19 pandemic, especially in border countries such as those in the Mediterranean, highlights the urgent need for a comprehensive, humane and cooperative approach to managing the migration and asylum situation in the EU. Finally, the institutions should adopt policies to prevent the use of crises—whether health crises such as the pandemic or other forms of emergency—as a justification for further violations of the rights of migrants and asylum seekers.

Acknowledgements The author, Anca Cretu, would like to acknowledge that the preliminary research and data collection for this chapter was carried out while she was a member of the Pedro Arrupe Human Rights Institute at the University of Deusto. However, the final drafting and finalisation of this chapter was carried out during her doctoral studies at the University of the Basque Country, supported by the Basque government under Grant Agreement PRE_2022_2_0132.

REFERENCES

AIDA. (2020a). Country report: Austria. Retrieved May 18, 2022, from https://asylumineurope.org/wp-content/uploads/2021/04/AIDA-AT_2020update.pdf.
AIDA. (2020b). Country report: Hungary. Retrieved May 19, 2022, from https://asylumineurope.org/wp-content/uploads/2021/04/AIDA-HU_2020update.pdf.
AIDA. (2020c). Country report: Italy. Retrieved May 16, 2022, from https://asylumineurope.org/wp-content/uploads/2021/06/AIDA-IT_2020update.pdf.

AIDA. (2020d). Country report: Malta. Retrieved December 29, 2022, from https://asylumineurope.org/wp-content/uploads/2021/05/AIDA-MT_2020update.pdf.

Bambra, C., Riordan, R., Ford, J., & Matthews, F. (2020). The COVID-19 pandemic and health inequalities. *Journal of Epidemiology and Community Health, 74*(11), 965. https://doi.org/10.1136/jech-2020-214401

Buades Fuster, S. J., Josep, Calderoni, M. V., Delpino, D. F.-M., & Castellano, D. M. (2020). *Seeking a way out. Report on the Southern border.* SJM.

Castles, S. (2003). The international policy of forced migration. *Migration and Development, 1*, 1–28.

Churruca-Muguruza, C. (2019). Shrinking protection space through gatekeeping and fencing strategies: The impact of EU's Migration Control on the Protection of Asylum Seekers and Forced Migrants at EU's External Borders. SYIL, 170–182; FRA, Migration: Fundamental Rights Issues at Land Borders. Publications Office of the European Union.

Ciudad Autónoma de Melilla - Consejería de Economía y Políticas Sociales. (2020). Orden n° 3221 de fecha 25 de agosto de 2020, relativa a medidas sanitarias preventivas de carácter coercitivo a aplicar en el término municipal de la Ciudad de Melilla, BOME EXTRA N° 41 - martes, 25 de agosto de 2020. https://bomemelilla.es/bome/BOME-BX-2020-4.

Civic Space Watch. (2020). Spain: Human rights and support networks in Spain in times of pandemic. https://civicspacewatch.eu/spain-human-rights-and-support-networks-in-spain-in-times-of-pandemic/

European Asylum Support Office. (2021). EASO asylum report 2021. Annual report on the situation of asylum in the European Union. Retrieved April 21, 2022, from https://euaa.europa.eu/sites/default/files/EASO-Asylum-Report-2021.pdf.

Eurostat. (2023a). Asylum and first time asylum applicants by citizenship, age and sex—Monthly data (rounded). Retrieved June 15, 2023, from https://ec.europa.eu/eurostat/databrowser/product/view/MIGR_ASYAPPCTZM

Eurostat. (2023b). Asylum and first time asylum applicants by citizenship, age and sex—Annual aggregated data (rounded). Retrieved June 15, 2023, from https://ec.europa.eu/eurostat/databrowser/view/MIGR_ASYAPPCTZA/default/table?lang=en

Fundamental Rights Agency. (2021). The coronavirus pandemic and fundamental rights. A year in review. European Union Fundamental Rights Agency. https://fra.europa.eu/sites/default/files/fra_uploads/fra-2021-fundamental-rights-report-2021-focus_en.pdf.

Gabrielli, L. (2015). Récurrence de la crise frontalière: l'exception permanente en Espagne. *Cultures & Conflicts, 99*(100), 75–98.

González-Páramo, A., del Rosal, C. G., Lejarza, A., Rodríguez, V., & Fanjul, G. (2019). Melilla y la excepcionalidad fronteriza. https://porcausa.org/wp-content/uploads/2019/02/MELILLA_y_la_excepcioanlidad_fronteriza_porCausa_FEB_2019.pdf.

Government of Malta. (2020). Statement—COVID-19. https://www.gov.mt/en/Government/DOI/Press%20Releases/PublishingImages/Pages/2020/April/09/pr200648/PR200648a.pdf.

Johnson, C., & Jones, R. (2016). The biopolitics and geopolitics of border enforcement in Melilla. *Territory, Politics, Governance, 6*(1), 61–80.

Jüneman, A., Fromm, N., & Scherer, N. (Eds.). (2019). *Fortress Europe? Challenges and failures of migration and asylum policies.* Springer.

Lemberg-Pedersen, M. (2012). Losing the right to have rights: EU externalization of borders control. In E. A. Andersen & E. M. Lassen (Eds.), *Europe and the Americas: Transatlantic approaches to human rights.* Brill.

Lo Coco, D., Ladan S., Cardona D., & Berrio A. G. (2021). Vulneraciones de Derechos En La Fronta Sur: Gran Canaria Y Melilla. Iridia. https://iridia.cat/wp-content/uploads/2021/01/INFORME-DDHH-FRONTERA-SUR-2021.pdf.

Ministerio de Asuntos Exteriores. (1992). Acuerdo entre el Reino de España y el Reino de Marruecos relativo a la circulación de personas, el tránsito y la readmisión de extranjeros entrados ilegalmente. https://www.boe.es/boe/dias/1992/04/25/pdfs/A13969-13970.pdf.

Ministerio del Interior. (2020). Orden INT/270/2020, de 21 de marzo, por la que se establecen criterios para la aplicación de una restricción temporal de viajes no imprescindibles desde terceros países a la Unión Europea y países asociados Schengen por razones de orden público y salud pública con motivo de la crisis sanitaria ocasionada por el COVID-19. Boletín Oficial del Estado Núm. 79 Sec. I, 26605. https://boe.es/boe/dias/2020/03/22/pdfs/BOE-A-2020-3972.pdf.

Moreno-Lax, V., & Lemberg-Pedersen, M. (2019). Border-induced displacement: The ethical and legal implications of distance-creation through externalization. *QIL, Zoom-in, 56*, 5–33.

Orchard, P. (2014). The non-entrée regime. In P. Orchard (Ed.), *A right to flee: Refugees, states, and the construction of international cooperation* (pp. 203–237). Cambridge University Press.

Pinyol-Jiménez, G., Caraballo S., & Espejo, S.. (2020). Situación de Las Personas En Necesidad de Protección Internacional Ante La COVID-19. Comisión Española de Ayuda al Refugiado (CEAR). https://www.cear.es/wp-content/uploads/2020/06/Informe-COVID_web.pdf.

Reches, D. (2022). Complying with international and regional law during the pandemic—Asylum seekers and COVID-19 emergency measures in EU member states Germany and Greece. *Social Sciences & Humanities Open, 6*(1), 100370. https://doi.org/10.1016/j.ssaho.2022.100370

Rijpma, J. J., & Cremona, M. (2007). The extra-territorialisation of EU migration policies and the rule of law. *EUI Law, 1.*

Soto, R.. (2020). Encharcados y confinados en tres carpas a las afueras de Melilla. *El Público.* https://www.publico.es/sociedad/melilla-COVID-19-encharcados-confinados-tres-carpas-afueras-melilla.html.

Tribunal Constitucional. (2021). Pleno. Sentencia 148/2021, de 14 de julio de 2021. Recurso de inconstitucionalidad 2054-2020.

World Bank. (2021). Is COVID-19 increasing global inequality? https://blogs.worldbank.org/opendata/COVID-19-increasing-global-inequality.

Zetter, R. (2014). *Protecting forced migrants: A state of the art report of concepts, challenges and ways forward.* Swiss Federal Migration Commission.

PART III

Non-Pharmaceutical Interventions

Stay at Home! A Comparative Analysis of the Implementation of Lockdowns as a Response to the COVID-19 Pandemic

Laura Chazel

INTRODUCTION

The year 2020 was marked by the implementation of lockdowns on a global scale to contain the COVID-19 pandemic by drastically minimizing human contact. This public health measure was instantly described as "medieval"[1] by several political actors but, facing the surge of the

---

[1] For instance, in France, François Ruffin, MP of *La France Insoumise* (radical left), declared on 9 April 2020 "confinement is a stopgap, it's what was done in the Middle Ages, we lock people up in their homes" in an interview in La Croix. Available online: https://www.la-croix.com/France/Politique/Ruffin-Le-gouvernement-transforme-nullite--doctrine-masques-tests-2020-04-09-1301088603?fbclid=IwAR2Kt943vdEPD50ZEpDOe57IFS-upswGqHRY7IWv00YGVfZsSRJpgfaNxLA.

L. Chazel (✉)
University of Grenoble Alpes, CNRS, Sciences Po Grenoble, Pacte, Grenoble, France

Department- École des hautes études hispaniques et ibériques (EHEHI), Casa de Velázquez, Madrid, Spain
e-mail: laura.chazel@sciencespo-grenoble.fr

© The Author(s) 2024   209
C. Egger et al. (eds.), *Covid-19 Containment Policies in Europe*, International Series on Public Policy,
https://doi.org/10.1007/978-3-031-52096-9_12

pandemic, many governments in Europe opted for this choice. The social science literature has already begun to analyse the attitudes of citizens towards lockdowns (Mariot et al., 2021), the impact of health measures on trust in governments (Glaurdić et al., 2021; Oude Groeniger et al., 2021), the responses of so-called "populist" parties to this restriction of freedom of movements (Katsambekis & Stavrakakis, 2020) and the political aspects of lockdowns that were presented as health measures during the first wave of COVID-19 (Bristielle, 2021). However, few studies have examined the different realities that were provoked by lockdown measures in different countries and the evolution of these measures over time. For instance, during the first lockdown, French citizens could not leave their home without a self-signed "derogation to travel" certificate proving a "compelling reason" to go out, while in Germany, the ban on leaving one's home was strongly recommended but not imposed.

This chapter has a dual objective. On the one hand, it aims to highlight differences in the stringency of lockdowns across countries. On the other hand, it seeks to identify some explanatory factors behind the observed differences. The comparative analysis builds on the EXCEPTIUS database and covers 20 countries in the first wave, and 15 in the second wave. The study period is from January 2020 to December 2020 and covers the first wave (January–June 2020) and the second wave (July–December 2020) of COVID-19. First, we distinguish between strict and flexible lockdowns, using an indicator of coerciveness of the lockdown by compiling different variables, such as the order to "stay home", the number of kilometres of travel allowed outside home, or the presence or self-completed forms for leaving home. Secondly, we look at whether the level of coerciveness of lockdown measures taken by governments was linked to the health situation in the country (circulation of the virus, number of deaths), and/or to political and economic criteria (wealth of the country, confidence of citizens in the institutions, party family of the ruling party) and if they had significantly impacted on the number of deaths.

STATE OF ART AND HYPOTHESES

Previous studies have already shown that several factors come into play when analysing the differences in the measures that governments adopted to deal with the COVID-19 pandemic in the first wave. For example, Engler et al. (2021) show that the quality of democracy in countries had an important impact on the restriction of individual freedom during the health crisis (see also Kuebler in this volume): the more governments protected freedom outside of crisis periods, the less restrictive measures they implemented during the COVID-19 crisis. Bristielle (2021) and Engler et al. (2021) show that, during the first wave, the measures depended largely on trust in institutions and political actors: the higher was the level of trust in political institutions, the less stringent the measures adopted. These works have highlighted the deeply political aspects of the measures put in place to curb the epidemic. Considering this political dimension, we formulate three hypotheses:

H1: During both waves, the coercive nature of the quarantine measures implemented in each country did not depend on the intensity of COVID-19 circulation.
H2: During both waves, the effectiveness of health policies was not related to the severity of lockdown measures.
H3: During both waves, countries with the highest levels of public trust in institutions implemented less restrictive quarantine measures than countries with low levels of trust in political institutions.

Lesschaeve et al. (2021) examined the economic dimension of the lockdown measures implemented to contain the COVID-19 epidemic. Their study showed that during the first wave in southern and eastern Europe, people were in favour of implementing these measures despite their "high economic costs". However, in the long run, countries with a low GDP would be less inclined to implement strong restrictive measures that affect the country's economy, which leads us to our fourth hypothesis:

H4: During the second wave, countries with the lowest GDP per capita implemented fewer lockdown measures than others.

Finally, this chapter looks at the effects of political party ideology on the response to the COVID-19 epidemic. Diverse ideologies— for example, liberalism, socialism, conservatism (Mudde, 2004)—can be associated with different positions that advocate both strong restrictions to protect the weakest and hospital care, and more flexible responses in order to guarantee individual freedom and collective rights. Katsambekis and Stavrakakis (2020) have shown that populist parties in Europe responded differently depending on national particularities, and that the right-left axis did not seem to have played a major role to explain their positions.

For example, in France, the radical left, represented by La France insou-mise (Unbowed France, LFI), and the radical right, represented by the Rassemblement National (National Rally, RN), assessed the situation dif-ferently, explaining that the COVID-19 crisis validated their respective ideologies. For LFI, the COVID-19 epidemic was the result of the eco-logical crisis, while for the RN it was linked to open borders and mass immigration (Chazel, 2020). However, during the first wave both parties defended the implementation of strong lockdown measures. This brings us to the fifth hypothesis:

H5: During both waves, the political ideology of the ruling party had no impact on the intensity of the lockdown measures.

To initially test these hypotheses, the chapter uses data coded in 20 European countries for the first wave and 15 countries for the second wave by the EXCEPTIUS project. We compiled an indicator of the stringency of lockdown measures put in place to contain the COVID-19 pandemic during the first and second waves, based on seven ordinal variables, each graduating from low to high the coercive intensity of single COVID-19 measures.

The aggregation of the indicator is done as follows: for each wave, and for each variable, we consider the most coercive measure taken by a coun-try whether at the national or subnational level, considering that, depend-ing on the state form of the countries, major decisions may have been taken mainly at one of the two levels (see Chap. 6).

We then divide each variable by the number of categories it contains, and then we divide the indicator by the number of variables (7) so that its value lies between zero and one. Thus, 0 corresponds to no coercive mea-sure at all and one corresponds to the maximum possible coercive mea-sures. Each value is the maximum of what a country has implemented during each wave (no matter if this score describes 1 day or 3 months); therefore, the indicator does not aim at capturing in which country the measures have been implemented the longest, but rather at capturing which are the maximum measures (in terms of severity) that have been implemented by the countries over a wave.

The indicator is then used to examine the correlation between the strin-gency of COVID-19 containment measures and contextual factors regard-ing health, political and economic conditions. Results provide insights into why such measures have been put in place in certain countries and enable to confront the working hypotheses. Respective variables (see respective distribution in appendixes 1 and 2) include:

- The number of deaths relative to population per million people: we rely on the dataset available on COVID Tracker.[2] On the one hand, we seek to determine whether there is a correlation between the intensity of the lockdown measures put in place during each wave and the number of deaths at the end of each wave (using as a basis the number of deaths relative to population per million people on 30 June 2020 for the first wave and on 31 December 2020 for the second wave) (H2). On the other hand, we aim to find out whether the measures implemented during each wave were implemented according to the circulation of the epidemic (H1). Considering that the detection of COVID-19 cases varied considerably from one country to another (e.g., depending on whether the tests were reimbursed or not), we look at the number of deaths relative to population per million people at the beginning of each wave to evaluate the circulation of the virus. For the first wave, as COVID-19 only appeared in Europe in March 2020, we use as a basis the number of deaths relative to the population on 31 March 2020,[3] and for the second wave on 1 July 2020.
- Confidence in national governments: we rely on the November 2019 Eurobarometer data to account for H3.
- Level of GDP per capita in 2019: we rely on the European Commission data to test H4.
- The ideology of the political party of the government in office in March 2020: we distinguish six types of parties in power to examine H5: far left (1), social democratic left and green parties (2), centre (3), liberal right and conservative right (4), far right (5). Regarding coalition governments, we have selected the party to which the president or prime minister belongs.

---

[2] Available online: https://COVIDtracker.fr/COVIDtracker-world/. The COVID Tracker website is based on Johns Hopkins University CSSE COVID-19 data (states' declarations of the number of deaths).

[3] In most countries, data are available from this date.

ANALYSIS AND RESULTS

Different Types of Lockdowns

Three groups of countries can be distinguished according to the intensity of the measures implemented: light lockdown (from 0 to 0.33), medium lockdown (from 0.33 to 0.66) and strict lockdown (from 0.66 to 1). The data show that two countries (out of 20) had light lockdowns in place in the first wave (Finland and Sweden), and five countries (out of 15) in the second wave (Denmark, Estonia, Finland, Poland, Sweden). The first group of countries is characterized by the fact that the governments in place relied primarily on the responsibility of citizens rather than on coercion: the injunctions to stay at home were primarily recommendations, and many shops remained open during the period. For example, in Finland, in the first and second waves (with a respective lockdown score of 0.24 and 0.17), the government recommended that cafés and restaurants be closed, and banned gatherings of more than ten people.

The Swedish case received particular attention. The indicator of coercive lockdown measures shows that there were no measures during the first wave (0) and a very light closure measure of non-essential shops during the second wave (0.07). The Swedish centre-left government led by Stefan Löfven (*Sveriges Socialdemokratiska Arbetareparti* [Swedish Social Democratic Party]) had announced during the first wave of COVID-19 that the fight against the virus was a "marathon, not a sprint". For instance, the Swedish government encouraged citizens to work from home, when possible, discouraged travel and going out for those who felt ill and for citizens aged 70 or older. During the first two COVID-19 waves, the Swedish government stood out by the trust it placed in its citizens to limit their contacts. When, in most European countries, masks started to become compulsory after the first wave (see de Saint Phalle's chapter in this volume), the government stood out again, as wearing masks never became compulsory. All over Europe, the Swedish case was taken as an example by the supporters of the lifting of sanitary restrictions (e.g., showing that another model was then possible), and it was mobilized by other political and scientific actors as an example not to be followed (e.g., showing the impasse of the search for herd immunity).

Regarding medium lockdowns, 14 countries out of 20 implemented them during the first wave (Austria, Belgium, Czech Republic, Denmark, Estonia, Germany, Greece, Hungary, Ireland, Luxembourg, Netherlands,

Poland, Portugal, United Kingdom) and 9 countries (out of 15) did so during the second wave (Austria, Belgium, Czech Republic, Hungary, Italy, Ireland, Portugal, Spain, United Kingdom). In most of these countries, governments have also called on citizens to take responsibility. This was the case in the Netherlands, for example, where the government declared relying on the "intelligence" and "self-discipline" of citizens. There was no form to fill in to leave home, no time limit and no space limit.

Finally, 4 countries (out of 20) implemented strict lockdown during the first wave (Spain, France, Italy, Romania) and only 1 (out of 15) during the second wave (France). During the first wave, countries such as Spain, Italy and France relied on coercion. In these three countries, citizens were forbidden to leave their homes except for essential reasons such as buying food or walking their pets. Very heavy fines could be imposed, and prison sentences could be incurred for non-compliance with lockdown (e.g., in France, up to 3750 euros and 6 months in prison). Citizens were required to carry a self-signed sworn statement/travel certificate every time they left their home to justify a compelling reason. In France, during the first lockdown, citizens were allowed to go out for 1 h/day, within a maximum radius of 1 km. France is a special case as during the second wave it implemented both strict lockdown measures and a strict curfew, while most other countries chose one or the other.

Initial Explanation of the Stringency of Lockdowns

When we look at the impact of the circulation of the virus on the lockdown measures, we can observe differences between the two waves (Figs. 12.1 and 12.2). In the first wave, a positive correlation between the circulation of the virus and the severity of the lockdown measures implemented is observed ($r = 0.53$): the higher the level of virus circulation (proxied by the number of deaths at the beginning of each phase), the stricter the lockdown measures—thus invalidating H1. However, for the second wave, if the correlation remains positive it appears much lighter and not significant ($r = 0.27$). As such, the posited relationship between the intensity of circulation of COVID-19 and the coerciveness of lockdown measures decorrelates and decreases over time.

Regarding the impacts of economic and political factors, the analysis of the first wave data reveals that only the level of institutional trust had a significant and negative impact on the types of lockdown measures implemented (Fig. 12.3). The lower the level of institutional trust, the higher

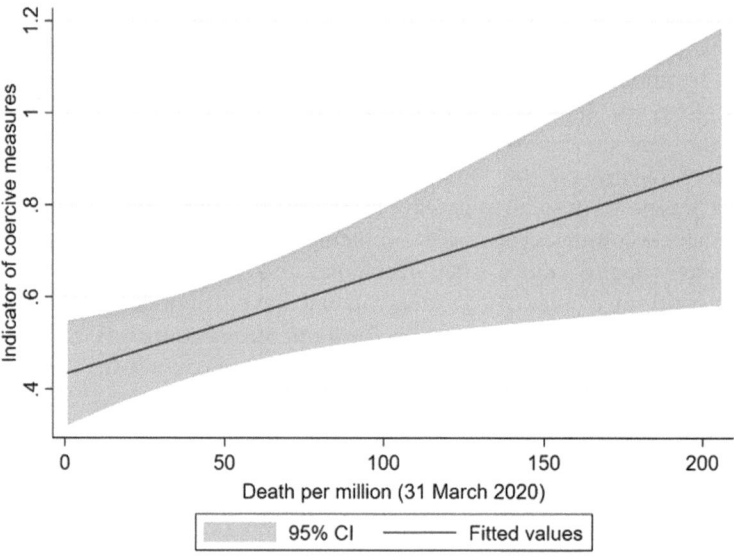

Fig. 12.1 Indicator of coercive measures and deaths per million habitants, beginning of the first wave

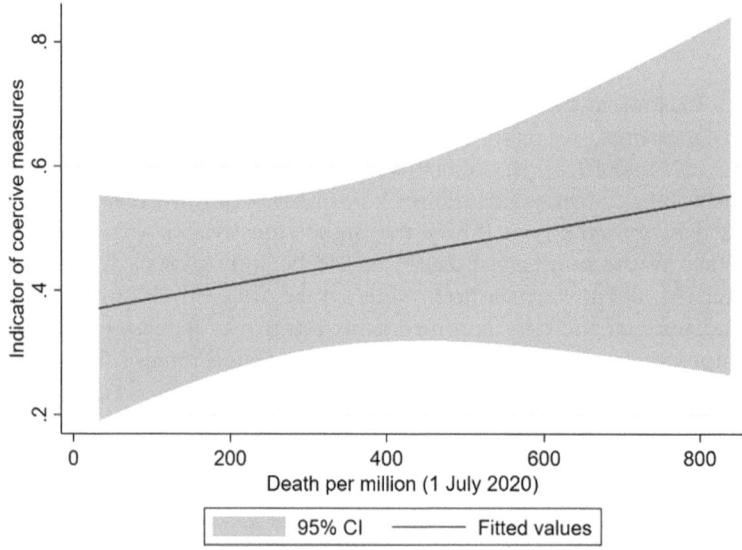

Fig. 12.2 Indicator of coercive measures and death per million habitants, beginning of the second wave

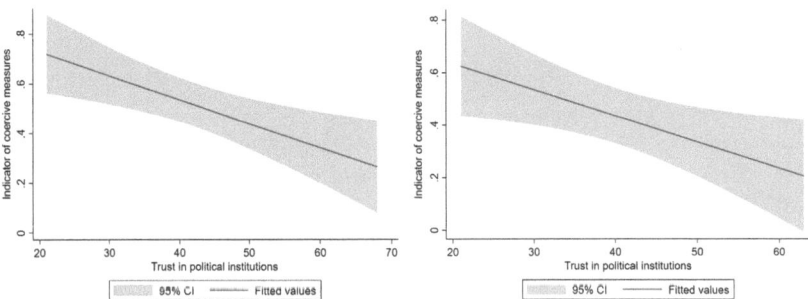

Fig. 12.3 (a) First (on the left) and (b) second (on the right) waves. Indicator of coercive measures and trust in political institutions

the intensity of coercive measures (r = -0.61). Similar results are observed in the second wave. The link between institutional trust and coercive measures is still significantly negative with a similar intensity (r = -0.59), thereby confirming H3 for the two waves.

Meanwhile, it seems that the GDP level, standing for the capacity of the countries' economy to cope with strong lockdown measures and the economic slowdown it implies is not linked with the coerciveness of implemented lockdowns (r = -0.24 with no significance for the first wave and r = 0.01 for the second wave). This result invalidates H4. In addition, the type of political party in power does not appear as a significant factor either to explain the decision to implement strong or weak lockdowns, neither during the first wave (r = 0.01) or the second wave (-0.16), here confirming H5 (Figs. 12.4 and 12.5).

Finally, regarding the impact of lockdown measures on mortality, during the first wave and the second wave, only a very low correlation exists with weak significance (r = 0.19 for the first wave, r = 0.34 for the second wave), partially validating the low impact of lockdown measures on mortality (H2) (Fig. 12.6).

Conclusion

This chapter has provided two main explanations for decision-making in times of crisis. On the one hand, while almost all European countries drastically restricted the movement of citizens and urged them to stay at home, there were also large differences between these countries. The lockdowns implemented to contain the circulation of COVID-19 have shown very different realities. On the other hand, only two of the four variables we

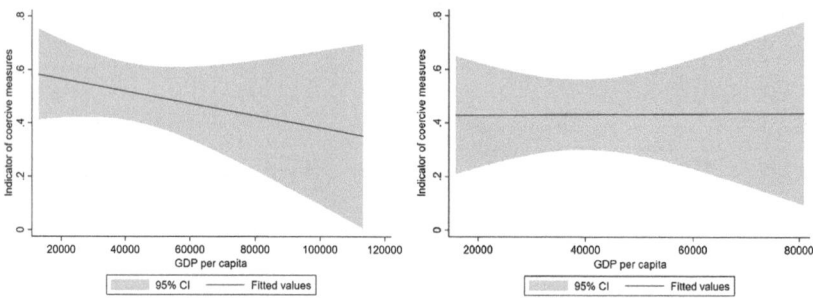

Fig. 12.4 (**a**) First (on the left) and (**b**) second (on the right) waves. Indicator of coercive measures and GDP per capita

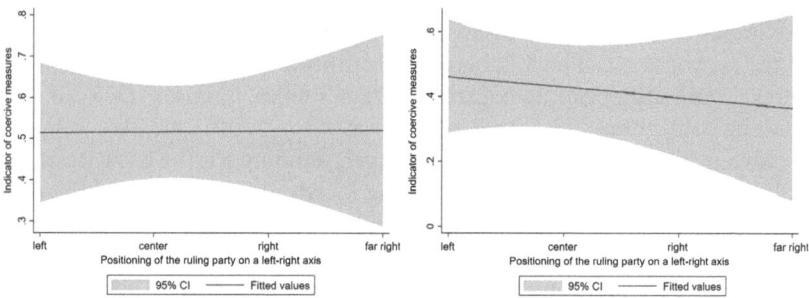

Fig. 12.5 (**a**) First (on the left) and (**b**) second (on the right) waves. Indicator of coercive measures and party in power

selected explain the level of severity of the lockdowns put in place. The circulation of the virus had a significant impact (the higher the circulation, the stricter the lockdowns) but only during the first wave, while the level of trust of citizens in political institutions was a much more robust explanatory factor during both waves (the lower the level of trust, the stricter the measures).

The chapter also showed that neither the level of GDP nor the incumbent political party explained the severity of the lockdown measures during the first two waves. Regarding the level of GDP, no correlation can be made between the latter and the indicator of coercive measures.

Regarding the ideological position of the governing party, it is interesting to note that the left-right axis does not seem to have had any impact on the position taken by the different political parties on lockdown

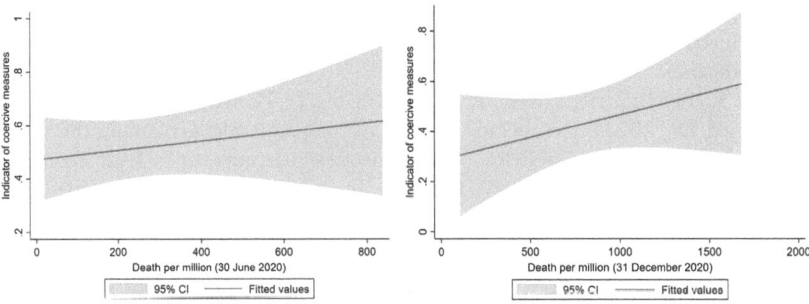

Fig. 12.6 (a) First (on the left) and (b) second (on the right) waves. Indicator of coercive measures and death per million (30 June/31 December 2020)

measures. For instance, the left was largely divided on the policy responses to the COVID-19 epidemic. In France, the main left-wing party, LFI opposed lockdown measures from the second wave onwards. The party proposed the reopening of essential and non-essential shops and the introduction of a "rolling society" (*société par roulement*). In Spain, Podemos (We Can), the Spanish counterpart of LFI, widely criticized the "laxity" of right-wing parties in some autonomous communities led by the conservative *Partido Popular* (Popular Party, PP), as in the Community of Madrid, and defended lockdown as a measure to protect the most vulnerable citizens.

To go further, it could be interesting to study the impact of complementary context variables such as democratic level of the country, hospital capacity or trust in the police. Furthermore, a double synchronic and diachronic analysis could be performed on the first and second wave (and also include the third wave) to categorize the countries according to the strictness of the lockdowns for each wave but also in an evolutionary way to perform an average over the study period.

Acknowledgements The author acknowledges Chloé Alexandre and Antoine Bristielle for their help and very valuable feedback on the chapter.

REFERENCES

Bristielle, A. (2021). *À Qui Se Fier? De La Crise de Confiance Institutionnelle à La Crise Sanitaire*. Monde En Cours. La Tour d'Aigues; Éditions de l'Aube ; Fondation Jean-Jaurès.

Chazel, L. (2020). French populism in time of COVID-19. In G. Katsambekis & Y. Stavrakakis (Eds.), *Populism and the pandemic, a collaborative report.* Populismus.

Engler, S., Brunner, P., Loviat, R., Abou-Chadi, T., Leemann, L., Glaser, A., & Kübler, D. (2021). Democracy in times of the pandemic: explaining the variation of COVID-19 policies across European democracies. *West European Politics, 44*(5–6), 1077–1102. https://doi.org/10.1080/0140238 2.2021.1900669

Glaurdić, J., Lesschaeve, C., & Mochtak, M. (2021). Coronavirus pandemic response and voter choice. *Communist and Post-Communist Studies, 54*(4), 197–214. https://doi.org/10.1525/j.postcomstud.2021.54.4.197

Katsambekis, G., & Stavrakakis, Y. (2020). *Populism and the pandemic: A collaborative report. 7.* Populismus Interventions.

Lesschaeve, C., Glaurdić, J., & Mochtak, M. (2021). Health versus wealth during the COVID-19 pandemic. *Public Opinion Quarterly, 85*(3), 808–835. https://doi.org/10.1093/poq/nfab036

Mariot, N., Mercklé, P., & Perdoncin, A. (Eds.). (2021). *Personne ne bouge: une enquête sur le confinement du printemps 2020. Carrefours des idées.* UGA éditions.

Mudde, C. (2004). The populist Zeitgeist. *Government and Opposition, 39*(4), 541–563. https://doi.org/10.1111/j.1477-7053.2004.00135.x

Oude Groeniger, J., Noordzij, K., van der Waal, J., & de Koster, W. (2021). Dutch COVID-19 lockdown measures increased trust in government and trust in science: A difference-in-differences analysis. *Social Science & Medicine, 275*(April), 113819. https://doi.org/10.1016/j.socscimed.2021.113819

CHAPTER 13

Masks and Social Distancing During COVID-19

Eugénie de Saint-Phalle

INTRODUCTION

During the COVID-19 pandemic, mask mandates emerged as key strategies to curb transmission and protect public health with social distancing measures (Chu et al., 2020).

In 2020, the World Health Organization (WHO) recommended the use of face masks in specific settings, particularly where physical distancing could not be maintained or where community transmission was high (WHO, 2020). European countries adopted mask-wearing policies with varying degrees of stringency and enforcement (Howard et al., 2021). While some countries mandated mask-wearing in public spaces early in the pandemic, others introduced them later or revised their guidance as additional evidence on mask effectiveness emerged (Fischer et al., 2021). Existing research on mask mandates has largely focused on assessing the efficacy of face masks in reducing viral transmission (Bundgaard et al.,

E. de Saint-Phalle (✉)
International Relations and International Organization, University of Groningen, Groningen, The Netherlands
e-mail: e.de.saint-phalle@rug.nl

© The Author(s) 2024
C. Egger et al. (eds.), *Covid-19 Containment Policies in Europe*,
International Series on Public Policy,
https://doi.org/10.1007/978-3-031-52096-9_13

2021; Chu et al., 2020). However, few studies have systematically compared the design, implementation, and impact of mask mandates across European countries (Fischer et al., 2021). Existing studies, such as Oxford COVID-19 response tracker (Hale et al., 2021) provides extensive information, which does not, however, go into the specifics of the responses (for example, the type of the mask-wearing mandate).

This chapter aims to provide a comprehensive overview of the mask mandates and social distancing measures implemented in European Union countries, as well as Switzerland and the UK, during the period from 2020 to early 2022.

The goals of this chapter are fourfold: (1) to outline the legal frameworks that allowed for the introduction of mask mandates and social distancing measures in European countries; (2) to map the implementation and retraction timelines of these measures across the region, identifying patterns and variations in policy strictness; (3) to explore the regional differences in implementing mask mandates, with a focus on Eastern, Central, Western, Southern, and Northern European countries; and (4) to analyse the national and regional differences in the implementation of mask mandates within individual countries.

By achieving these goals, we intend to contribute to the existing body of literature on the response to the COVID-19 pandemic in Europe, while offering insights into the factors that influenced the design and implementation of mask mandates and social distancing measures. Some of the existing works have already addressed how governments responded to the pandemic (e.g., Greer et al., 2020). Furthermore, we aim to provide policymakers and public health officials with valuable information that may inform future decision-making in times of crisis, as well as highlight the limitations and directions for future research in this area.

The Effectiveness and Implications of Mask Mandates

State-of-Art Research

Previous studies shed light on the role and effectiveness of mask mandates in slowing down the spread of COVID-19. A comprehensive evidence review conducted by Howard et al. (2021) highlighted the importance of mask-wearing in conjunction with other preventive measures in containing the virus' spread. The researchers pointed to various pieces of evidence, including laboratory studies, asymptomatic transmission reports, and super-spreading events, to argue for widespread mask usage given its minimal costs and potential substantial benefits. Lyu and Welby's (2020) research further reinforces the effectiveness of mask mandates. Using a natural experiment design, the authors showed that state-level mask mandates in the United States led to a significant slowdown in the daily COVID-19 growth rate, implying that such mandates can considerably curb the community spread of the virus. Based on these findings, the authors estimated that between 230,000 and 450,000 cases were possibly prevented by May 22, 2020, due to these mandates.

However, the effectiveness of mask mandates cannot be considered in isolation, as they are influenced by a myriad of factors including public compliance, demographic attributes, socio-economic conditions, and the broader public health environment, including the pandemic's state and other protective measures' implementation. A global study by Islam et al. (2020) underscores this point by demonstrating that physical distancing interventions, presumably inclusive of mask-wearing, were associated with a decrease in COVID-19 incidence. Nevertheless, the correlation's strength varied by country and over time, implying that local factors and adherence to measures can significantly affect the success of these interventions.

The findings of these studies have economic implications as well. Fowler et al. (2021) have shown that the implementation of stay-at-home orders, a visible public health measure similar to mask mandates, had a noticeable effect on COVID-19 cases and fatalities in the United States. This suggests that such measures may play a role in controlling disease, shaping public perceptions, and potentially mitigating the pandemic's economic impacts. In summary, mask mandates appear to be a key tool in controlling COVID-19's spread. Nevertheless, their effectiveness hinges on several factors, such as timely implementation, public compliance, and integration with other public health measures.

Influence of Rising Cases on the Implementation of Mandates

Figure 13.1 illustrates the implementation of mask mandates in selected countries, based on the number of weekly cases preceding the decision, and shows the differences among the three waves.

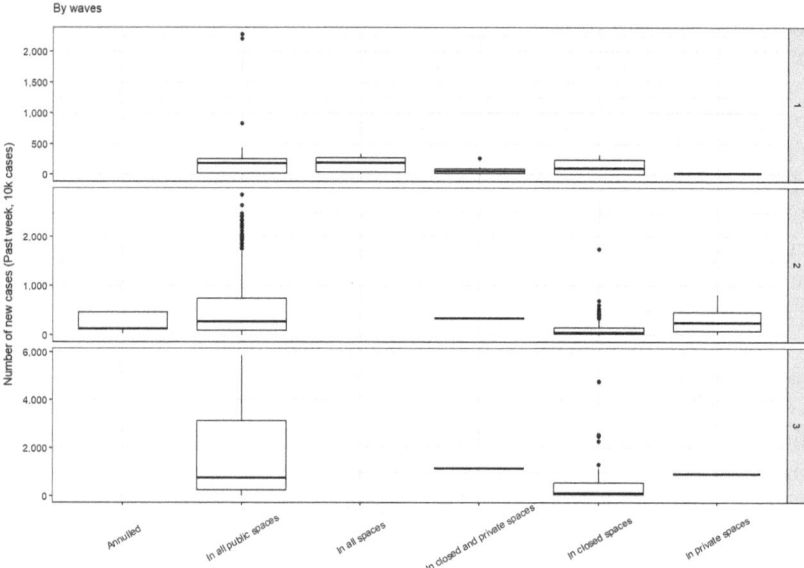

Fig. 13.1   Distribution of weekly COVID-19 cases by mask mandate category, by wave. Source: EXCEPTIUS data, own rendering. Note: The data presented may be non-exhaustive

Based on the graph, we can conclude the following. First, the number of cases it took to implement mask mandates differs among waves: in the first wave, most mandates were passed when the infection rates were relatively low, with some notable exceptions. The second wave has seen several annulments of masks, and most countries stuck to using masks in either all public or in private spaces.[1] By the third wave, the use of masks in public spaces, both closed and open, has become the most popular measure for most countries. However, no annulments were registered in the dataset for this period (January–April 2021). Other measures, such as use of masks in only closed or private spaces, were significantly less popular. This also may indicate that by the third wave of the pandemic, most countries have

---

[1] It is important to note that mandates for private spaces do not mean that no masks are used in public spaces. Usage of masks in private spaces (e.g., at home or in cars) often was implemented separately from other mask mandates and depended on how country managed the issue in general.

established similar approaches to mask management, as more information and experience was acquired during 2020.

LEGAL FRAMEWORKS FOR MASK MANDATES IN EUROPEAN COUNTRIES

The introduction of mask mandates and social distancing measures across European countries was facilitated through different legal frameworks, broadly categorized as emergency powers or existing crisis-management legislation.

Emergency Powers Versus Existing Legislation

Emergency powers refer to the temporary authority granted to governments to address extraordinary situations, such as pandemics or natural disasters (Ferejohn & Pasquino 2004, see also Egger's chapter in this volume). They often involve the suspension or modification of ordinary legal processes, allowing for the swift implementation of public health measures. In contrast, existing legislation encompasses the pre-existing laws and regulations that provide a legal basis for introducing public health measures without resorting to emergency powers (Habibi et al., 2020). Sometimes, emergency powers were deemed necessary to respond to the fast-evolving situation, while in others, existing legislation provided sufficient legal authority to implement mask mandates and social distancing measures.

Countries That Used Emergency Powers to Introduce Mandates

Several European countries, including France, Italy, and Spain, relied on emergency powers to introduce mask mandates and social distancing measures in the early stages of the pandemic. Being hit the first among European countries, Italy enacted a nationwide state of emergency on January 31, 2020, enabling the government to adopt a series of decrees and ordinances that imposed mask requirements and social distancing rules. Similarly, in France, the government declared a state of health emergency on March 23, 2020, under the Public Health, granting the executive branch extensive powers to impose various containment measures, including mask mandates. In Spain, the government declared a state of alarm on March 14, 2020, under the Organic Law 4/1981, giving the executive branch the authority to impose restrictions on movement and social interactions, including the use of face masks in public spaces.

Countries That Used Existing Legal Frameworks to Introduce Mandates

Other European countries relied on existing legal frameworks to implement mask mandates and social distancing measures. For instance, Germany used the Infection Protection Act (*Infektionsschutzgesetz*) to grant federal states the authority to introduce mask requirements and social distancing rules. The Netherlands implemented mask mandates through the Temporary Measures COVID-19 Act, which provided a legal basis for restrictions on public gatherings and mask-wearing in designated areas. In Belgium, the government relied on the Law on Civil Security (*Loi relative à la sécurité civile*) to impose mask mandates and social distancing measures (Belgium 2007). Similarly, Switzerland implemented mask requirements and social distancing rules through the Epidemics Act (*Epidemiengesetz*), which grants the Federal Council the authority to take necessary measures to combat communicable diseases.

In summary, European countries adopted a mix of emergency powers and existing legislation to introduce mask mandates and social distancing measures. The choice of legal framework depended on the specific circumstances in each country and the perceived need for rapid action. The use of emergency powers has been subject to critique by scholars and civil society organizations, who argue that such powers can lead to the centralization of decision-making, lack of transparency, and potential erosion of civil liberties (Ginsburg & Versteeg, 2021; Habibi et al., 2020).

Critics contend governments might exploit emergencies to increase executive authority, bypass legislative oversight, and undermine democratic checks and balances (Ferejohn & Pasquino, 2004; Gostin et al., 2020). Proponents of emergency powers emphasize the need for swift and decisive action to address public health crises, arguing that the flexibility offered by emergency powers can facilitate more effective responses to rapidly developing situations (Dodds et al., 2020). Thus, the choice of legal framework for implementing mask mandates and social distancing measures in European countries reflects not only the specific conditions of the pandemic but also broader debates surrounding the balance between executive authority, democratic accountability, and public health imperatives during times of crisis.

TIMELINE OF THE IMPLEMENTATION AND RETRACTION OF MASK MANDATES AND SOCIAL DISTANCING MEASURES

In this section, we examine three distinct groups of countries based on their approach to mask mandates and social distancing measures: strict, moderate, and lenient. These categories reflect the varying degrees of stringency, comprehensiveness, and duration of the public health policies implemented in response to the COVID-19 pandemic.

Strict Countries Strict countries are those that have implemented comprehensive and stringent mask mandates and social distancing measures, often enforcing these policies with penalties for non-compliance. These countries typically introduced mask mandates early in the pandemic, requiring the use of face coverings in various public settings and maintaining strict social distancing rules. Strict countries have also periodically reinforced these measures as the pandemic evolved, responding to changing transmission rates and emerging evidence. The strict approach is hypothesized to prioritize public health and safety, with the aim of minimizing the spread of the virus and protecting vulnerable populations. In such countries, fines for not following the rules were generally high and enforced by the police.

Moderate Countries Moderate countries are characterized by a more balanced approach to mask mandates and social distancing measures, adopting policies that are less stringent than those in strict countries but still aimed at reducing transmission. These countries may have introduced mask mandates and social distancing rules with more flexibility, allowing for regional variations or exemptions based on local conditions. Governments took into account the trade-offs between public health, economic, and social considerations, seeking a balance between controlling the spread of the virus and mitigating the disruptive effects of these measures on society and the economy.

Lenient Countries Lenient countries are those that have implemented relatively relaxed mask mandates and social distancing measures, relying more on voluntary compliance and personal responsibility. These countries may have introduced mask mandates and social distancing rules later in the pandemic or limited their scope to specific settings or situations. Governments in such countries might have prioritized individual freedoms and economic concerns over strict public health measures, considering the

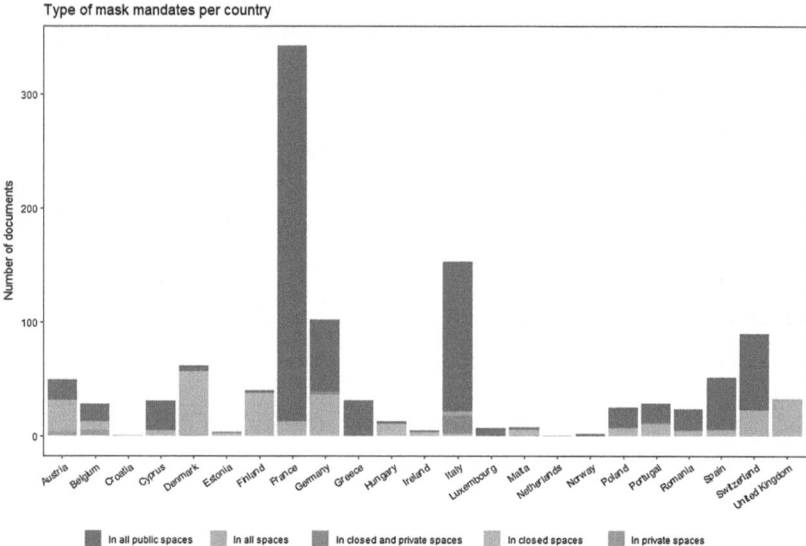

Fig. 13.2 Type of mask mandates implemented in selected EU countries (including Switzerland and the UK). Source: EXCEPTIUS data, own rendering

potential negative consequences of prolonged or stringent restrictions on society and the economy.

Figure 13.2 visualizes the types of responses in terms of mask mandates. We observe that while some countries had a varying response, like Italy, which was the first one to be hit by the pandemic in February 2020. The use of masks appears to be quite strict: not only were the masks required in all public spaces most of the time, but several decrees were passed that required wearing masks in all public and private spaces. On the contrary, countries like Denmark or Finland mostly required the masks only in closed spaces (with Finland simply recommending the use).

Timeline for Strict Countries

Strict countries in Europe enforced rigorous mask mandates and social distancing measures early in the pandemic, maintaining them for extended durations, with retractions and reintroductions as needed. Italy, for instance, executed a nationwide lockdown on March 9, 2020, and required mask-wearing in public spaces beginning April 26. The Italian government upheld mask mandates and social distancing rules, modifying them based on the epidemiological situation. Some restrictions were eased in the summer of 2020, but were later reintroduced as the pandemic worsened. Greece swiftly imposed a lockdown on March 23, 2020, and introduced mask mandates in public spaces on June 29, 2020. Greece sustained these measures throughout the pandemic, adjusting them according to regional differences and epidemiological trends. Mask mandates were partially lifted during low transmission periods but were reinstated as cases surged. France also pursued a strict approach, initiating a nationwide lockdown on March 17, 2020, followed by mask mandates in public spaces from May 11, 2020. The French government relaxed some restrictions in the summer of 2020, only to reimpose them later in response to subsequent waves of the pandemic.

Timeline for Moderate Countries

Moderate countries in Europe adopted more gradual approaches to mask mandates and social distancing measures, adjusting their implementation based on the epidemiological situation. Germany, for example, did not impose a nationwide lockdown but instead implemented regional lockdowns and mask mandates depending on the infection rates in each federal state. Mask-wearing became compulsory in public transportation and shops across all federal states by April 27, 2020, with each state setting its own timeline for enforcement and easing (Robert Koch Institute, 2020). Retractions and reintroductions of these measures were subject to regional decisions. In the Czech Republic, the government initially enforced a lockdown on March 16, 2020, and mandated mask-wearing in public spaces on March 18. Although the government eased some restrictions in May 2020, it reintroduced them later as the pandemic continued. Masks were no longer required outdoors from May 25, 2020, but were later reinstated as cases increased.

The Netherlands implemented an "intelligent lockdown" on March 15, 2020, which included social distancing measures but no compulsory mask mandates. However, the government later introduced mask mandates in public transportation on June 1, 2020, and expanded it to indoor public spaces on December 1, 2020. The Netherlands temporarily lifted the indoor mask mandate during low transmission periods, only to reimpose it when cases rose again. Similarly, the United Kingdom adopted a diverse approach to managing the pandemic, with England, Scotland,

Wales, and Northern Ireland implementing their own measures. Overall, the UK favoured voluntary guidance and targeted restrictions over blanket lockdowns and mask mandates. However, mask-wearing became compulsory in public transport and indoor public spaces in England from July 24, 2020, and was later rescinded on July 19, 2021, as part of the UK's broader reopening strategy.

Timeline for Lenient Countries

Lenient countries in Europe typically adopted less stringent mask mandates and social distancing measures, often relying on voluntary guidelines and recommendations. They were relatively late into the pandemic (often in the second wave) to introduce masks in public spaces. For instance, Denmark implemented a partial lockdown on March 11, 2020, but did not mandate masks in public spaces until August 22, 2020. The Danish government later lifted the mask mandate on September 10, 2021, following a decline in COVID-19 cases. Finland never introduced an official mask mandate, instead issuing only a recommendation. An anecdotic explanation circulated a lot, explaining that two meters of distance is too close for Finns.

Estonia followed a similar approach, enacting social distancing recommendations without imposing a full lockdown or widespread mask mandates. In Estonia, mask-wearing was only required in public transportation and in healthcare facilities. Restrictions were gradually lifted as the pandemic situation improved.

Spillover Effects Between Countries

As the pandemic unfolded, spillover effects between countries became apparent, with neighbouring nations often influencing each other's policy decisions. The implementation or relaxation of mask mandates and social distancing measures in one country sometimes prompted similar actions in nearby countries, either due to epidemiological trends or political considerations. For example, when Germany implemented regional lockdowns and mask mandates, several neighbouring countries, such as Austria and Poland, followed suit by adopting similar policies. The success or failure of these measures in one country often informed policy decisions in others.

Moreover, the European Union's coordination efforts, such as the European Centre for Disease Prevention and Control (ECDC) guidelines and recommendations, played a role in harmonizing some public health measures across member states (ECDC, 2020). The exchange of information and best practices facilitated evidence-based policymaking and contributed to a more unified approach to managing the pandemic. Additionally, spillover effects were evident in the coordination of travel restrictions between countries. As nations implemented or lifted mask mandates and social distancing measures, they often adjusted their travel policies accordingly, allowing or limiting the movement of people based on the epidemiological situation in adjacent countries.

To sum up, the implementation and retraction of mask mandates and social distancing measures across European countries were influenced not only by their unique policy approaches and epidemiological situations but also by spillover effects resulting from the interconnectedness of the continent and the need for coordinated action to address the pandemic (Fig. 13.3).

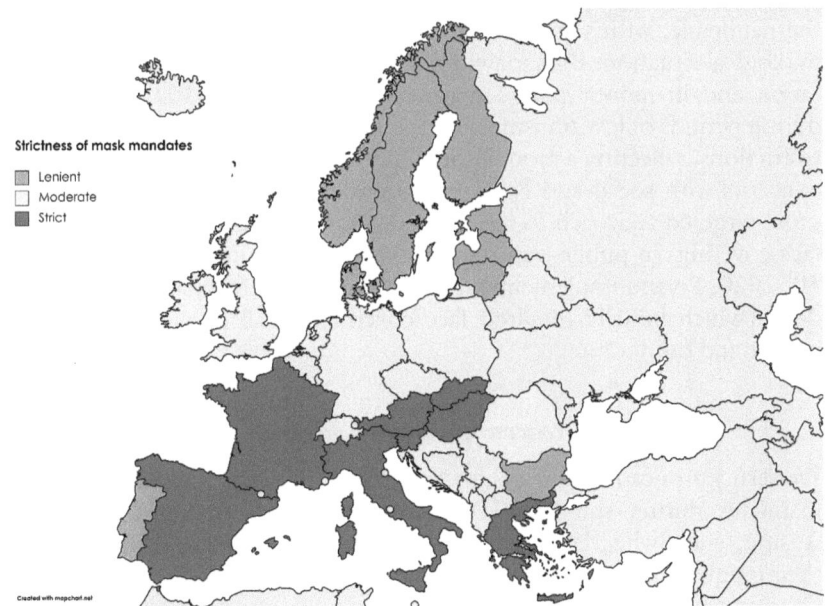

Fig. 13.3 Mapping of mask mandates' strictness

REGIONAL DIFFERENCES IN THE IMPLEMENTATION
OF MASK MANDATES

The implementation of mask mandates across Europe showcased a mosaic of strategies, reflecting the unique social, political, and epidemiological contexts of each region. From Eastern to Northern Europe, countries exhibited diverse approaches to mask mandates, with some enforcing strict nationwide policies, while others favoured regional or voluntary guidelines. This variety indicates that there were no one-size-fits-all solutions in response to the pandemic.

Eastern European Countries

Eastern European countries exhibited a wide array of strategies when it came to implementing mask mandates. Countries, such as Romania, Bulgaria, Poland, and Lithuania, each adopted different policies, reflecting their distinct public health priorities and evolving understanding of the virus. For example, Romania instituted mandatory mask-wearing in public spaces on May 15, 2020, and continued to enforce this policy throughout the pandemic, with varying levels of strictness depending on the epidemiological situation. Bulgaria enforced mask-wearing on public transportation and in indoor public spaces starting May 14, 2020. However, during periods of low transmission, the Bulgarian government eased these restrictions, reflecting a more flexible approach that balanced public health concerns with social and economic considerations. Lithuania adopted a more targeted approach to mask mandates, introducing requirements for face coverings in public transportation and indoor public spaces on April 10, 2020. Poland implemented a nationwide mask mandate on April 16, 2020, which initially required face coverings in all public spaces, both indoor and outdoor.

Western European Countries

Western European countries also exhibited a range of responses to mask mandates during the COVID-19 pandemic. For example, Germany, Austria, and Switzerland each adopted distinct strategies that reflected their unique political structures, public health systems, and social contexts. Germany employed a regional approach to mask mandates, allowing each of its 16 federal states to determine their own timeline for implementing and lifting mask requirements. This decentralized strategy was consistent with Germany's federal system, which grants significant autonomy to individual states in areas such as public health. Austria, in contrast, opted for a more centralized strategy. The Austrian government imposed a nationwide mask mandate on April 6, 2020, requiring masks in public transportation, shops, and indoor public spaces. As the pandemic evolved, Austria adapted its mask policy based on the prevailing epidemiological situation, tightening or easing restrictions in response to fluctuations in case numbers and other relevant indicators.

Switzerland took a somewhat mixed approach to mask mandates. The Swiss government initially recommended, rather than required, the use of masks in public spaces when physical distancing of 2 m could not be maintained. However, as the pandemic progressed and case numbers increased, the Swiss Federal Council implemented a nationwide mask mandate on October 19, 2020, which applied to public transportation, indoor public spaces, and shops. Despite this central decision, cantonal governments were given the authority to impose additional mask requirements or relax them based on local conditions. This approach struck a balance between nationwide consistency and regional adaptability.

Central European Countries

Slovenian government chose to implement a nationwide mask mandate on March 30, 2020, requiring individuals to wear masks in enclosed public spaces, such as shops, and on public transportation. The decision to apply this mandate uniformly across the country was driven by a desire for consistency in policy and messaging, as well as a recognition of the potential for rapid spread of the virus if left unchecked. Slovakia's approach to mask mandates evolved over time. Initially, the government enforced a nationwide mask mandate on March 25, 2020, requiring the use of masks in public transportation and indoor public spaces. This early action was taken to prevent the healthcare system from becoming overwhelmed by a surge in cases. However, as the pandemic progressed and more data became available, the Slovak government modified the policy to focus on specific regions with higher infection rates. This targeted approach allowed for a more efficient allocation of resources and a tailored response to the varying levels of risk across the country.

Southern European Countries

Approaches in the Southern Europe varied, mostly based on the epidemiological situation and the number of infections. Italy introduced a nationwide mask mandate on April 26, 2020, and sustained this requirement, with modifications based on the epidemiological context. Portugal mandated mask-wearing in public transportation and enclosed spaces from May 4, 2020, and later expanded the requirement to outdoor public spaces where social distancing was impractical. Conversely, Malta implemented a nationwide mask mandate on October 17, 2020, requiring face coverings in all public spaces, both indoor and outdoor. This approach was influenced by the island nation's dense population and the need to minimize transmission in close quarters. In Croatia, the government enforced mask-wearing in indoor public spaces and on public transportation starting July 13, 2020. This approach was taken in response to the rising number of cases in the country. Additionally, the Croatian government recommended the use of masks in outdoor public spaces, particularly when physical distancing could not be maintained. This guidance was aimed at reducing transmission of the virus while allowing for greater flexibility in outdoor settings, where the risk of transmission is generally lower.

Northern European Countries

Northern European countries took varied but generally lenient approaches to mask mandates. As previously mentioned, Denmark did not impose mask-wearing in public spaces until August 22, 2020, and eventually lifted the mandate on September 10, 2021. This relatively late introduction of mask rules and subsequent lifting demonstrated the Danish government's evolving approach based on the changing epidemiological situation. In Finland, the Finnish Institute for Health and Welfare advised wearing masks in situations where social distancing was unattainable, such as on public transportation, but never mandated masks on a nationwide scale. This guidance-based approach aimed to empower individuals to make informed decisions about mask-wearing, without imposing strict requirements. Norway, similar to Finland, did not impose a nationwide mask mandate. The Norwegian Institute of Public Health recommended the use of masks in situations where maintaining social distancing was difficult, such as on public transportation or in crowded indoor spaces. The Norwegian government focused on promoting other preventive measures like physical distancing and maintaining good hygiene to limit the spread of the virus.

Sweden, known for its distinct approach to the pandemic, did not implement a nationwide mask mandate. Instead, the Swedish Public Health Agency recommended mask-wearing in specific situations, such as during peak hours on public transportation, while emphasizing the importance of other preventive measures like social distancing and good hygiene practices. This strategy was consistent with Sweden's overall approach to the pandemic, which relied on voluntary compliance and individual responsibility.

NATIONAL AND REGIONAL DIFFERENCES IN THE IMPLEMENTATION OF MASK MANDATES

The implementation of mask mandates also varied in terms of the level at which these measures were enacted. Some countries chose to enforce mask mandates exclusively at the national level, while others opted for a combination of national and regional approaches. Several factors, including political systems, regional autonomy, epidemiological trends, cultural factors, and the need for adaptability influenced the decision to govern the situation at.

Political Systems The political structure of a country plays a significant role in determining the level at which mask mandates are implemented. Countries with centralized political systems, such as Denmark and Greece, were more likely to implement national-level mandates, whereas those with more decentralized or federal systems, such as Germany and Spain, opted for a combination of national and regional approaches.

Regional Autonomy In countries with strong regional governments, such as the United Kingdom and Spain, regional authorities played a more prominent role in implementing and adjusting mask mandates. This allowed for a greater degree of autonomy in responding to local conditions and needs, while still adhering to overarching national guidelines (see Chap. 5 on territorial powers).

Epidemiological Trends The distribution of COVID-19 cases and the severity of outbreaks varied considerably across regions within individual countries. As a result, some governments opted for regional approaches to mask mandates, allowing them to tailor their policies to local infection rates and trends. This flexibility enabled a more targeted response to the pandemic.

Need for Adaptability The rapidly evolving nature of the COVID-19 pandemic, with frequent changes in infection rates, transmission patterns, and the emergence of new virus variants, necessitated a high degree of adaptability in public health measures. For some countries, a regional approach to mask mandates provided the flexibility to adjust policies quickly in response to changing circumstances, whereas others preferred a uniform national approach to maintain consistency and avoid confusion among the public (Fig. 13.4).

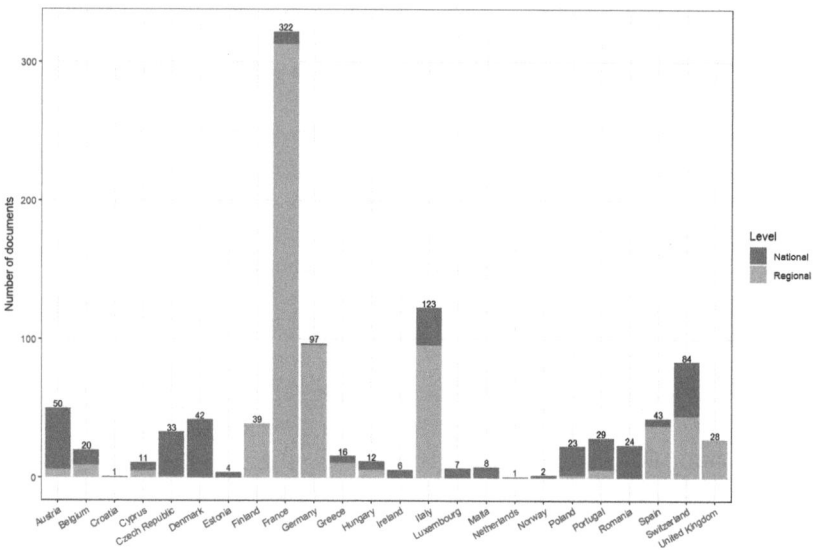

Fig. 13.4 Total number of mask mandate-related legislation in European countries. Source: EXCEPTIUS data, own rendering. Notes: The list may be non-exhaustive

Countries That Implemented Mandates Only on the National Level

Most countries across Europe, such as Slovakia, Slovenia, Poland, Portugal, Baltic states and others, opted for a purely national-level mandates, mostly due to the specifics of political systems and the centralized governmental approach to the crisis management. Mask mandates were enforced at the national level, with a uniform approach across all regions. One primary factor is the need for a unified and consistent approach to public health policy. By implementing mask mandates at the national level, governments can ensure that the entire population adheres to the same set of guidelines, which helps to streamline public health messaging and reduce confusion. This consistent approach is particularly important during a pandemic, as it enables clear communication of expectations and guidelines, fostering public trust and compliance with public health measures.

Additionally, national-level mask mandates can be more effective in controlling the spread of infectious diseases such as COVID-19, as they are not limited by regional boundaries or differences in policy implementation. Viruses do not respect borders, and a patchwork of regional policies can create loopholes that facilitate the spread of the virus. A nationwide mandate allows for a more coordinated and comprehensive response to the pandemic, ensuring that all regions are working together to mitigate transmission and protect public health. Furthermore, national governments typically have greater resources and expertise to monitor and evaluate the impact of mask mandates, enabling them to adapt policies as needed based on the evolving epidemiological situation.

Countries That Implemented Mandates on National and Regional Levels

Some countries, such as Germany, Spain, the United Kingdom, and Switzerland, have opted for a mixed approach to mask mandates, implementing them at both national and regional levels. This strategy allowed for more flexibility and adaptability in response to local conditions. Moreover, it reflects the recognition that different regions may face varying levels of risk and unique challenges in managing the pandemic. By allowing regional or municipal authorities to tailor mask mandates to local conditions, governments can create more targeted and flexible public health policies that address the specific needs of each area.

A mixed approach also acknowledges the importance of balancing nationwide consistency with regional autonomy. In countries with federal or decentralized political systems, regional or municipal authorities often have greater knowledge of local conditions and more direct access to relevant data. This familiarity with the local context enables them to make more informed decisions about the appropriate public health measures to implement in their jurisdiction. Furthermore, by involving regional or municipal authorities in the decision-making process, national governments can promote collaboration and encourage the sharing of best practices and lessons learned. This cooperative approach fosters a more effective and adaptive response to the pandemic, ensuring that public health policies remain responsive to the evolving epidemiological situation in each region.

In the United Kingdom, governments of England, Scotland, Wales, and Northern Ireland each set their own mask-wearing policies, reflecting the devolved nature of the UK's political system. While these policies were similar in many respects, they were tailored to the specific needs and circumstances of each region. Similarly, in Hungary, the national government introduced a nationwide mask mandate on April 27, 2020, requiring masks on public transportation and indoor public spaces. Despite this national level policy, regional governments were permitted to adjust the rules according to the local situation. This allowed for more targeted responses to outbreaks and changing infection rates.

Insights and Conclusions

Upon examining the various approaches to mask mandates across Europe, several patterns emerge. Firstly, countries that opted for nationwide mandates, such as Austria, France, or Italy, tended to adjust their policies in response to the changing epidemiological situation. This suggests that these countries valued a centralized approach, ensuring consistent application of the mandates while remaining adaptable to the fluctuations in transmission rates. Secondly, countries with more decentralized political systems, like Germany or Spain, preferred to allow regional or local authorities to determine the specifics of mask mandates. This approach illustrates the importance of regional autonomy and decision-making in tailoring pandemic responses to the unique circumstances of each area. Drawing conclusions from these patterns, it is evident that various factors played a role in shaping a country's approach to mask mandates. In some cases, the preference for nationwide mandates or voluntary guidelines may be indicative of trust in government and public health authorities, as well as societal attitudes towards individual liberties and collective responsibility. Furthermore, the varied approaches to mask mandates underscore the complex interplay between public health objectives and the need to balance economic, social, and psychological considerations during a crisis.

CONCLUSION

This chapter has examined the various legal frameworks, timelines, regional differences, and national and regional implementations of mask mandates in European countries during the period of 2020–early 2022. The analysis revealed that countries utilized a mix of emergency powers and existing legislation to introduce mask mandates and social distancing measures, depending on the specific circumstances and perceived need for rapid action. The study also identified three broad categories of countries in terms of strictness, with strict, moderate, and lenient countries displaying different timelines for the implementation and retraction of these measures. Additionally, the investigation uncovered distinct regional patterns in the enforcement of mask mandates, with Eastern, Central, Western, Southern, and Northern European countries exhibiting diverse approaches. Lastly, the research highlighted the differences between countries implementing mandates solely at the national level and those employing a combination of national and regional approaches.

The findings of this chapter have several implications for future policies related to public health measures. Understanding the legal frameworks and the diverse approaches employed across Europe provides valuable insights for policymakers in the event of future public health crises. By examining the effectiveness of different strategies, authorities can identify best practices and adopt more targeted, context-sensitive policies. Furthermore, the recognition of regional differences and the potential benefits of a combined national-regional approach can contribute to more efficient and adaptable policy responses to evolving epidemiological situations.

This study has some limitations, such as the focus on mask mandates and social distancing measures, which may not encompass the full range of public health policies enacted during the pandemic. Additionally, the analysis is primarily descriptive and does not provide a comprehensive assessment of the effectiveness of these measures in controlling the spread of the virus.

Future research could build upon this study by exploring the effectiveness of mask mandates and social distancing measures in reducing transmission rates and preventing outbreaks. Moreover, researchers could examine the interplay between public health measures, public compliance, and cultural factors, and investigate how these elements influence the success of different policy approaches.

REFERENCES

Bundgaard, H., Bundgaard, J. S., Raaschou-Pedersen, D.E.T., von Buchwald, C., Todsen, T., Norsk, J.B., Pries-Heje, M. M., et al. (2021). Effectiveness of adding a mask recommendation to other public health measures to prevent SARS-CoV-2 infection in Danish mask wearers: a randomized controlled trial. *Annals of internal medicine, 174*(3), 335–343.

Chu, D. K., Akl, E. A., Duda, S., Solo, K., Yaacoub, S., Schünemann, H. J., & COVID-19 Systematic Urgent Review Group Effort (SURGE) Study Authors. (2020). Physical distancing, face masks, and eye protection to prevent person-to-person transmission of SARS-CoV-2 and COVID-19: A systematic review and meta-analysis. *Lancet, 395*(10242), 1973–1987.

Dodds, K., Broto, V. C., Detterbeck, K., Jones, M., Mamadouh, V., Ramutsindela, M., Varsanyi, M., Wachsmuth, D., & Woon, C. Y. (2020). The COVID-19 pandemic: Territorial, political and governance dimensions of the crisis. *Territory, Politics, Governance, 8*(3), 289–298.

ECDC. (2020). Guidelines for non-pharmaceutical interventions to reduce the impact of COVID-19 in the EU/EEA and the UK. 24 September 2020. ECDC: Stockholm.

Ferejohn, J., & Pasquino, G. (2004). The law of the exception: A typology of emergency powers. *International Journal of Constitutional Law, 2*(2), 210–239.

Fischer, C. B., Adrien, N., Silguero, J. J., Hopper, J. J., Chowdhury, A. I., & Werler, M. M. (2021). Mask adherence and rate of COVID-19 across the United States. *PloS one, 16*(4), e0249891.

Fowler, J. H., Hill, S. J., Levin, R., & Obradovich, N. (2021). Stay-at-home orders associate with subsequent decreases in COVID-19 cases and fatalities in the United States. *PloS one, 16*(6), e0248849.

Ginsburg, T., & Versteeg, M. (2021). The bound executive: Emergency powers during the pandemic. *International Journal of Constitutional Law, 19*(5), 1498–1535.

Gostin, L. O., Hodge, J. G., & Wiley, L. F. (2020). Presidential powers and response to COVID-19. *JAMA, 323*(16), 1547–1548.

Greer, S. L., King, E. J., da Fonseca, E. M., & Peralta-Santos, A. (2020). The comparative politics of COVID-19: The need to understand government responses. *Global Public Health, 15*(9), 1413–1416.

Habibi, R., Burci, G. L., De Campos, T. C., Chirwa, D., Cinà, M., Dagron, S., Eccleston-Turner, M., Forman, L., Gostin, L. O., Meier, B. M., Negri, S., Ooms, G., Sekalala, S., Taylor, A., Yamin, A. E., & Hoffman, S. J. (2020). Do not violate the international health regulations during the COVID-19 outbreak. *The Lancet, 395*(10225), 664–666.

Hale, T., Angrist, N., Goldszmidt, R., Kira, B., Petherick, A., Phillips, T., Webster, S., Cameron-Blake, E., Hallas, L., Majumdar, S., & Tatlow, H. (2021). A global panel database of pandemic policies (Oxford COVID-19 government response tracker). *Nature Human Behaviour, 5*(4), 529–538.

Howard, J., Huang, A., Li, Z., Tufekci, Z., Zdimal, V., van der Westhuizen, H. M., von Delft, A., Price, A., Fridman, L., Tang, L. H., Tang, V., Watson, G. L., Bax, C. E., Shaikh, R., Questier, F., Hernandez, D., Chu, L. F., Ramirez, C. M., & Rimoin, A. W. (2021). An evidence review of face masks against COVID-19. *Proceedings of the National Academy of Sciences, 118*(4), e2014564118.

Islam, N., Sharp, S. J., Chowell, G., Shabnam, S., Kawachi, I., Lacey, B., Massaro, J. M., D'Agostino, R. B., Sr., & White, M. (2020). Physical distancing interventions and incidence of Coronavirus disease 2019: Natural experiment in 149 countries. *British Medical Journal, 370*, m2743.

Lyu, W., & Wehby, G. L. (2020). Community use of face masks and COVID-19: Evidence from a natural experiment of state mandates in the US. *Health Affairs, 39*(8), 1419–1425.

Robert Koch Institute. (2020). Covid-19 Infektionen, General Website (NPGEO Corona Hub). https://npgeo-coronanpgeo-de.hub.arcgis.com/

WHO, (2020). WHO/2019-nCoV/IPC_Masks/2020.5

CHAPTER 14

Education in Times of COVID-19

Olga Litvyak

INTRODUCTION

The COVID-19-induced policy responses in the education sector were particularly diverse, often with distinct approaches adopted not only across Europe but even at the regional level within one country, for example, in Spain (Díez-Gutiérrez & Gajardo Espinoza, 2021) or Germany (Freundl et al., 2021). Furthermore, countries introduced a variety of measures depending on the level of education. While universities largely switched to digital or hybrid learning, daycare and primary schools that initially also faced restrictions on face-to-face learning became crucial in providing support to workers in essential professions and, in the later stage of the pandemic, to parents working from home.

School closures during the lockdown periods largely disrupted education, leading to potential long-term consequences (Blaskó et al., 2022), especially for young children (Fuchs-Schündeln et al., 2020), and increasing existing educational inequalities (Dimopoulos et al., 2021; Engzell

O. Litvyak (✉)
Department of Communication, University of Vienna, Vienna, Austria

Department for E-Governance and Administration, University for Continuing Education Krems, Krems an der Donau, Austria
e-mail: olga.litvyak@donau-uni.ac.at

© The Author(s) 2024   243
C. Egger et al. (eds.), *Covid-19 Containment Policies in Europe*,
International Series on Public Policy,
https://doi.org/10.1007/978-3-031-52096-9_14

et al., 2020). Emerging research on the impact of the COVID-19 pandemic on the education sector has shown that suspension of in-person learning has contributed to learning loss, exacerbating achievement gaps in several European countries (Maldonado & De Witte, 2022), and negatively impacted students' well-being (Grewenig et al., 2021). It also challenged the capacities and abilities of parents, who often had to combine their work responsibilities with home schooling (Hank & Steinbach, 2020; Hipp & Bünning, 2021).

At the same time, the transition to distance and hybrid learning accelerated the digitalisation of education institutions and education systems across Europe, amplifying economic disparities across the countries (Arday, 2022). With digital learning becoming the dominant policy measure, especially in higher education sector, supranational actors, such as the EU and the UN intensified competition for global education governance, proposing own policy solutions (Symeonidis et al., 2021; Williamson et al., 2020; Wulff, 2021).

This chapter discusses differences and similarities in education policy measures adopted during the COVID-19 pandemic in the countries of the European Economic Area and Switzerland and the role of supranational actors. It addresses the differences between crisis policymaking process in the field of education, contrasting them with the COVID-19-related developments, such as epidemiological data and the introduction of lockdowns or other restrictions. Thus, it aims at providing an in-depth comparative examination of the emergency policymaking in the field of education during the COVID-19 pandemic.

Diversity of Policy Responses in the Field of Education Across Europe

The COVID-19 pandemic forced millions of people to stay at home, leaving educational institutions closed for months and, as in other spheres of life in pandemic, often moving everyday life and, as an essential part of it, learning and teaching, into the digital realm. High fragmentation of education governance in the European countries and absence of the EU-wide education policies hindered an effective and coordinated response to the challenges emerging during the pandemic (Symeonidis et al., 2021). In the situation of high uncertainty and growing number of cases and COVID-related deaths, initial crisis-management measures led to closure

of educational institutions and often immediate switch to online education. As a result, educational professionals had to cope with the changing
mode of teaching and adopt to the challenges of new learning environment, often compromising own physical and mental health (Baker et al.,
2021; Košir et al., 2022).

Early childhood education and care sector serves as crucial support
mechanisms for parents and constitutes the first stage of a child's educational journey. The Eurostat data (2022a) reveals that on average 92.9% of
children from age three in the EU were enrolled into early childhood
education in 2020, though enrolment rates vary between 70 and 100%. In
Norway, the share of children attending early childcare facilities was about
95%, whereas in Switzerland this figure drops to 50%. There are also differences between the financial support in this sector, as some countries or
even regions provide state support for early childhood education, even
from the age of one (e.g., in Vienna state in Austria), whereas other countries have no or limited state-funded kindergarten places.

Primary and secondary schools are the cornerstone of education in
Europe. According to the Eurostat statistics (2022b), in 2020 there were
23.3 million primary school pupils with on average 87.3% of them attending public schools. Secondary education still largely constitutes compulsory education in the EEA countries, as children are obliged to attend
school until the age of 14–16 (Eurostat, 2022c), with only 2–5% of this
age group not attending secondary education institutions. As in the case
of primary education, the majority of pupils are educated in public schools.

In 2020, there were 18 million students enrolled in tertiary education
programmes in the EU (Eurostat, 2022d), corresponding to on average
70% rate, though there are large discrepancies among countries with lower
attendance rates (less than 50%) in the CEE countries (World Bank Group,
2022). These data reflect the existing inequalities in the access to higher
education. Though some countries provide state support for tertiary education, disparities in social and economic opportunities often render
higher education inaccessible, unlike compulsory primary and secondary
education. Levels of educational inequality vary across regions, with
Nordic and Western European countries demonstrating lower levels, while
Mediterranean and Eastern European countries report higher inequality
levels (Palmisano et al., 2022).

As in the other aspects of life in times of the COVID-19 pandemic,
education was also impacted, when most countries introduced measures
limiting the transmission consequently bringing social life to a standstill.

Italy, Spain, Austria, the UK, and the Netherlands imposed lockdowns of various intensity (see Chazel's contribution to this volume) in March 2020 that with brief phases of reopening lasted until 2022. The Nordic countries, despite similarities in health and welfare systems, adopted various policies: as Finland, Denmark, and Norway enforced lockdowns, Sweden became known for an alternative approach aiming at herd immunity (Pierre, 2020). The Central and Eastern European countries initially followed Western European countries implementing preventive lockdowns early on and limiting the spread of the COVID-19 in the spring of 2020 (Bohle & Eihmanis, 2022). Educational institutions often had to follow suit and either close completely or provide opportunities for hybrid or digital learning.

However, in the later stages of the crisis, most of the CEE countries failed to implement effective vaccination policies and confront increasing mistrust into the governmental decisions. Hungary, Poland, and Slovakia took advantage of the situation, strengthening illiberal democratic practices (Bohle et al., 2022; Popic & Moise, 2022). In the Baltic countries, on the contrary, early restrictive measures and centralised response provided an opportunity to prepare and preserve the health systems (Webb et al., 2022).

An overview of policy responses in the field of education across countries, provided in Fig. 14.1, reflects the results of the EXCEPTIUS project legislative data analysis. The maps demonstrate how often the measures were mentioned in the legal documents and, therefore, the extent of specific measures in the period between January 2020 and May 2021.

The dataset includes six different types of policy measures: distance learning, hybrid learning, full closure, partial closure, minimal service for essential professions, and finally reopening. The first two measures entail the provisions for either distance learning, such as the use of diverse communication tools, existing and specifically developed online learning platforms or other instruments allowing to provide distance education. Given the extensive range of tools used to ensure distance learning, this chapter does not aim to enumerate the exact tools deployed in each country. Universities had been incorporating online learning platforms into their classroom teaching long before the pandemic; however, other educational sectors often had to implement ad-hoc developed tools (Barberi et al., 2020; Katić et al., 2021; Williamson et al., 2020).

Hybrid learning, a blend of remote and face-to-face instruction, could supplement distance learning or occasionally act as a transitional phase

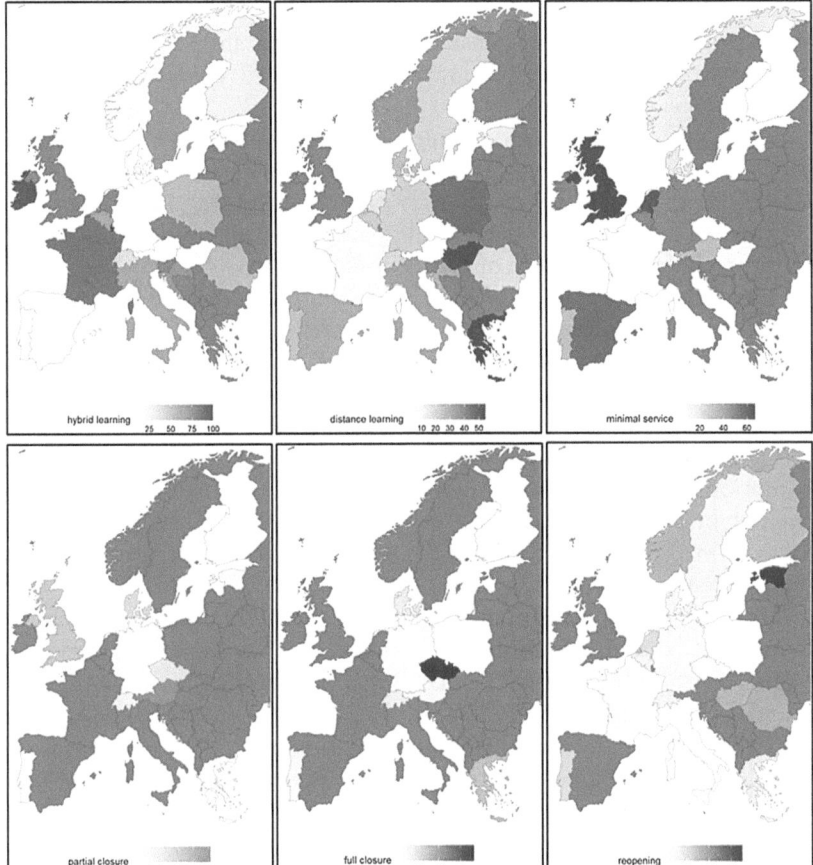

Fig. 14.1   Policy responses in the field of education across countries, January 2020–May 2021. *Source*: EXCEPTIUS dataset, own rendering, demonstrating the salience of the measures in legislative documents by country in percent

between in-person education and remote learning, either prior to or following lockdowns. Full and partial closures of educational institutions encompass restrictions on in-person instruction. Yet, even in the times of full closure of education institutions some countries maintained minimal service for essential professions, offering support for people unable to transition to remote work, such as, for example, doctors, nurses, and police. All the measures could complement each other and be implemented simultaneously, for example, closures, minimal service, and distance learning, and therefore may be referenced concurrently in the analysed legal documents.

Finally, provisions for reopening educational institutions, though primarily put forth when restrictions were being eased, could also be debated alongside discussions about closures or hybrid learning. Therefore, the presence of one of the measures within a legal document does not necessarily preclude the presence of the others.

Table 14.1 provides an overview of the number of coded measures for each country and serves as a basis for interpretation of the results demonstrated in Figs. 14.4, 14.5, 14.6, 14.7, 14.8, and 14.9 in the following sections. In case no legislative documents in a country mentioned specific measures, these countries were excluded from the analysis.

Figure 14.1 reveals important patterns in policy measures in the field of education, elucidating the differences and similarities between the countries. Hybrid and digital learning provisions dominated the policy response and were to some extent introduced in almost all the countries analysed within the project.

However, only a small number of countries implemented full or partial closures of education institutions. Among these countries are Germany, Denmark, the UK, Austria, Czech Republic, Estonia, and Finland that opted for strict lockdowns in the early days of the pandemic. These countries are also among those who maintained minimal educational service for essential professions, aiming to support the crucial workforce. The data demonstrates the lack of this policy measure in the CEE countries except for Hungary and the Czech Republic.

As the pandemic evolved, the policy focus shifted towards relaxing measures in education sector. Despite the positive effect of the closures on the infection transmission, increasing number of expert advice highlighted the negative impact of the closures on socio-emotional well-being of children, youth, educational professionals, and parents (Brooks et al., 2020; Viner et al., 2020), the long-term learning losses (Blaskó et al., 2022) and inequalities between the countries and regions (Esteban-Navarro et al., 2020; Mitescu-Manea et al., 2021). Contrary to the restrictions, relaxing measures contributed to positive emotions (Eisele et al., 2021). Therefore, the prevalence of educational reopening provisions across Europe found in the analysed legal documents is not surprising.

Table 14.1 Overview of the policy measures data by country

	Full closure	Partial closure	Minimal service	Hybrid learning	Distance learning	Reopening
Austria	13	84	49	14	3	
Belgium				24	9	5
Croatia				5	2	
Cyprus					53	32
Czech Republic	63	16	3		1	4
Denmark	38	59	40	21	62	24
Estonia		2		4	3	21
Finland	2	1	2	26	39	29
France			1	38	3	2
Germany	15	19	160	41	74	27
Greece	49	7			92	21
Hungary			2	4	19	11
Ireland				3		
Italy				204	106	4
Luxembourg				4		
Malta				8		8
Netherlands			12		3	4
Norway			4	4	9	8
Poland	1			71	59	2
Portugal	4	2	16	6	13	10
Romania				16	5	10
Spain			153	39	87	
Sweden				7	2	1
Switzerland	19	18	14	57	31	21
United Kingdom		3	6			
Total	204	211	462	596	675	244

Source: EXCEPTIUS data

The comparison of the WHO epidemiological data (WHO, n.d.) on the new cases of the COVID-19 and total deaths for all the countries (Figs. 14.2 and 14.3) generally demonstrates the link between the negative health dynamics during the pandemic and the measures restricting in-person education. Given the existence of significant outliers, such as days with a high number of newly registered cases, for instance, with a maximum of 57,506 in Italy, Fig. 14.2 amplifies the core findings of the comparison for up to 5000 new cases per day, disregarding the outliers. As the figures show, decrease in the number of new cases and fatalities aligns

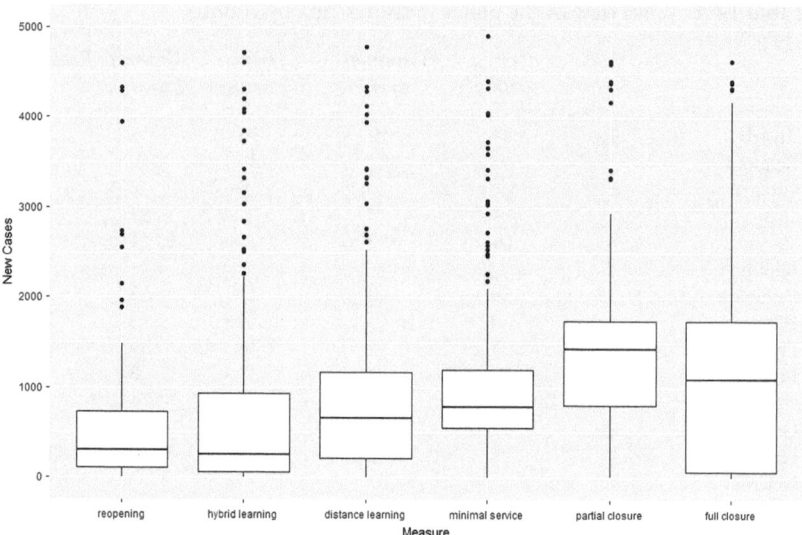

Fig. 14.2 Association between the daily number of new COVID-19 cases limited to maximum 5000 and mentions of policy measures, January 2020–May 2021. *Source*: EXCEPTIUS data, own rendering

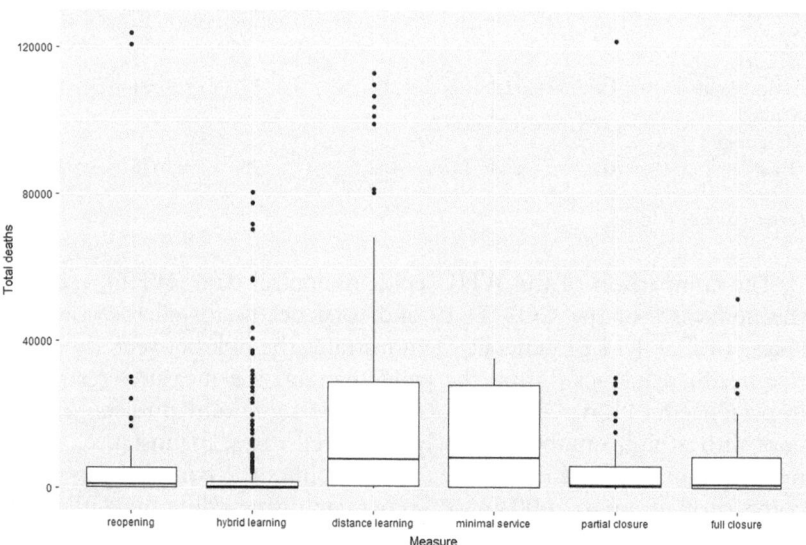

Fig. 14.3 Association between the daily total number of deaths and mentions of policy measures, January 2020–May 2021. *Source*: EXCEPTIUS dataset, own rendering

with legislation on reopening measures and the shift towards hybrid education. There is, however, a large range in the daily number of cases when it comes to the introduction of the full closure measures. The boxplots that link distance learning and the provision of minimal service to total deaths in Fig. 14.3 reveal comparable trends.

Table 14.2 provides an overview of the measures within the dataset concerning different educational fields. It reveals that legislative attention to primary, secondary, and tertiary education is relatively equal, while the portion of documents addressing early childhood education constitutes approximately half of that dedicated to each of the other sectors.

Table 14.2 Policy measures by country and education sector

	Early childhood education	Primary education	Secondary education	Higher education
Austria	19	56	56	32
Belgium	5	10	12	11
Croatia	1	2	2	2
Cyprus	N/A	22	43	20
Czech Republic	8	27	26	26
Denmark	21	122	30	71
Estonia	1	9	11	9
Finland	11	21	44	23
France	12	14	11	7
Germany	87	91	94	64
Greece	37	44	44	44
Hungary	13	5	5	13
Ireland	0	1	1	1
Italy	68	80	86	80
Luxembourg	1	1	1	1
Malta	4	4	4	4
Netherlands	5	6	4	4
Norway	6	6	6	7
Poland	18	22	26	67
Portugal	13	17	16	5
Romania	4	6	12	9
Spain	17	87	88	87
Sweden	2	3	4	1
Switzerland	32	32	48	48
United Kingdom	2	3	3	1
Total	387	691	677	637

Source: EXCEPTIUS data

Wide range of policy responses adopted by nations within the EEA reflects the variety of educational institutions, the distinct characteristics of different educational levels, and their societal roles. The next part of the chapter focuses on the in-depth discussion of the measures introduced within the educational sectors, from early childhood education to primary and secondary schools and, finally, university sector.

DISTANCE AND HYBRID LEARNING MEASURES

Distance and hybrid learning measures dominated the policy response in the field of education (see Figs. 14.4 and 14.5). Almost all the countries investigated within the EXCEPTIUS project made legal provisions for either one or both measures. However, the extent of these measures across different levels of education varies.

Compared to all other education fields, both distance and hybrid learning measures prevail in the field of tertiary education. Due to their age, students at this level typically exhibit greater independence. Coupled with the high level of digital skills they were often considered capable to, often almost immediately, transition to digital learning. Indeed, the Eurostat data (Eurostat, 2020) reveals that in 2019 about 80% of European youth aged between 16 and 24 had basic or above basic digital skills.

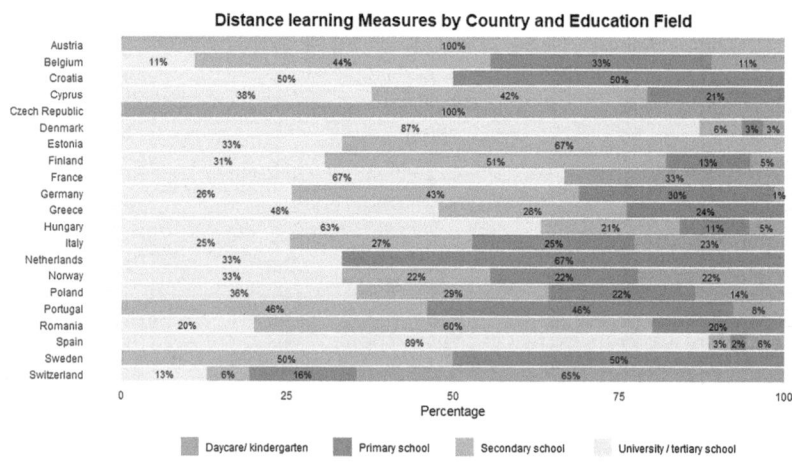

Fig. 14.4 Distance learning measures by country and education field introduced from January 2020 to May 2021. *Source*: EXCEPTIUS data, own rendering

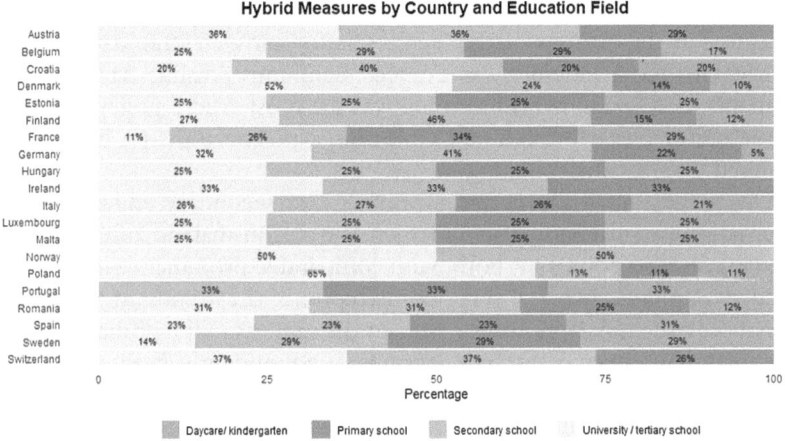

Fig. 14.5 Hybrid learning measures by country and education field introduced from January 2020 to May 2021. *Source*: EXCEPTIUS data, own rendering

Analysis of legislative documents revealed that distance learning was the sole policy response for tertiary education in Greece and neighbouring Cyprus. In Spain, Hungary, Denmark, Finland, Norway, Croatia, and Germany, distance learning emerged as the dominant response in the higher education sector, supplemented by hybrid learning. The data shows that, notably, only Austria, Portugal, and Czech Republic did not make any distance learning provisions for higher education in the legislation analysed, with the latter adopting the measure only in the field of early childhood education and care, that is, daycare and kindergarten. However, both Austria and Portugal largely employed hybrid learning in higher education, resulting in students primarily using online tools for learning and attending exams physically.

On the contrary, distance learning is seldom used in early childhood education and care, a sector pivotal in supporting the workforce by alleviating childcare responsibilities. Considering comparatively high occurrence of the early childhood education mentions in legal documents in Switzerland (see Table 14.2), extensive focus on distance learning in early childhood education is remarkable. In Switzerland, 65% of the documents discussing distance learning provide legal provisions for early childhood education sector. Predictably, most European countries channelled their efforts into creating hybrid possibilities for early childhood education. In case of Croatia, Sweden, and Luxembourg, these were the only identified measures in the analysis of the legal basis for early childhood education policies in the pandemic. In France, Belgium, Poland, Malta, Italy, Romania, and Spain, hybrid learning was the most crucial policy response in the sector of early childhood education with more than a half of the analysed documents legislating its use.

Given the similarities between primary and secondary education sectors, it is not surprising that emergency decision-making often yielded similar policy responses for both, with comparable prominence in the analysed documents. With a very few exceptions the trends in pandemic response in secondary education remain the same as in the primary education, with hybrid and distance learning predominantly used across the EEA countries. In Germany, Cyprus, Hungary, Poland, Portugal, and Greece, distance learning was the prevailing measure in secondary education sector, though, as discussed later, the school closures are seldom mentioned in the countries' legislation. Although the data suggests that distance and hybrid learning provisions are important in Romania, Norway, and Sweden, the limited number of documents coded for these countries precludes definitive interpretations.

CLOSURES AND PROVISION OF THE MINIMAL SERVICE FOR ESSENTIAL PROFESSIONS

Overall full or partial closures (see Figs. 14.6 and 14.7) were rather rare with fewer than half of all the European countries examined within the EXCEPTIUS project opting for these approaches. Even when these measures were implemented, in Finland, Estonia, Poland, Portugal, and the UK, the overall number of mentions of these measures in the data was fewer than 10, thereby making any resulting conclusions somewhat tentative. The measures often complement each other or are used at different times during the pandemic. However, the exact timing is not the focus of this overview. This section largely addresses the closures in combination with the minimal service for essential professions.

The analysis of closures in education corresponds to the trends revealed in the previous section. A distinguishing factor in higher education was the greater prevalence of full or partial closures complemented by distance or hybrid learning provisions discussed earlier. Consistent with its approach in other education sectors, the Czech Republic outlined measures for

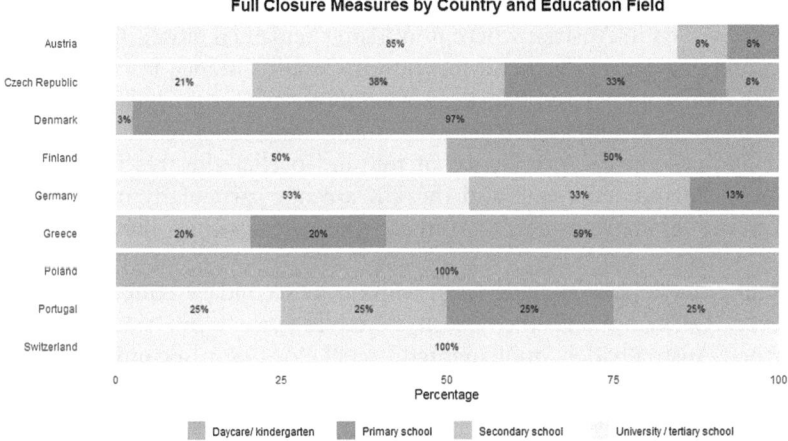

Fig. 14.6 Full closure measures by country and education field introduced from January 2020 to May 2021. *Source*: EXCEPTIUS data, own rendering

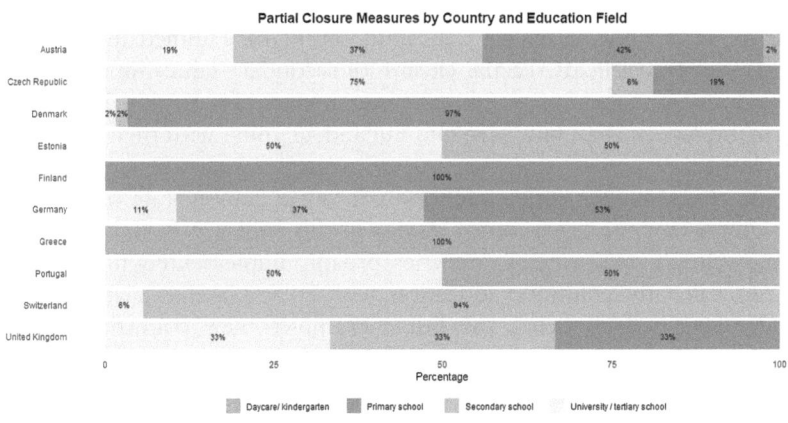

Fig. 14.7 Partial closure measures by country and education field introduced from January 2020 to May 2021. *Source*: EXCEPTIUS data, own rendering

comprehensive and partial closures of tertiary institutions. Similar trends were observed in Austria, where universities remained closed for nearly 2 years, relying on regional and institution-specific distance learning tools. Switzerland notably used full closure measures only for universities, paired with hybrid learning that essentially meant long-term remote learning. The findings on the prevalence of full and partial closures in Finland, Estonia, Poland, Portugal, and the UK are not particularly meaningful, given the limited instances of these measures within the legislative documents.

Full closure policies were less common in secondary education, with Greece, Germany, and the Czech Republic once again standing out. Further, Austria widely implemented partial closures in secondary education. This strategy complemented full closures in Germany, a variation potentially attributable to the specifics of educational decision-making in Germany. It is worth noting that legislative power in the educational sector in Germany is often decentralised, residing more often with the German states than the federal government.

The full closure measures for primary education institutions were rare, though Denmark represents a distinct exception with about 97% of the full closure legislation targeting primary schools. Other countries like Greece and Czech Republic implemented this measure to some extent both in primary and secondary education, opting for a unified approach to these educational fields. Partial closure of secondary educational institutions dominated legislative responses in countries like Austria, Denmark, Germany, Czech Republic, UK, and Finland, aligning with their stringent lockdowns.

The results on the early childhood education demonstrate once again how important the provision of service in this field was during the pandemic. Only a minority of countries broadly implemented full closure measures in early childhood education, with Poland, and to a large extent Greece and Finland being the prime examples. Few countries largely adopted full closure of the early childhood education. Two countries, however, stand out in this regard: Greece and the Czech Republic. Though the latter had provisions for minimal service for essential professions and some distance learning, the COVID-19 response in the country largely entailed the complete closure of early childhood education. In Greece, the governmental response to the pandemic was even more drastic, as almost all the legislation analysed focused on either the full closure or partial closure of early childhood education institutions.

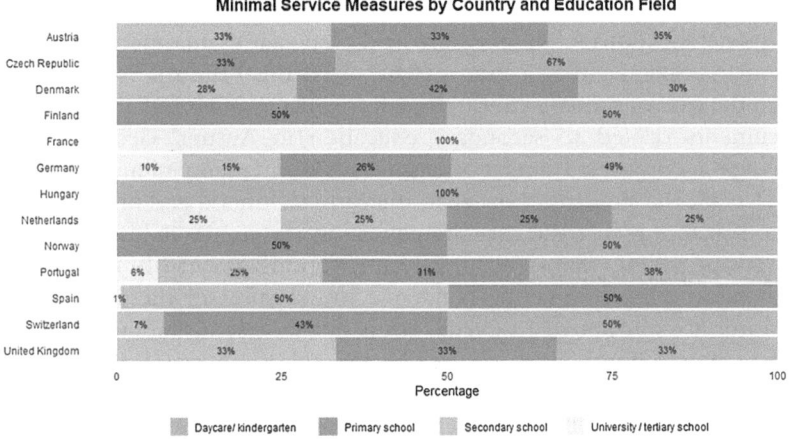

Fig. 14.8 Minimal service provision for essential workers by country and education field introduced from January 2020 to May 2021. *Source*: EXCEPTIUS data, own rendering

When it comes to the provisions of minimal educational services (Fig. 14.8), most measures target early childhood, primary, and secondary education sectors. Large percentage of the provisions for the university education in France and the Netherlands translates to a small number of instances when viewed in absolute terms. Germany stands out as a country that to some extent preserved minimal service in all the fields of education.

The EXCEPTIUS data demonstrates that countries enforcing strict lockdowns, such as Austria, UK, the Netherlands, Denmark, Portugal, and Germany, enacted significant legislative measures to preserve early childhood education and care for essential workers. As discussed earlier, this educational sector was also rarely affected by the closures. The overall approaches to early childhood and primary education highlight their importance for society, particularly for working parents. The pandemic-induced closures, as discussed earlier, added pressure on such parents, thus making minimal service maintenance or distance learning provisions crucial for sustaining the economy and health systems.

Though children in secondary school require less caring as children of pre-school and primary school age, secondary education programmes are more challenging for parents that had to adopt to home schooling. Therefore, providing minimal secondary school service for essential professions remained one of the main legislative priorities for the countries with strict lockdowns. This measure held particular significance in the UK, Denmark, Spain, and to a lesser extent, in Portugal and the Netherlands. As in the case of primary education, approximately a third of all legislative documents related to secondary education in Austria, Germany, and Portugal incorporated similar provisions for maintaining minimal service.

Overall, the similarities between the early childhood and primary education sectors reflect the role the education for young children plays in society, providing important support for working parents. In the time of high uncertainty during the pandemic the closures of these education institutions contributed to overall stress put on parents, some of whom had to juggle home office with childcare and education (Spinelli et al., 2020). Thus, the maintenance of minimal service or at least some provisions for distance or hybrid learning observed in the most EEA countries were necessary to preserve economic performance of adult population, but also to reduce the strain on the health systems.

REOPENING MEASURES

The variety of measures employed by the European countries to navigate the educational implications of the COVID-19 crisis has been substantial, and reopening measures tied directly to the level of restrictions, closures, and limitations on face-to-face instruction. In line with the findings discussed above, legislating reopening of educational institutions (Fig. 14.9) was crucial for countries that underwent closure or transitioned to distance learning.

Yet, the level of attention towards these measures in many countries (see Table 14.1) should be taken in consideration, when interpreting the results. Cyprus, Finland, Denmark, Estonia, Germany, Greece, and Switzerland demonstrated the greatest legislative focus, with mentions of reopening exceeding 20 instances in their legal documents.

The results indicate that reopening legislation across countries mostly focused on the primary and secondary school education, followed by the early childhood education and care, and, finally, to a lesser extent by higher education. The findings reveal a relatively uniform attention patterns across countries, with only a handful of exceptions prioritising a particular educational sector.

With respect to early childhood education and to a lesser extent primary education, Hungary's prominence in attention to reopening

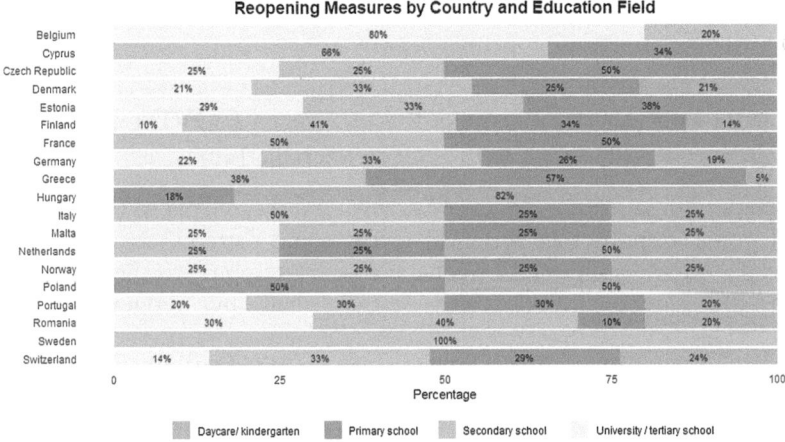

Fig. 14.9 Reopening measures by country and education field introduced from January 2020 to May 2021. *Source*: EXCEPTIUS data, own rendering

measures reflects both the pandemic fatigue and scepticism towards the crisis exhibited by the nation's right-wing government. Primary education was dominating legislative documents on reopening in Greece, and to some extent in Czech Republic and Poland. These measures also highlight the exacerbation of existing gender inequalities during the COVID-19 crisis, especially prominent in Central and Eastern European countries.

Considering the critical role secondary education plays in granting access to higher education and improving life prospects (Grewenig et al., 2021; Hammerstein et al., 2021; Maldonado & De Witte, 2022; Reimers, 2022), it is understandable it often receives equal or even greater attention in reopening-related legislation compared to primary education. Cyprus, Finland, Italy, Romania, and Sweden notably prioritised the reopening measures pertaining to secondary education.

Finally, regarding higher education, reopening measures have been less prominent as universities mainly operated in a distance or hybrid learning mode. Belgium stands out with more than 80% of legislation addressing reopening measures focusing on the university sector. Though other countries, such as Estonia or Romania, target about one-third of their reopening policy measures towards higher education, emphasis on this sector is relatively low. Consequently, these results should be interpreted considering the general lower legislative attention towards higher education, when it comes to reopening measures.

Conclusion: Lessons Learnt from COVID-19 Policymaking in Education Field

Though both salience of education across legal acts related to COVID-19 and policy responses in this field differ, some patterns emerge across Europe, often conditioned by general country response to the pandemic and the extent of restrictions rather than by geographical or cultural factors.

Overall, the EEA countries largely made use of digital and hybrid learning, especially in the primary, secondary, and higher education fields. The countries that had imposed strict lockdowns and closure of early childhood and primary education institutions often aimed to provide support to the parents working in essential professions, offering minimal service in such cases. To some extent, the same trend pertained to secondary education, whereas in higher education minimal service was rather rare.

The analysis has revealed overall consistency in the pandemic policy response in the fields of primary and secondary education sectors across the EEA countries, as measures in the two sectors often converge. Articulation of reopening provisions was important for the sectors that placed additional strain on parents, such as early childhood and primary education.

A challenge to the education systems around the world, the COVID-19 pandemic became a critical juncture that has led to re-evaluation of existing policies and practices in education. Fostering the digitalisation in higher education, it has highlighted the existing inequalities in the access to education, social and geographical digital divides (e.g., between rural and urban regions, see Esteban-Navarro et al., 2020), as well as generational differences among teaching professionals (Webb et al., 2021). In the aftermath of the pandemic, the educational institutions, especially in the field of higher education, returned to the new normal with the changes in teacher training (Baker et al., 2021; Díez-Gutiérrez & Gajardo Espinoza, 2021) and increasing use of digital means in education.

Though overall focus of the EU education policies remained on upskilling and sustainable development, the lessons learned during the pandemic contributed to acceleration of digitalisation in education policies

(Symeonidis et al., 2021). Focus on digitalisation would allow to make education more resilient to new crises and decrease inequalities in access to education, especially in primary and secondary sector, as the future generations of students and education professionals become more proficient in digital skills.

REFERENCES

Arday, J. (2022). COVID-19 and higher education: The times they are a'changin. *Educational Review, 74*(3), 365–377. https://doi.org/10.1080/0013191 1.2022.2076462

Baker, C. N., Peele, H., Daniels, M., Saybe, M., Whalen, K., Overstreet, S., & Trauma-Informed Schools Learning Collaborative The New Orleans. (2021). The experience of COVID-19 and its impact on teachers' mental health, coping, and teaching. *School Psychology Review, 50*(4), 491–504. https://doi.org/10.1080/2372966X.2020.1855473

Barberi, A., Grünberger, N., & Schmölz, A. (2020). Editorial 2/2020: Nähe(n) und Distanz(en) in Zeiten der COVID-19-Krise. *Medienimpulse, 58*(02), Article 02. https://doi.org/10.21243/mi-02-20-32

Blaskó, Z., da Costa, P., & Schnepf, S. V. (2022). Learning losses and educational inequalities in Europe: Mapping the potential consequences of the COVID-19 crisis. *Journal of European Social Policy, 32*(4), 361–375. https://doi.org/10.1177/09589287221091687

Bohle, D., & Eihmanis, E. (2022). East Central Europe in the COVID-19 crisis. *East European Politics, 38*(4), 491–506. https://doi.org/10.1080/2159916 5.2022.2122051

Bohle, D., Medve-Bálint, G., Šćepanović, V., & Toplišek, A. (2022). Riding the COVID waves: Authoritarian socio-economic responses of East Central Europe's anti-liberal governments. *East European Politics, 38*(4), 662–686. https://doi.org/10.1080/21599165.2022.2122044

Brooks, S. K., Webster, R. K., Smith, L. E., Woodland, L., Wessely, S., Greenberg, N., & Rubin, G. J. (2020). The psychological impact of quarantine and how to reduce it: Rapid review of the evidence. *The Lancet, 395*(10227), 912–920. https://doi.org/10.1016/S0140-6736(20)30460-8

Díez-Gutiérrez, E.-J., & Gajardo Espinoza, K. (2021). Educational policies during the lockdown: Measures in Spain after COVID-19. *Center for Educational Policy Studies Journal, 11*(Sp.Issue), 117–140. https://doi.org/10.26529/cepsj.1017

Dimopoulos, K., Koutsampelas, C., & Tsatsaroni, A. (2021). Home schooling through online teaching in the era of COVID-19: Exploring the role of home-related factors that deepen educational inequalities across European societies.

European Educational Research Journal, 20(4), 479–497. https://doi.org/10.1177/14749041211023331

Eisele, O., Litvyak, O., Brändle, V. K., Balluff, P., Fischeneder, A., Sotirakou, C., Syed Ali, P., & Boomgaarden, H. G. (2021). An emotional rally: Exploring commenters' responses to online news coverage of the COVID-19 crisis in Austria. *Digital Journalism, 10*, 1–24. https://doi.org/10.1080/21670811.2021.2004552

Engzell, P., Frey, A., & Verhagen, M. D. (2020, October 29). Learning inequality during the COVID-19 pandemic. *SocArXiv.* https://doi.org/10.31219/osf.io/ve4z7.

Esteban-Navarro, M. A., García-Madurga, M. A., Morte-Nadal, T., & Nogales-Bocio, A. I. (2020). The rural digital divide in the face of the COVID-19 pandemic in Europe—Recommendations from a scoping review. *Informatics, 7*(4), 54. https://doi.org/10.3390/informatics7040054

Eurostat. (2020). Do young people in the EU have digital skills? https://ec.europa.eu/eurostat/web/products-eurostat-news/-/edn-20200715-1.

Eurostat. (2022a). Early childhood education statistics. https://ec.europa.eu/eurostat/statistics-explained/index.php?title=Early_childhood_education_statistics.

Eurostat. (2022b). Primary education statistics. https://ec.europa.eu/eurostat/statistics-explained/index.php?title=Primary_education_statistics.

Eurostat. (2022c). Secondary education statistics. https://ec.europa.eu/eurostat/statistics-explained/index.php?title=Secondary_education_statistics.

Eurostat. (2022d). Tertiary education statistics. https://ec.europa.eu/eurostat/statistics-explained/index.php?title=Tertiary_education_statistics.

Freundl, V., Lergetporer, P., & Zierow, L. (2021). Germany's education policy during the COVID-19 crisis. *Zeitschrift Für Politikwissenschaft, 31*(1), 109–116. https://doi.org/10.1007/s41358-021-00262-7

Fuchs-Schündeln, N., Krueger, D., Ludwig, A., & Popova, I. (2020). *The long-term distributional and welfare effects of COVID-19 school closures.* National Bureau of Economic Research.

Grewenig, E., Lergetporer, P., Werner, K., Woessmann, L., & Zierow, L. (2021). COVID-19 and educational inequality: How school closures affect low- and high-achieving students. *European Economic Review, 140*(November), 103920. https://doi.org/10.1016/j.euroecorev.2021.103920

Hammerstein, S., König, C., Dreisörner, T., & Frey, A. (2021). Effects of COVID-19-related school closures on student achievement—A systematic review. *Frontiers in Psychology, 12*, 746289.

Hank, K., & Steinbach, A. (2020). The virus changed everything, didn't it? Couples' division of housework and childcare before and during the Corona crisis. *Journal of Family Research, 33*(1), 99–114.

Hipp, L., & Bünning, M. (2021). Parenthood as a driver of increased gender inequality during COVID-19? Exploratory evidence from Germany. *European Societies,* 23(supl), S658–S673. https://doi.org/10.1080/1461669 6.2020.1833229

Katić, S., Ferraro, F. V., Ambra, F. I., & Iavarone, M. L. (2021). Distance learning during the COVID-19 pandemic. A comparison between european countries. *Education Sciences,* 11(10), 595

Košir, K., Dugonik, Š., Huskić, A., Gračner, J., Kokol, Z., & Krajnc, Ž. (2022). Predictors of perceived teachers' and school counsellors' work stress in the transition period of online education in schools during the COVID-19 pandemic. *Educational Studies,* 48(6), 844–848.

Maldonado, J. E., & De Witte, K. (2022). The effect of school closures on standardised student test outcomes. *British Educational Research Journal,* 48(1), 49–94. https://doi.org/10.1002/berj.3754

Mitescu-Manea, M., Safta-Zecheria, L., Neumann, E., Bodrug-Lungu, V., Milenkova, V., & Lendzhova, V. (2021). Inequities in first education policy responses to the COVID-19 crisis: A comparative analysis in four Central and East European countries. *European Educational Research Journal,* 20(5), 543–563.

Palmisano, F., Biagi, F., & Peragine, V. (2022). Inequality of opportunity in tertiary education: Evidence from Europe. *Research in Higher Education,* 63(3), 514–565. https://doi.org/10.1007/s11162-021-09658-4

Pierre, J. (2020). Nudges against pandemics: Sweden's COVID-19 containment strategy in perspective. *Policy and Society,* 39(3), 478–493. https://doi.org/ 10.1080/14494035.2020.1783787

Popic, T., & Moise, A. D. (2022). Government responses to the COVID-19 pandemic in Eastern and Western Europe: The role of health, political and economic factors. *East European Politics,* 38(4), 507–528. https://doi.org/ 10.1080/21599165.2022.2122050

Reimers, F. M. (2022). *Primary and secondary education during COVID-19: Disruptions to educational opportunity during a pandemic.* Springer Nature.

Spinelli, M., Lionetti, F., Pastore, M., & Fasolo, M. (2020). Parents' stress and children's psychological problems in families facing the COVID-19 outbreak in Italy. *Frontiers in Psychology, 11.* https://www.frontiersin.org/articles/10.3389/fpsyg.2020.01713

Symeonidis, V., Francesconi, D., & Agostini, E. (2021). The EU's education policy response to the COVID-19 pandemic: A discourse and content analysis. *Center for Educational Policy Studies Journal,* 11(Sp. Issue). https://doi.org/10.26529/cepsj.1137

Viner, R. M., Russell, S. J., Croker, H., Packer, J., Ward, J., Stansfield, C., Mytton, O., Bonell, C., & Booy, R. (2020). School closure and management practices during coronavirus outbreaks including COVID-19: A rapid systematic review.

The Lancet Child & Adolescent Health, 4(5), 397–404. https://doi.org/10.1016/S2352-4642(20)30095-X

Webb, C. L., Kohler, K. L., & Piper, R. E. (2021). Teachers' preparedness and professional learning about using educational technologies during the COVID-19 pandemic. *Journal of Online Learning Research, 7*(2), 113–132.

Webb, E., Winkelmann, J., Scarpetti, G., Behmane, D., Habicht, T., Kahur, K., Kasekamp, K., Köhler, K., Miščikienė, L., Misins, J., Reinap, M., Slapšinskaitė-Dackevičienė, A., Võrk, A., & Karanikolos, M. (2022). Lessons learned from the Baltic countries' response to the first wave of COVID-19. *Health Policy, 126*(5), 438–445. https://doi.org/10.1016/j.healthpol.2021.12.003

WHO. (n.d.) WHO Coronavirus (COVID-19) dashboard | WHO Coronavirus (COVID-19) dashboard with vaccination data. Retrieved April 15, 2023, from https://COVID19.who.int/data.

Williamson, B., Eynon, R., & Potter, J. (2020). Pandemic politics, pedagogies and practices: Digital technologies and distance education during the coronavirus emergency. *Learning, Media and Technology, 45*(2), 107–114. https://doi.org/10.1080/17439884.2020.1761641

World Bank. (2022). School enrollment, tertiary (% gross)—European Union | Data. https://data.worldbank.org/indicator/SE.TER.ENRR?end=2020&locations=EU&start=2020&view=map.

Wulff, A. (2021). Global Education Governance in the Context of COVID-19: Tensions and Threats to Education as a Public Good. *Development, 64*(1), 74–81. https://doi.org/10.1057/s41301-021-00293-1

CHAPTER 15

Compulsory Medical Examinations and "Green Pass"

Clara Egger and Raul Magni-Berton

INTRODUCTION

To manage the COVID-19 pandemic, European governments have combined restrictive measures with a close monitoring of the epidemiological
situation. The most stringent measures—such as the imposition of lockdowns, curfews and the closure of national borders—have always been
justified by epidemiological indicators, in particular the evolution of
COVID-19 cases and deaths. At the same time, the relaxing of containment measures has often come with the requirement to undergo compulsory medical examinations. In the summer of 2020, bars and restaurants

C. Egger (✉)
Public Administration and Sociology,
Erasmus University Rotterdam, Rotterdam, The Netherlands
e-mail: egger@essb.eur.nl

R. Magni-Berton
European School of Political and Social Sciences, ESPOL-LAB Université
Catholique de Lille, Lille, France
e-mail: raul.magniberton@univ-catholille.fr

© The Author(s) 2024   265
C. Egger et al. (eds.), *Covid-19 Containment Policies in Europe*,
International Series on Public Policy,
https://doi.org/10.1007/978-3-031-52096-9_15

in Belgium, Italy and Cyprus reopened only to people able to show evidence of a negative COVID-19 test. Later in 2021, as COVID-19 vaccines became available to the public and vaccination the leading strategy to contain the pandemic, COVID-19 passes became widespread across Europe—with the notable exceptions of Luxembourg, Malta and Sweden. Under various names, such as the Green Pass in Italy, the 2 or 3 G Pass in Germany, the Immunity Pass in Hungary or the Freedom ID in Lithuania, these documents linked the restoration of daily freedoms to a negative COVID-19 test, proof of vaccination or full recovery from the disease. Much has been written about the role of vaccination policy in containing the COVID-19 pandemic (see Charrier et al., 2022 for a review).

Several datasets document the vaccination plans adopted, how different target groups were prioritised for access to vaccination, and whether vaccination policies were compulsory or not (Cameron-Blake et al., 2023; Cheng et al., 2020). However, most of these datasets begin their coverage in 2022 (Cameron-Blake et al., 2023), when controversies about the merits of vaccine mandates became heated in both the academic and public spheres (see, among others, Karaivanov et al., 2022; Kuznetsova et al., 2022). Moreover, we know little about the compulsory medical examinations that took place before then. The tracking of COVID-19 health surveillance measures before 2022 mostly concerns internal and external border restrictions and the availability of testing facilities (Cheng et al., 2020) but does not examine how compulsory medical procedures were used to relax restrictions on mass gatherings, allow access to public and private services, and various socio-cultural activities.

This chapter aims to fill this gap and focuses on two main medical procedures: the mandatory testing policy implemented before the mass roll-out of COVID-19 vaccines, and the implementation of COVID-19 passes. Our descriptive analysis is divided into three main sections. First, we map how different European countries relied on mandatory testing and green passes and show that, unlike other non-pharmaceutical policies, the implementation of such policies is quite homogeneous across (see the other chapters gathered in Part III of this volume). Main differences concern the territorial level of implementation of COVID-19 passes and their date of introduction. Second, we focus on the use of COVID-19 passes and examine whether their adoption is associated with a deterioration of the public health situation in a country or with the overall stringency of the crisis response. In other words, we ask whether COVID-19 passes are yet another policy instrument used by restrictive governments, or whether they are part of a different approach to public health monitoring. Finally, we conclude our chapter with some insights into the effectiveness of COVID-19 passes in generating support for vaccination policies.

Strengthening Control Measures to Ease Restrictions: Comparing Mandatory Testing and COVID-19 Passes

The EXCEPTIUS data allow to trace how compulsory medical examinations have been used together with other types of restrictive measures. A typical and well-documented example concerns the use of compulsory medical examinations at international and internal borders. In the summer of 2020, all European countries reopened their external borders (and internal borders in the case of federal states) to people who can prove their immunity, either through vaccination, recovery status or negative COVID-19 tests. What is less well documented, however, is how compulsory medical procedures have been used at the domestic level, not to control the free movement of individuals, but to guarantee other types of fundamental or everyday freedoms—such as the freedom of association or the use of public and private facilities. In this section, we focus on two of the most commonly used medical procedures: compulsory testing and the COVID-19 passes.

Prior to the release of COVID-19 vaccines to the public, EXCEPTIUS data show that very few countries relied on compulsory testing to grant access to mass gatherings or closed public and private spaces. Compulsory testing procedures condition access to some spaces and participation to mass events to evidence of a negative COVID-19 test. In most cases, large gatherings were banned, shops and restaurants were closed, or strict social distancing was enforced. Figure 15.1 shows the countries that implemented compulsory testing policies during the three COVID-19 waves covered by EXCEPTIUS data (from January 2020 to April 2021). Note that coverage ends shortly after the start of mass vaccination campaigns in Europe and before the introduction of the EU COVID-19 digital certificate in July 2021.

Three groups of countries can be distinguished. The first—consisting of Denmark and the Czech Republic—includes countries that started implementing mandatory testing in the first wave and continued to do so throughout the three waves. Mandatory testing for access to closed spaces

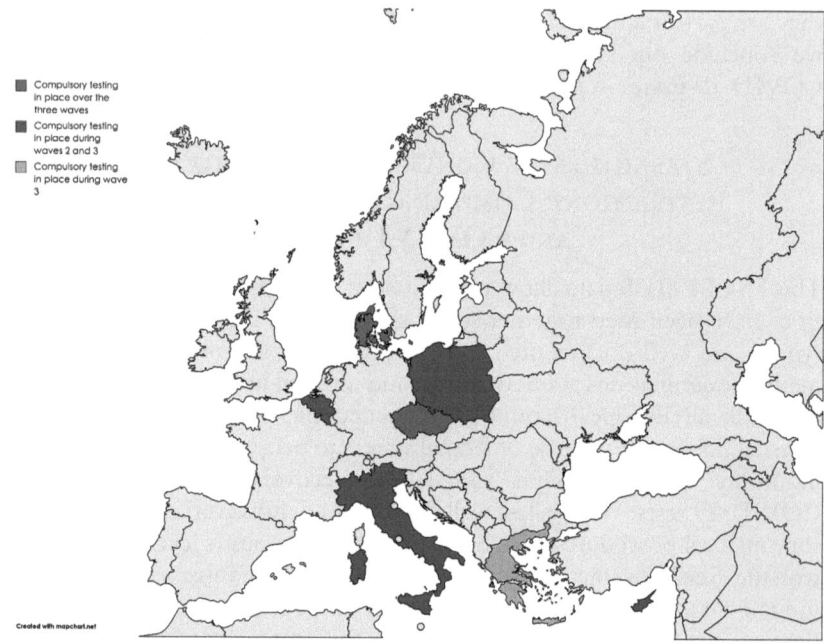

Fig. 15.1 Compulsory testing to access mass events and public and private facilities. *Source*: EXCEPTIUS, own rendering

and mass gatherings was introduced in Denmark as early as on 17 March 2023. Czechia followed a month later, on 23 April 2020. Initially, mandatory testing was only required to access closed spaces but was extended to mass gatherings on 17 May 2021. Belgium, Cyprus, Italy and Poland started enforcing mandatory testing in the second wave, but with a very different timing. While Cyprus adopted regulations on 14 July 2020, the other countries did so only in the autumn (30 November for Italy, 30 October for Poland) or winter of 2020 (Christmas Eve for Belgium). In these countries, a negative test was required to access every closed space. Only one country in our dataset, Greece, required a mandatory test to access closed spaces only during wave 3 and implemented as of 10 April 2021.

In contrast, the introduction of a COVID-19 pass concerned a much larger number of countries in Europe. This pass required individuals to show proof of some form of immunity to COVID-19 before entering public or private spaces and attending mass events. Most of the countries in our sample accepted different types of evidence, such as a negative COVID-19 test less than 48 h old, a complete vaccination scheme or a recovery status. In some cases—described below—the COVID-19 pass was restricted to vaccinated persons only. This widespread use can be explained by two factors: the mass availability of vaccines, but also the decision of the European Union to enforce an EU-wide COVID-19 digital certificate, which facilitated its adoption by many countries. Table 15.1 shows the timing of the introduction of the COVID-19 pass in Europe and does not suggest any specific patterns of diffusion of the pass, for example, in relation to neighbouring countries. Instead, each country seems to have followed its own strategy, although some explicitly mentioned that the EU digital certificate provided strong incentives for them to develop their own pass.

As with the compulsory testing policy, Denmark—together with Hungary—pioneered the movement. However, the enforcement of the

Table 15.1 Month of enforcement of the COVID-19 pass per country

Month of enforcement	Country
Mar/21	Hungary
Apr/21	Denmark
May/21	Austria
May/21	Cyprus
May/21	Lithuania
May/21	Czech Republic
Jun/21	Italy
Jun/21	Latvia
Jul/21	France
Jul/21	Ireland
Aug/21	Estonia
Sep/21	Slovenia
Sep/21	Malta
Sep/21	Switzerland
Oct/21	Belgium
Oct/21	Bulgaria
Oct/21	Finland
Nov/21	Netherlands
Nov/21	Portugal
Nov/21	Croatia

Source: EXCEPTIUS, own rendering

COVID-19 pass in Denmark was suspended 6 months after its introduction, in September 2021, while the Hungarian immunity pass was converted to a vaccine-only pass in February 2022. Both countries were closely followed by Austria, Cyprus, Lithuania—called Freedom ID—and the Czech Republic in May 2021. In Cyprus, a recovery status was not sufficient to issue a "safe pass". Austria made the headlines with the adoption of a general COVID-19 vaccination mandate in the country on 5 February 2022. This COVID-19 Mandatory Vaccination Ordinance stipulated that anyone who did not comply with the vaccination mandate after 15 March 2022 could be fined up to 3600 euros, depending on their income level. The fine could be waived if a person was vaccinated within 2 weeks of being reminded, and a person could only be fined four times in a calendar year for non-compliance. Latvia and Italy introduced the pass in June 2021, but in Italy only one dose of vaccine was required. France, Ireland and Estonia followed suit in July and August, immediately introducing the EU COVID-19 digital pass. In Ireland, the pass was only required to access indoor spaces where social distancing could not be maintained.

The other countries in our sample adopted the COVID-19 pass in the autumn, with some national specificities. In Portugal, high-risk municipalities were offered the possibility to request a COVID-19 pass in July 2021, except on Friday evenings, weekends and national holidays. Its use was extended nationally in November 2021. However, vaccinated persons could only obtain a pass if they could provide evidence of a recent negative COVID-19 test. In Croatia, the use of the pass was restricted to public buildings. Although not shown in Table 15.1, Greece introduced a pass as well, but we were unable to collect data on the date of its introduction.

Other countries were characterised by a more decentralised approach (see Magni-Berton in this volume for a more detailed analysis). In Spain, despite high infection rates, only the tourist regions of Galicia and the Canary Islands adopted it. In Germany, the rules for mandatory testing varied from place to place and state to state. Bade-Württemberg accepted the usual three types of proof (3G for "geimpft, getestete, gennesen"). In Rhineland-Palatinate and Saarland, 2G rules restricted the issue of the pass to vaccinated or recovered people, while in the latter region a negative test was required on top of either document to access nightclubs and Christmas markets. However, on 7 April 2022, the German Bundestag rejected a national vaccination mandate (Gehrke, 2022). In the UK, only England

and Scotland required a pass to attend mass gatherings from September 2021, while enforcement was left to venues in Sweden and cities in Norway.

PUBLIC HEALTH CONCERNS VERSUS OVERALL STRINGENCY OF CRISIS RESPONSE: WHAT DRIVES THE ADOPTION OF THE COVID-19 PASS?

To further explain the rationale behind the different strategies adopted by European governments, this section examines the relationship between the adoption of the COVID-19 pass, the evolution of the severity of the COVID-19 pandemic on the national territory and the overall stringency of the crisis response. Our reasoning is as follows. On the one hand, COVID-19 passes can be seen as a way of preserving some daily freedoms while limiting their impact on public health indicators in a high-risk epidemiological context characterised, for example, by an increase in cases and deaths. The timeline of COVID-19 adoption in Europe—see Table 15.1— provides some evidence to support this interpretation. More than half of the countries in our sample introduced the pass before the winter season— when people's promiscuity is high—or at the peak of the tourist season (France, Portugal, Spain). On the other hand, we can expect the introduction of the COVID-19 passes to be associated with the overall stringency of the crisis response in a country. As documented in previous studies (Egger et al., 2021; Engler et al., 2021, Vulcano in this volume), some governments were caught in a vicious circle of distrust when designing their COVID-19 management policies. Public trust is key to ensuring compliance with COVID-19 measures. The higher the level of public trust, the less the need for authorities to rely on very stringent measures to ensure compliance. Conversely, governments facing low levels of public trust are forced to rely on very stringent policies to enforce containment measures. In doing so, however, governments further erode their (limited) trust capital and must always go the extra mile to ensure a minimum level of compliance with sanitary measures. According to this interpretation, we should see that COVID-19 passes are adopted by countries that do not necessarily face higher epidemiological risks but are characterised by very stringent policies. To explore the validity of both explanations, we rely only on descriptive data, due to the limited size of our sample. We used the data of Mathieu et al. (2021) and calculated the monthly evolution (in percentage) of the number of COVID-19 cases and deaths 1 month before the implementation of the COVID-19 laws in each country. We had to rely on monthly indicators because for more than half of the countries in our sample the exact date of enforcement of the COVID-19 pass was not available. Nevertheless, we believe that these indicators provide a first indication of some of the drivers of such a government decision. The results of this descriptive analysis are presented in Table 15.2.

Four groups of countries can be distinguished. The first group—in bold-includes countries that adopted the COVID-19 pass in a context of marked deterioration in epidemiological indicators. The second group— in bold italics—includes countries that experienced an increase in the number of cases and deaths before adopting the pass, but to a lesser extent. Estonia could be included in the first group for the increase in the number

Table 15.2 Evolution of the COVID-19 epidemiological indicators 1 month before the enforcement of the COVID-19 pass

Country	Month of enforcement of COVID-19 pass	Monthly evolution of COVID-19 cases (m-1)	Monthly evolution of COVID-19 deaths (m-1)
Slovenia	**Sep/21**	**82%**	**52%**
Switzerland	**Sep/21**	**75%**	**79%**
Netherlands	**Nov/21**	**60%**	**55%**
Croatia	**Nov/21**	**53%**	**48%**
Cyprus	**May/21**	**44%**	**56%**
Bulgaria	**Oct/21**	**33%**	**71%**
Lithuania	*May/21*	*46%*	*10%*
Latvia	*Jun/21*	*20%*	*16%*
Belgium	*Oct/21*	*5%*	*36%*
Estonia	*Aug/21*	*7%*	*88%*
Denmark	Apr/21	42%	–327%
Ireland	Jul/21	30%	–96%
Portugal	Nov/21	26%	–8%
Hungary	Mar/21	26%	–22%
Finland	Oct/21	–43%	27%
Austria	May/21	14%	5%
Italy	*Jun/21*	*–120%*	*–112%*
Czech Republic	*May/21*	*–200%*	*–128%*
France	*Jul/21*	*–379%*	*–336%*

Source: EXCEPTIUS data; Mathieu et al. (2021)

of deaths, but not for the number of cases. A third group of countries showed a more mixed pattern. In some cases (e.g. Denmark, Hungary, Ireland and Portugal) the number of cases increased but this was not yet associated with an increase of the lethality of the disease. In this case, the adoption of the COVID-19 pass can be seen as a precautionary measure to anticipate a possible increase in the number of deaths, for example, due to overcrowding in hospitals. In Finland, the pass was introduced when the number of cases was falling sharply, but after an increase in the number of deaths. In Austria, the number of cases and deaths increased, but the increase was close to zero. The last group of three countries (in italics) is characterised by a reverse and less expected trend. In these countries, the pass was introduced at a time when there was no evidence of a deterioration in public health.

According to the index presented by Chazel in this volume, the last group of countries scores highly in terms of non-pharmaceutical policy stringency. In particular, France, which has implemented the COVID-19 pass in a situation where infections and deaths are decreasing, has been classified as the most stringent country in Europe. Italy was the second. The case of the Czech Republic is less clear, although it was ranked quite high (seventh) in each wave. Only Austria and Spain are identified as more stringent than the Czech Republic in the first two waves. As we have seen, Austria implemented the COVID-19 pass without any risk of infection or death. Unfortunately, no vaccination data are available for Spain.

Globally, therefore, we can conclude that the motivation to introduce the COVID-19 pass was generally due to a deterioration of epidemiological indicators, except in countries where non-pharmaceutical restrictions were already particularly high.

Does COVID-19 Pass Boost Vaccination?

A key argument used by policymakers to justify the introduction of the COVID-19 pass is the need to create incentives for people to be vaccinated in a context where mass vaccination was considered as the safest and most effective strategy to contain the pandemic. Although most countries accepted different types of evidence of immunity status, vaccination was the simplest and least demanding way to obtain an indefinite COVID-19 pass. In contrast, relying on COVID-19 testing meant that people had to be tested almost every time they wanted to enter a public or private space, as the validity of the tests often expired after 48 h. A key question is whether the introduction of the COVID-19 pass convinced more people to be vaccinated for the first time. Previous studies have provided mixed evidence on this question. While COVID-19 mandates have not been shown to be particularly effective in reducing vaccine hesitancy among the adult population in Europe (Kuznetsova et al., 2022) and the USA (Mello et al., 2022), proof of COVID-19 vaccination requirements for access to public places and non-essential businesses contributed to an increase in vaccine uptake in Canada, France, Germany and Italy (Karaivanov et al., 2022). To contribute to such debates, Fig. 15.2 compares the proportion of the population primo-vaccinated one month before and after the introduction of COVID-19 passes, using vaccination data from Mathieu et al. (2021). Note that we do not take into account differences in the type of passes used, as the variation between European countries is rather limited, as explained in section "Strengthening Control Measures to Ease Restrictions: Comparing Mandatory Testing and COVID-19 Passes". Looking at the figure, two findings emerge. First, passes do not appear to be particularly effective in countries that are already characterised by a high uptake of COVID-19 vaccines, such as Belgium, the Netherlands, Finland and the European record holder, Portugal.

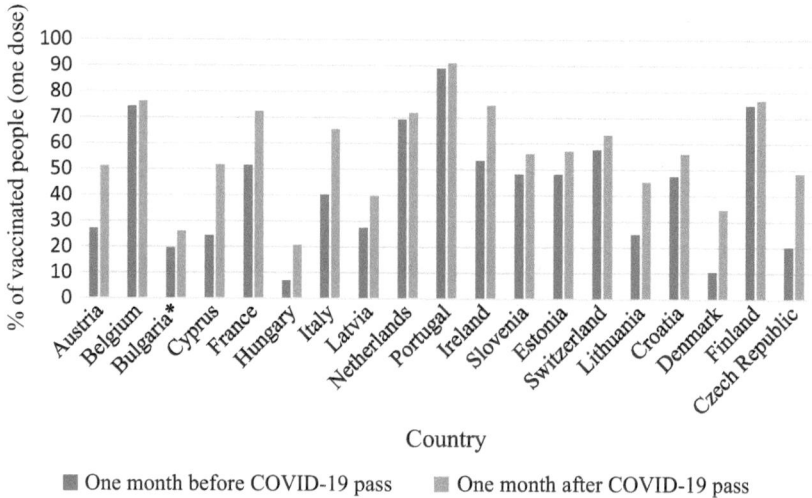

Fig. 15.2 Vaccination rate before and after the implementation of the COVID-19 pass. *Source*: EXCEPTIUS and Mathieu et al. (2021)

Second, in Austria, Cyprus, France, Hungary, Italy, Latvia, Ireland, Lithuania, Denmark and the Czech Republic, the introduction of COVID-19 passes was followed by a notable increase in vaccination coverage, despite large differences in the proportion of vaccinated persons before the measure was introduced. Third, in Bulgaria, Estonia, Slovenia and Switzerland, the enforcement of passes did not lead to a massive decrease in vaccine hesitancy in a context of low to moderate vaccine uptake. Taken together, this descriptive evidence suggests that COVID-19 passes alone are not sufficient to increase vaccination coverage. Their impact is more likely to depend on the initial level of vaccination and people's attitudes towards vaccination.

We conclude this chapter by examining these attitudes. Attitudes to the COVID-19 vaccine may vary according to general attitudes to vaccination and the specific context of the pandemic, which was characterised by emergency and restrictive policies. The Vaccine Confidence Project, funded by the European Commission, provides bi-annual surveys of public attitudes to vaccines across the EU. Their most recent report (de Figueiredo et al., 2022) introduced the question of confidence in the COVID-19 vaccine in almost all EU countries except the Czech Republic.

To capture the specificity of the COVID-19 vaccine, we compare the level of confidence in it to the confidence in the flu vaccine. Confidence is measured in terms of potential side effects (% of people who think the vaccine is safe). Overall, while the flu vaccine is considered safe by 81.4% of Europeans, the COVID 19 vaccine is considered safe by 73.5% of respondents. In each country, confidence in the COVID-19 vaccine is lower than in the flu vaccine. The difference is particularly small in Denmark and Portugal, where confidence is particularly high. On the contrary, in Eastern countries, where vaccine confidence is generally the lowest, the difference between flu and COVID-19 vaccines is particularly large. This is particularly the case in Bulgaria, Croatia, Lithuania, Romania, Slovakia and Slovenia. In Latvia, the difference is smallest because confidence in flu vaccine is already particularly low. These differences in confidence are not associated with the month in which the COVID-19 passes are administered. However, we find an association between the relative lack of confidence and the epidemiological context: the more the latter worsened when the pass was introduced, the lower the confidence, both in absolute terms and relative to the confidence in flu vaccines. This correlation could be interpreted as follows: governments in countries with low confidence in vaccines have to wait for an emergency to implement the pass in a consensual way. This is not the case for governments in countries with high confidence in vaccines. However, there are some exceptions. Governments in Austria, France and Hungary implement passes without facing a particular public health emergency, despite relatively low levels of confidence in vaccines. On the other hand, Cyprus implemented the COVID-19 pass in a worsened epidemiological context, despite a high level of confidence in vaccines.

Conclusion

In contrast to the variants of compulsory testing, the COVID-19 pass has been widely implemented in Europe with similar modalities. Our data cover 23 EU countries plus Norway, Switzerland and the United Kingdom. Data are not available for Romania, Poland and Slovakia. Only three countries do not use it: Luxembourg, Malta and Sweden. Some countries have implemented it at sub-national level, including Germany, Norway, Spain and the United Kingdom. The date of implementation varies from March 2021 (Hungary) to November 2021 (Croatia, the Netherlands and Portugal). The impact on the vaccination rate also varies between countries: in Austria, Cyprus, the Czech Republic, Denmark and Italy, the vaccination rate increased by more than 20% after the introduction of the pass. In Belgium, the Netherlands, Finland and Portugal, on the other hand, the vaccination rate remained almost the same.

The implementation of COVID-19 passes also varied according to the epidemiological context. In most countries, the pass was introduced after an increase in infections or deaths due to COVID-19. Three countries (Czech Republic, France and Italy) introduced their passes when the number of infections and deaths was falling sharply. In France and Italy, this could be explained by the calendar, just before the tourist season. Another complementary explanation could be the fact that they were among the countries that implemented the most stringent non-pharmaceutical measures. Austria could be included in this group, as it introduced the pass in a stable epidemiological context. This suggests that these governments are following their own preferences rather than adapting their policies. Finally, we also observe that the countries that waited for the epidemiological indicators to deteriorate are usually those where confidence in vaccines is lower. In high-confidence contexts, the introduction of the pass was not clearly associated with such a deterioration. However, in the case of Austria, France, Hungary and possibly the Czech Republic, the pass was introduced in non-emergency situations despite relatively low confidence in vaccines.

In the light of these findings, we conclude with some suggestions. Vaccination in the context of a pandemic can help to create personal benefits for people who help to reduce the spread of the virus. However, it can also create huge disadvantages for those who refuse to be vaccinated, leading to protests, polarisation or economic stagnation. To avoid these side effects, vaccination should be used in countries with high levels of trust (including trust in vaccines) but low vaccination rates. Denmark is a typical case. Given the moderate impact of the vaccination rate, the opposite case—a country with relatively low confidence in vaccines and the political system and high vaccination rates should find alternative ways to encourage people to vaccinate themselves. The Netherlands is a typical case. In the intermediate context, it is debatable and probably right for many countries to introduce a vaccination pass if the spread of the virus is worrying. On the other hand, a vaccination pass should be avoided when the vaccination rate is above 60%.

References

Cameron-Blake, E., Tatlow, H., Andretti, B., Boby, T., Green, K., Hale, T., Petherick, A., Phillips, T., Pott, A., Wade, A., & Zha, H. (2023). A panel dataset of COVID-19 vaccination policies in 185 countries. *Nature Human Behaviour.* https://doi.org/10.1038/s41562-023-01615-8

Charrier, L., Garlasco, J., Thomas, R., Gardois, P., Bo, M., & Zotti, C. M. (2022). An overview of strategies to improve vaccination compliance before and during the COVID-19 pandemic. *International Journal of Environmental Research and Public Health, 19*(17), 11044.

Cheng, C., Barceló, J., Hartnett, A. S., Kubinec, R., & Messerschmidt, L. (2020). COVID-19 government response event dataset (CoronaNet v.1.0). *Nature Human Behaviour, 4*(7), 756–768. https://doi.org/10.1038/s41562-020-0909-7

de Figueiredo, A., Eagan, R. L., Hendrickx, G., Karafillakis, E., van Damme, P., & Larson, H. J. (2022). *State of vaccine confidence in the European Union.* Publications Office of the European Union.

Egger, C. M., Magni-Berton, R., Roché, S., & Aarts, K. (2021). I do it my way: Understanding policy variation in pandemic response across Europe. *Frontiers in Political Science, 3*, 622069.

Engler, S., Brunner, P., Loviat, R., Abou-Chadi, T., Leemann, L., Glaser, A., & Kübler, D. (2021). Democracy in times of the pandemic: explaining the variation of COVID-19 policies across European democracies. *West European Politics, 44*(5–6), 1077–1102.

Gehrke, L. (2022). German parliament rejects mandatory coronavirus vaccination. *Politico.* Retrieved June 1, 2023, from https://www.politico.eu/article/german-parliament-rejects-mandatory-coronavirus-vaccination/

Karaivanov, A., Kim, D., Lu, S. E., & Shigeoka, H. (2022). COVID-19 vaccination mandates and vaccine uptake. *Nature Human Behaviour, 6*(12), 1615–1624.

Kuznetsova, L., Diago-Navarro, E., Mathu, R., & Trilla, A. (2022). Effectiveness of COVID-19 vaccination mandates and incentives in Europe. *Vaccines, 10*(10), 1714.

Mathieu, E., Ritchie, H., Ortiz-Ospina, E., Roser, M., Hasell, J., Appel, C., Giattino, C., & Rodés-Guirao, L. (2021). A global database of COVID-19 vaccinations. *Nature Human Behaviour, 5*(7), 947–953.

Mello, M. M., Opel, D. J., Benjamin, R. M., Callaghan, T., DiResta, R., Elharake, J. A., Flowers, L. C., Galvani, A. P., Salmon, D. A., Schwartz, J. L., Brewer, N. T., Buttenheim, A. M., Carpiano, R. M., Clinton, C., Hotez, P. J., Lakshmanan, R., Maldonado, Y. A., Omer, S. B., Sharfstein, J. M., … , Caplan, A. (2022). Effectiveness of vaccination mandates in improving uptake of COVID-19 vaccines in the USA. *The Lancet, 400*(10351), 535–538.

CHAPTER 16

Lockdowns and Mobility Rate Variation in the COVID-19 Era

Rossella Vulcano

INTRODUCTION

In March 2020, governments were faced with the need to implement restrictive measures to reduce social coming closer and promote public behaviour change in social distance (Pedersen & Favero, 2020). Such non-pharmaceutical interventions included several containment measures whose most typical examples were lockdowns. In this chapter, lockdowns are conceptualised as a cluster of heterogeneous interventions according to the categories used in the EXCEPTIUS dataset (Egger et al., 2022).

As a result of the restrictive measures, European Member States experienced different rates of compliance, conceptualised in this case as the change in the rate of mobility for retail and recreation, which differs across countries.

R. Vulcano (✉)
Faculty of Social and Behavioural Science, University of Groningen, Groningen, The Netherlands

Political Science, SHPT, PACTE, University of Grenoble Alpes, Grenoble, France
e-mail: r.vulcano@rug.nl

© The Author(s) 2024   279
C. Egger et al. (eds.), *Covid-19 Containment Policies in Europe*,
International Series on Public Policy,
https://doi.org/10.1007/978-3-031-52096-9_16

At the onset of the pandemic, academic attention focused on investigating possible triggers for compliance with social distancing measures. However, there is no comprehensive narrative describing the variability of mobility rates due to restrictive measures and providing a comparative description of possible compliance triggers across Europe. Therefore, this chapter aims to contribute to the literature on mobility rate variability in COVID-19 by elucidating the mobility rate variability during the first strict national lockdown in 15 EU Member States, and to identify possible research clues focused on improving crisis-management strategies for future possible crises and enhancing public safety.

Indeed, although the effectiveness of lockdowns in containing the spread of COVID-19 is still controversial (Dainton & Hay, 2021), this chapter follows the empirical findings of Mégarbane et al. (2021) and Alfano and Ercolano (2020), which positively correlate restrictive social mobility policies with rule compliance and public safety.

In addition, the importance of contextual factors in shaping citizens' rule compliance (lower mobility rates) is considered, such as the level of stringency of containment measures (Caselli et al., 2022), modalities of public enforcement (Mills et al., 2021), government trust (Bargain & Aminjonov, 2020), risk perception (Xie et al., 2020) and the influence of time (Six et al., 2021).

MOBILITY RATE AND COMPLIANCE

The extant literature highlights how societal and institutional macro-level factors, such as the stringency of restrictions, the modalities of public enforcement and government trust, are important triggers of rule compliance towards lockdowns. As lockdowns aim to reduce the mobility rate, authors such as Dainton and Hay (2021) and Caselli et al. (2022) analysed the variation in mobility rate to estimate the level of compliance with COVID-19 containment measures.

Caselli et al. (2022) and Sun et al. (2021) demonstrate how a higher level of lockdown stringency leads to a greater decrease in mobility rate. However, despite the robustness of the authors' results, the former focuses only on three EU Member States while the latter focuses only on the US. Similar to the deterrent logic of higher stringency, another macro element such as rule enforcement has been shown to be influential in reducing the mobility rate during lockdowns. Indeed, Huntley et al. (2020) and Jennings and Perez (2020) provide empirical evidence on how stronger enforcement, in this case higher fines and a higher number of police officers on the street, leads to a greater decrease in the mobility rate. Nevertheless, there is no analysis focusing on the whole European continent that differentiates between the stringency of legislation and the depth of control of enforcement modalities nor is there a comparative analysis of the enforcement rate during the COVID-19 per EU Member State.

In addition, not only macro factors directly related to the regulations implemented, but also public perceptions of government reliability, such as higher public trust, lead people to comply more (Bargain & Aminjonov, 2020; Sarracino et al., 2022). In addition, previous literature on preventive behaviour and COVID-19 has highlighted how higher levels of risk perception leads to higher compliance (Xie et al., 2020).

This chapter aims to contribute to current research on compliance with COVID-19 regulations by providing a descriptive analysis of the above factors. A novelty is the use of risk perception at the macro level. It also aims to identify the most influential dimension of compliance, be it policy or public opinion.

MEASURING COMPLIANCE AND ITS DRIVERS

This chapter uses the Google Mobility Rate dataset (2022) to operationalise the dependent variable (compliance with social distancing measures). The dataset collects aggregated and anonymised data from Google Maps, which reports mobility trends per country and region on a daily basis from February 2020 to October 2022. In addition, these trends are divided into six main categories (1) retail and recreation, (2) food and pharmacy, (3) parks, (4) transit stations, (5) workplaces, (6) and residential. Finally, the variability of mobility rates is calculated based on a baseline, which is the median of a five-week period between 3 January 2020 and 6 February 2020. Nevertheless, in the current chapter, only the mobility category retail and recreation is considered, as it was the one that was first targeted by various lockdown policies. Therefore, when using the term 'mobility rate', the current chapter only refers to the mobility rate towards retail and recreational places such as bars and clubs.

Second, this chapter uses EXCEPTIUS data (Egger et al., 2022) as an independent variable of the stringency of social distancing measures adopted by governments. However, the EXCEPTIUS dataset does not include a dedicated category on lockdowns as this terminology was used by most European members only in official government press conferences and mass media, and not in the relevant legislative decrees (see Chazel in this volume). Specifically, the current chapter uses seven measures falling under the lockdowns umbrella as presented by Chazel in this chapter and aggregates them into a single stringency score.

In order to operationalise 'regulatory enforcement', this chapter uses Eurostat's Government Expenditure (2020) dataset. The dataset collects the annual expenditure as a percentage of GDP of each government by function, some of which are health, public services, education, defence, public order and safety from 2012 to 2021 in all European Member States. In this case, the chapter only analyses annual government expenditure on 'public order and safety', which includes expenditure on 'police, fire brigade, courts, prisons, R&D related to public order and safety' as well as expenditure classified elsewhere (Eurostat, 2021).

Furthermore, in the absence of a longitudinal dataset on risk perception, this chapter draws upon a proxy for risk perception by using the number of COVID-19 cases and deaths per day at the national level. Indeed, a linear statistical correlation has already been observed between a higher rate of recorded COVID-19 cases and an increase in individual risk perception (Vulcano, 2025).

For this purpose, the current chapter uses the "Coronavirus (COVID-19) cases" of Our World in Data (data collected in 2023), which collects the number of COVID-19 deaths, cases, tests, hospitalisations and vaccinations worldwide on a daily basis until today (Edouard et al., 2020).

Finally, to measure public trust in government, this chapter uses the European Parliament COVID-19 Survey—Round 1 (GESIS, 2021). The survey aims to collect data on the general satisfaction of the public with the COVID-19 responses. The survey was carried out in April and May 2020 in 24 EU Member States. The current paper uses the mean of the answers given by people per nation using an ordinal scale (1 = I do not trust the government at all to 4 = I really trust the government).

General Analysis of Lockdown and Mobility Rates

In general, across all three waves of COVID-19, the Czech Republic and Austria have implemented the highest number of national lockdowns, followed by Belgium, France, Hungary, Ireland, Italy and Portugal (see Table 16.1). Croatia, Malta and Finland are the countries with the lowest number of implemented lockdowns. France, Germany, Italy and Portugal have implemented the most restrictive measures, followed by Austria, the

Table 16.1 Comparison between the level of stringency of the first implemented lockdown and mobility rates

Country	Number of lockdowns	Mobility rate before first lockdown	Mobility rate after first lockdown mean	First lockdown stringency mean
Austria	5	-8.07	-80.875	2.06
Belgium	4	-16.28	15	0.8
Croatia	1	-3	-68.8	1.2
Czech Republic	5	1.84	-58.46	2.46
Denmark	1	13	-33.8	0.46
Estonia	2	3.85	-37.43	0.46
France	4	-10.7	-83.66	13.26
Germany	3	-17.8	-59.8	8.56
Greece	3	-42.2	-77.2	8.33
Hungary	4	-36.8	-56.33	0.35
Italy	4	-13.66	-76.33	7.93
Luxembourg	3	-9.66	-64.8	0.6
Malta	1	-63.86	-67.46	0.86
Poland	2	4.14	-55.14	0.71
Portugal	4	-33.35	-64.92	7.46

Source: EXEPTIUS and Google Mobility Reports. In the second column, the table shows the mean of the 15-day mobility rate before the implementation of the first lockdown. Since the Google Mobility dataset uses the median of a five-week period between 3 January 2020 and 6 February 2020 as the baseline for the mobility rate, the numbers are relative. The third column shows the average mobility rate over the 15 days following the lockdown

Czech Republic and Croatia. On the other hand, Estonia, Denmark, Belgium and Luxembourg have the least restrictive measures. By simply subtracting the mean mobility rate before the ban from the mean mobility rate after the ban, it is possible to grasp the variation of mobility rates before and after the ban. France, Austria, Croatia and Italy are the countries where the mobility rate decreased the most, while Hungary and Malta experienced the smallest decrease in the mobility rate. Finally, Belgium is the only country where the mobility rate increased after the introduction of the lockdown.

Analysis of Compliance

The following analysis considers the previously mentioned macro factors: (1) stringency, (2) enforcement (security expenditure), (3) trust in government, (4) risk perception by considering only the first national lockdown per country and 15 days pre- and post-lockdown. As the dataset includes 15 EU Member States[1] with 30 observations each, the total number of observations is 450.[2] Finally, as the European Parliament's COVID-19 survey is based on a large sample of individuals per country, the mean of the answers per country is used in this chapter.

The following graphs show the multivariate OLS regression with mobility rate as the dependent variable and security expenditure, government trust, stringency and risk perception as independent variables. These data are collected 15 days before and 15 days after the first lockdown to observe its impact. Some data, such as stringency or risk perception, are collected every day and do not require special processing. Other measures, such as security expenditure and government trust, are collected annually. Their impact on mobility is, therefore, expected to be conditional on the implementation of the lockdown. This is why a dummy variable (pre-lockdown implementation = 0 and post-lockdown implementation = 1) was introduced to create an interaction term for the variables that have identical observations.

The scatterplot (Fig. 16.1) shows the relationship between mobility rate and security expenditure before and after the implementation of the lockdown, while the fitted line values highlight the coefficient relationship between the two variables. The linear regression shows a negative relationship between enforcement and mobility rate with a coefficient of -732. However, the relationship is not significant ($p = 0.280$). Looking at the relationship between mobility rate and security expenditure with the interaction term (after the introduction of the lockdown), there is a significant ($p < 0.01$) and stronger negative correlation with a coefficient of -1466.

Figure 16.2 shows the scatterplot with line-fitted values of mobility rate and trust in government. The OLS shows a positive but not significant correlation between trust in government and mobility rate before the lockdown, with a coefficient of 2.2 and a p-value of 0.08. After the

[1] Austria, Belgium, Croatia, Czech Republic, Denmark, Estonia, France, Germany, Greece, Hungary, Italy, Luxembourg, Malta, Poland, Portugal.

[2] As the EXCEPTIUS dataset does not contain all 15 days before and after the first national lockdown of each country, the actual number of observations is 436.

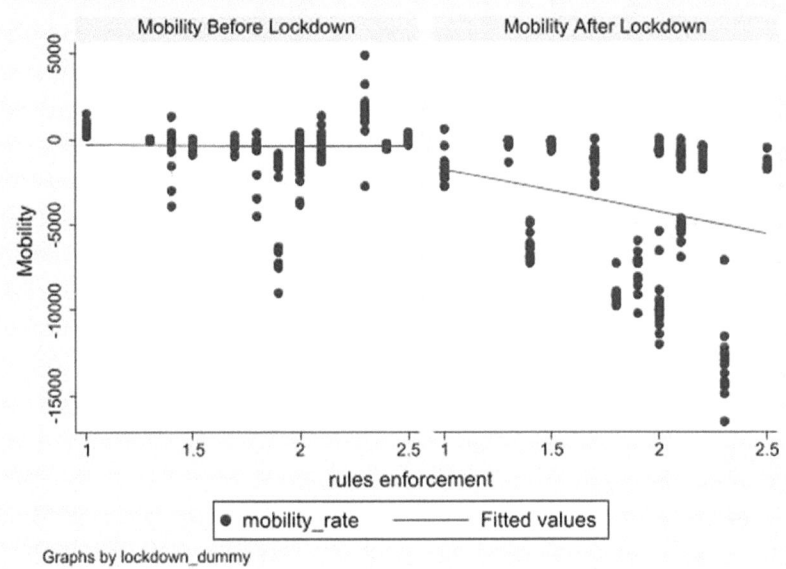

Fig. 16.1 Relationship between security expenditure and mobility rate before and after the first lockdown. *Source*: EXCEPTIUS, Google Mobility Report

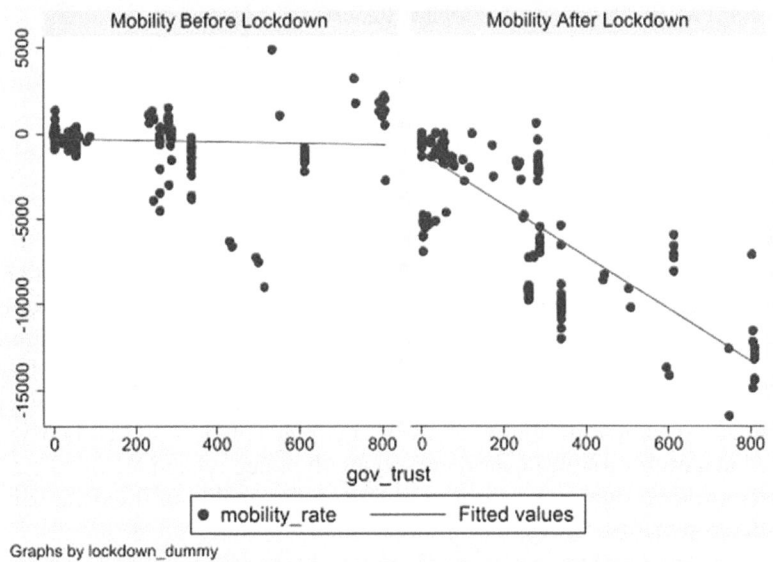

Fig. 16.2 Relationship between trust in government and mobility rate before and after the first lockdown. *Source*: EXCEPTIUS, Google Mobility Report

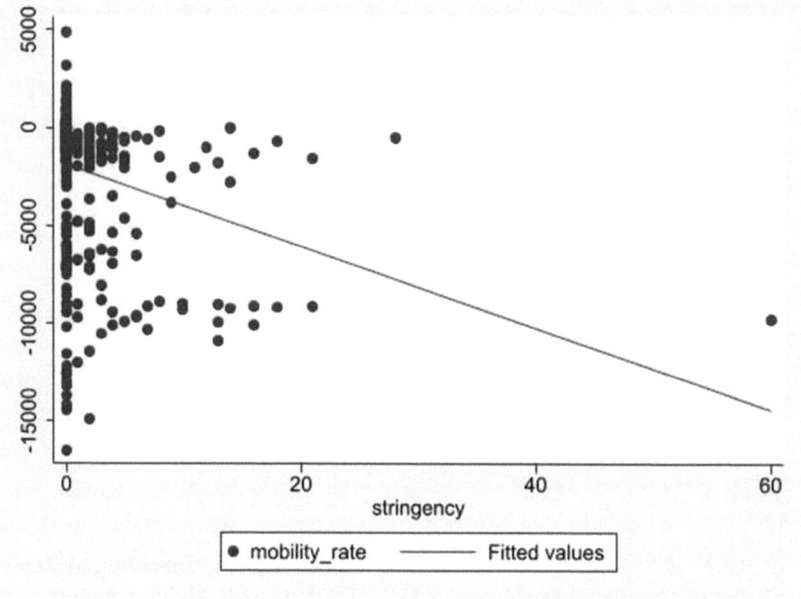

Fig. 16.3 Relationship between social distancing stringency and mobility rate. *Source*: EXCEPTIUS, Google Mobility Report

lockdown, however, there is a statistically significant negative correlation with a coefficient of -14.6948.

Figure 16.3 shows the correlation between mobility rate and stringency. The lockdown dummy was not used as an interaction term because the stringency observations are daily collected and most of them start with the first lockdown. OLS shows a significant and negative correlation between the two variables ($p = 0.07$) with a correlation coefficient of -51.

Figure 16.4 shows the relationship between mobility rate and risk perception. When analysed alone, risk perception has a negative and significant correlation with a decrease in the mobility rate. However, OLS shows a positive but not significant relationship ($p = 0.166$) between risk perception and decline in mobility rate, with a coefficient close to 0, when analysed in a multivariable linear regression with policy-related factors. Finally, the lockdown dummy was not used due to the quality of the data, which is heterogeneous throughout the year.

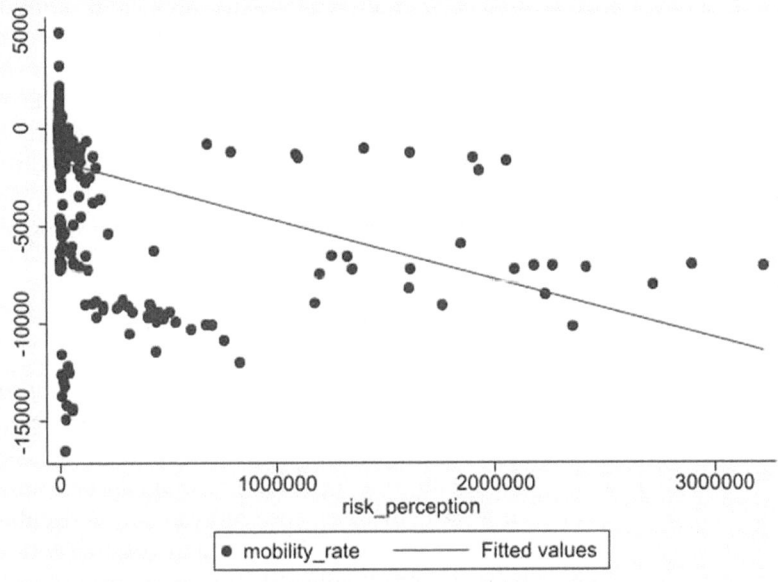

Fig. 16.4 Relationship between risk perception and mobility rate

CONCLUSION

Empirical evidence collected by the Google Mobility Rate showed how the decline in mobility rate during the COVID-19 lockdowns varied significantly across European countries. Such a phenomenon boded well for a comparative and macro-level analysis across EU member states. Indeed, previous research identified how a loyal citizen fearing to be infected by the COVID-19 virus in an emergency context of high regulation and strong rule enforcement is the scenario with higher public rule compliance. However, previous studies focused on risk perception as a micro-level factor, did not compare the EU Member States or distinguished between how citizens' attitudes and perception and rule stringency shape compliance. This left open the question of why people in different countries have responded differently to the implementation of lockdown and what are the most important factors for the institution to consider.

According to the empirical results, rule enforcement is not statistically significant before the introduction of lockdown, but after its introduction it is the most influential variable in reducing mobility rates and promoting compliance. Similarly, the stringency of the lockdown and trust in the government lead to lower mobility rates. These initial results are consistent with past studies. The results regarding the influence of COVID-19 risk perception on mobility rates are, however, new. Indeed, according to the empirical findings of Xie et al. (2020), risk perception has a positive influence on compliance that we don't observe in our macro analyses. The limitation of the current chapter may be the use of COVID-19 cases as a proxy for risk perception, while Xie et al. (2020) used an ad hoc 22-question online survey with 317 Chinese participants. Therefore, it is promising to investigate other variables as a proxy for risk perception, such as COVID-19 death rate, COVID-19 case percentage, COVID-19 relative growth.

In conclusion, this research engaged with a comparative analysis of the different rates of compliance with the lockdown measures with different levels of stringency across the EU. Consequently, the research investigated two influential dimensions in the development of compliance, namely policy-related factors such as stringency versus enforcement, and public opinion-related factors such as trust in government and risk perception. Enforcement is found to be the most influential factor in reducing the mobility rate after the introduction of lockdowns, followed by regulatory stringency. Trust in government is important but less influential. Highlighting the importance of policy-related factors across the EU may be important to provide insights for policy makers in formulating effective regulations in terms of compliance in possible future crises, and to better understand the social dynamics of compliance.

REFERENCES

Alfano, V., & Ercolano, S. (2020). The efficacy of lockdown against COVID-19: A cross-country panel analysis. *Applied Health Economics Health Policy, 18*(4), 509–517. https://doi.org/10.1007/s40258-020-00596-3

Bargain, O., & Aminjonov, U. (2020). Trust and compliance to public health policies in times of COVID-19. *Journal of Public Economics, 192*, 104316. https://doi.org/10.1016/j.jpubeco.2020.104316

Caselli, F., Grigoli, F., Sandri, D., & Spilimbergo, A. (2022). Mobility under the COVID-19 pandemic: Asymmetric effects across gender and age. *IMF Economic Review, 70*(1), 105–138. https://doi.org/10.1057/s41308-021-00149-1

Dainton, C., & Hay, A. (2021). Quantifying the relationship between lockdowns, mobility, and effective reproduction number (Rt) during the COVID-19 pandemic in the Greater Toronto Area. *BMC Public Health, 21*(1), 1658. https://doi.org/10.1186/s12889-021-11684-x

Edouard, M., Hannah, R., Lucas, R.-G., Cameron, A., Charlie, G., Joe, H., Bobbie, M., Saloni, D., Diana, B., Esteban, O.-O., & Max, R. (2020). Coronavirus Pandemic (COVID-19). Our World in Data. https://ourworldindata.org/covid-cases

Egger, C. M., de Saint Phalle, E., Magni-Berton, R., Aarts, C., & Roché S. (2022). EXCEPTIUS dataset v2.0. https://doi.org/10.34894/TTS0MF

European Parliament, Directorate-General for Communication, Public Opinion Monitoring Unit. (2021). European Parliament COVID-19 survey—Round 1. GESIS Data Archive, Cologne. ZA7736 Data file Version 1.0.0. https://doi.org/10.4232/1.1370

Eurostat. (2021). Government expenditure on public order and safety. Statistics Explained. European Commission. Retrieved from https://ec.europa.eu/eurostat/statistics-explained/index.php?title=Government_expenditure_on_public_order_and_safety.

Google. (2022). Google COVID-19 community mobility reports. https://www.google.com/covid19/mobility/

Huntley, K. S., Mintz, J., Wahood, W., Raine, S., Dicaro, M. V., Hardigan, P. C., & Haffizulla, F. (2020). Enforcement of stay-at-home orders associated with improved COVID-19 population outcomes. *Annals of Epidemiology, 52*, 104–105. https://doi.org/10.1016/j.annepidem.2020.08.026

Jennings, W. G., & Perez, N. M. (2020). The immediate impact of COVID-19 on law enforcement in the United States. *American Journal of Criminal Justice: AJCJ, 45*(4), 690–701. https://doi.org/10.1007/s12103-020-09536-2

Mégarbane, B., Bourasset, F., & Scherrmann, J. M. (2021). Is curfew effective in limiting SARS-CoV-2 progression? An evaluation in France based on epidemiokinetic analyses. *Journal of General Internal Medicine, 36*, 2731–2738. https://doi.org/10.1007/s11606-021-06953

Mills, F., Symons, C., & Carter, H. (2021). Exploring the role of enforcement in promoting adherence with protective behaviours during COVID-19. *Policing: A Journal of Policy and Practice*. Advance online publication. https://doi.org/10.1093/police/paab079

Pedersen, M. J., & Favero, N. (2020). Social distancing during the COVID-19 pandemic: Who are the present and future noncompliers? *Public Administration Review, 80*(5), 805–814. https://doi.org/10.1111/puar.13240

Sarracino, F., Greyling, T., O'Connor, K., Peroni, C., & Rossouw, S. (2022). Trust predicts compliance with COVID-19 containment policies: Evidence from ten countries using big data. *SSRN Journal (SSRN Electronic Journal)*. https://doi.org/10.2139/ssrn.4114731

Six, F., de Vadder, S., Glavina, M., Verhoest, K., & Pepermans, K. (2021). What drives compliance with COVID-19 measures over time? Explaining changing impacts with goal framing theory. *Regulation & Governance*. Advance online publication. https://doi.org/10.1111/rego.12440.

Sun, J., Kwek, K., Li, M., & Shen, H. (2021). Effects of social mobility and stringency measures on the COVID-19 outcomes: Evidence from the United States. *Frontiers in Public Health, 9*, 779501. https://doi.org/10.3389/fpubh.2021.779501

Vulcano, R. (2025). Rule acceptance in the Covid-19 era [Unpublished doctoral dissertation]. University of Groningen and University of Grenoble Alpes.

Xie, K., Liang, B., Dulebenets, M. A., & Mei, Y. (2020). The impact of risk perception on social distancing during the COVID-19 pandemic in China. *International Journal of Environmental Research and Public Health, 17*(17). https://doi.org/10.3390/ijerph17176256

CHAPTER 17

Conclusion: Learning from the COVID-19 Cases for Future Emergencies

*Clara Egger, Raul Magni-Berton, and
Eugénie de Saint-Phalle*

As a final stop in our descriptive journey into the variety of COVID-19 policies in Europe, this concluding chapter is drawing, from our analysis, some take-aways for the future of emergency policymaking in Europe. Although EXCEPTIUS focuses on the specific case of Covid-19, our

C. Egger (✉)
Public Administration and Sociology,
Erasmus University Rotterdam, Rotterdam, The Netherlands
e-mail: egger@essb.eur.nl

R. Magni-Berton
European School of Political and Social Sciences, ESPOL-LAB Université
Catholique de Lille , Lille, France
e-mail: raul.magniberton@univ-catholille.fr

E. de Saint-Phalle
International Relations and International Organization,
University of Groningen, Groningen, The Netherlands
e-mail: e.de.saint-phalle@rug.nl

© The Author(s) 2024
C. Egger et al. (eds.), *Covid-19 Containment Policies in Europe*,
International Series on Public Policy,
https://doi.org/10.1007/978-3-031-52096-9_17

results also inform crisis-management strategies at large, in a context where climate change as well as the growing interdependence of economies and societies are likely to make large-scale hazards more frequent. Whether such hazards generate a crisis however depends on the level of vulnerability and preparedness of societies as well as on the nature of the policy responses adopted. In many cases, policy responses have been found exacerbate the vulnerability of societies to the pandemic (Bjørnskov & Voigt, 2022; Kelman, 2020; Lundgren et al., 2020). Seconding global calls for action encapsulated, for example, in the 2015 Sendai Framework for Disaster Risk Reduction, our analyses show the importance for government to invest in efficient, fair and accountable disaster governance. The current moment is particularly ripe for such exploration as many of the countries studied in the EXCEPTIUS project are currently evaluating to effectiveness of their COVID-19 policy responses. At the time of writing these lines, in late December 2023, such processes are ongoing at the national and international levels. For example, the Organization of Economic Co-Operation and Development (OECD)'s Directorate for Public Governance released the first evaluation reports of its work on "government evaluations of OECD COVID-19 responses". The present edited volume intends to contribute new evidence to such processes by identifying some key lessons learned and take-aways from our analyses.

Our ambition is to provide the first descriptive and comparative mapping of COVID-19 containment policies. Scholars focusing on decision-making and public policy rarely take a broad comparative approach, and when they do, they aim to provide a typology of institutions or policies using cross-national aggregated data, rather than an analysis of what decisions were taken in specific circumstances to solve specific problems. Decision-making itself is, therefore, usually studied using case-specific approaches or comparisons limited to two or three countries. This is mainly due to the fact that the problems that reach the political agenda in each country are different, and similar problems are dealt with in different time periods. In this respect, the COVID-19 pandemic is rather unique: many governments had to solve the same problem at the same time. This allows scholars to analyse decision-making in an unusually broad comparative perspective. This is done in this volume for 23 European countries. Given the novelty of this perspective, our priority was to provide a descriptive account of the policies adopted as collected in an open access database, to identify general trends and to contribute new evidence that could be used to assess traditional policy-making theories.

Two aspects in particular have been analyzed. The first is the impact of neighbors' experiences on domestic decision-making. Interestingly, agenda setting—the process by which problems gain or lose attention among decision-makers—was of secondary importance during the pandemic because, as in many emergency situations, the problems were largely defined exogenously. This could help supranational institutions, especially the European Union, to achieve policy convergence through recommendations and guidelines without creating legally binding constraints. Despite the activation of several EU coordination mechanisms, this convergence has not been observed. The second aspect is a global re-evaluation of old issues. While we do not provide a rigorous analysis of each of these issues, we do provide preliminary evidence throughout the volume. First, we find no compelling evidence for ideological styles of fighting the pandemic. The question of whether parties matter is answered in the negative. Second, the problem-solving approach does not seem to be congruent with what is observed. The severity of the pandemic only partially explains the degree of political exceptionalism. Third, the responsiveness to public opinion also seems to have been quite low. In short, there is even a negative relationship between public demand for more restrictions and the stringency of the measures taken. On the other hand, the data globally confirm the path dependency approach. The type of policy chosen is strongly related to what has been done before, even in the long run. Democratic practices and traditions have shaped the way in which the level of stringency, the role of parliament, subnational power and many other policies have been designed.

Individual contributions to this volume provide new insights into emergency policymaking as well as confirm previous findings. Our ambition to document how—behind semantic proximity—COVID-19 policies vary across countries calls for a stronger emphasis on the value of theoretically informed descriptive analysis for the study of policymaking. EXCEPTIUS taxonomy contributes a new conceptual framework to the analysis of crisis policy-making that could be applied to the management of other large scale transnational crises—such as the ongoing war in Ukraine. Moving beyond what governments declare to study how each policy is legally designed and enforced allows revealing new patterns of similarities and variations. This is especially the case of the contributions gathered in Parts II and III of this volume that show how governments opted for applying in their own way of common strategy—such as the implementation of a lockdown, the adaptation of education services or the restriction of specific rights. The methodological approach followed to collect EXCEPTIUS data (see introduction for a detailed presentation) also opens new avenues for interdisciplinary research. Grasping in such a fine-grained manner the modalities of implementation of rapidly evolving COVID-19 policies would have been impossible without the support of computation linguists, expert in the automated processing of textual data.

Overall, this volume complements the predominant focus on crisis decision-making to cover an equally relevant dimension of crisis management, the design and implementation of crisis-management policies. So far, policymaking theories have mainly been developed under business-as-usual situations (Wenzelburger & Wolf, 2015). While testing these theories is beyond the descriptive scope of this chapter, we believe that our volume provides new evidence allowing for theory testing and development in policy (making) theories. In terms of agency, our volume gives justice to the variety of actors involved in crisis policymaking. While the first part of the volume mainly focuses on the role of political actors, Parts II and III broadens the scope of the analysis and presents in a fine-grained how various political, administrative actors and experts played a role in shaping the policy outcome observed in each of our country case.

Crisis management policies are only partially dictated by the characteristics of the crisis at hand, and the COVID-19 pandemic is no exception. Our chapters show that even when faced with a very similar set of challenges, countries opted for a variety of policy options. Analysing the rationale behind such diverse policies has long been a focus of the literature. So far, scholars have mainly considered leadership styles as a crucial factor shaping the effectiveness of crisis policies (see, among others Boin et al., 2016 as well as the introduction for a review). Our volume complements this focus by considering the role of slow-evolving structural factors. In many countries, COVID-19 containment policies appeared to be shaped by institutional and historical factors. Countries with a high level of institutional trust, a strong quality of democracy and a high degree of legal preparedness were also able to maintain a higher degree of democratic continuity in the management of COVID-19. The different waves of the COVID-19 pandemic also allowed us to see how much governments learned from managing one wave to the next. Our answer to this important question is rather pessimistic. On the one hand, governments do seem to learn from the effects of their past policies, as their policies evolved through the different COVID-19 waves. On the other hand, the evolution of containment policies does not converge toward a similar approach.

This suggests three conclusions. First, European governments have failed to collectively develop an evidence-based approach to managing the pandemic. Comparative data are scarce, and there has been no systematic collaboration to improve information and evaluate policies. Second, governments also failed to provide a consistent ethical standard for managing the pandemic. Behind technical terms such as "lockdown" or "curfew," different restrictions were implemented and different levels of protection of individual freedoms were required. Third, despite the clear impact of the WHO recommendations, each government tended to respond more to domestic debates and specific legal opportunities than to the performance of its neighbors.

THE COVID-19 PANDEMIC: A GAME CHANGER IN EMERGENCY POLICYMAKING?

Most of the scholarly and media accounts of the policy responses to the COVID-19 stress the unprecedented challenge it created for European governments. Our analysis shows that—while this statement holds some truth—one should not overestimate the extraordinary nature of the governmental reactions to it. On the one hand, European governments had—in comparison with, for example, their Asian counterparts—little experience of coronavirus-induced pandemic. They hence had to improvise policy responses—sometimes mimicking each other; sometimes following their own pandemic containment strategy. This fueled a trial-and-error process which saw some countries adopting a very restrictive approach—such as Austria, France or Hungary—while others opted for a more gradual introduction of measures—the Netherlands, the United Kingdom and, to some extent, Germany. Over time and although our data only partially capture such time evolution, policies converged across the European policy space. For example, and following the lead of the European Union, most countries adopted, for example, a COVID-19 pass to allow for the re-opening of public spaces, restaurants and entertainment venues. The COVID-19 pandemic also accelerated the digitalization of public services, notably in the field of education. On the other hand, variation in COVID-19 policy responses reflect the weight of long-term structural patterns characterizing European countries. Patterns of emergency decision-making examined in the first part of this volume reveals that countries with high degree of democratic quality managed to safeguard it during the pandemic much better than countries which were already experiencing some loss in democratic quality. By the same token, the reliance on COVID-19 apps highlights a broader appeal of technosolutionism that was already in place before the pandemic.

The game changing nature of the pandemic is, therefore, all relative. In many respects, the pandemic exacerbated trends that date back to well before. Our analyses suggest that the trajectory that countries followed during the pandemic could have somehow been predicted by looking at the quality of their democratic governance and the strength of their human rights protection apparatus before the pandemic. Evidence suggests the existence of strong path dependence patterns.

Escaping the Vicious Circle of Distrust: The Importance of Proportionality

As many contributors to this volume note, an effective crisis-management strategy results in the use of proportionate emergency measures. While the spectrum of pandemic management policies is very large and diverse (including public health, economic and social policies), EXCEPTIUS focuses specifically on exceptional measures, namely measures imposing extraordinary restrictions on democratic governance, fundamental rights and daily liberties. Our focus comes from the fact that the exercise of exceptional powers come with several democratic and political costs such as: (1) The weakening of the rule of law, (2) The reduction of institutional predictability (triggering a perception of arbitrariness) and (3) An increased social and political polarization (through increasing the choices to be decided upon and limiting the adoption of policy options in a consensual manner). In the short run, exceptional measures also have a strong impact on the effectiveness of crisis management policies. Exceptional measures—especially as they extend in time as in the case of the COVID-19 pandemic—have a strong and negative effect on institutional trust. Yet, institutional trust is one of the key factors of the effectiveness of crisis management policies as it favors cooperation and coordination (Győrffy, 2018). Overall, our results show that the lower the institutional trust, the more stringent exceptional measures and that the more policymakers based their pandemic management policies on exceptional measures, the more they lost the trust of the population. Policymakers should hence be concerned with not falling in what we identified as the "vicious circle of exceptionalism". Such a vicious circle leads policymakers to adopt exceptional measures to compensate for low initial levels of political trust while the use of exceptional measures during the crisis trigger, in turn, an erosion of political trust and a further vulnerability to future crises. Avoiding this trap is even more important as political trust is hard and slow to build.

Many contributors to our volume call policymakers for adopting measures proportionate to the severity of the public health posed by the pandemic. Neves, Merrill, Miguel and Forte advocate, for example, for the adopting a "balanced harm principle" restricting speeches that can cause direct harm (e.g., dangerous health advice), while being cautious about overreach that may stifle legitimate expression. Brzozowski, Hau and Rybczyńska call for preferring light restrictions that preserve religious freedoms in a non-discriminatory manner.

Investing in Legal Preparedness

Safeguarding the principle of proportionality amid a large-scale crisis is, however, challenging. Faced with an emergency, policymakers are likely to fall into an *action bias* leading them to overestimate the benefits of exceptional decision-making in the absence of credible and legitimate alternatives (Voigt, 2022). To avoid this trap, our results call for learning from the COVID-19 pandemic to invest in legal preparedness to disasters. This recommendation is consistent with previous studies showing that countries that had legal arrangements in place before the pandemic reacted in more proportionate and managed to balance better public health needs with socio-economic and democratic ones (Lundgren et al., 2020).

Legal preparedness ensures the adoption of proportionate measures at several levels. First and foremost, it allows for the preservation of high standards of democratic decision-making in emergency situations. The chapters from Egger and de Saint Phalle and Chazel show that governments that relied on emergency powers to contain the pandemic were particularly heavy-handed in the adoption of restrictive measures. In contrast, governments that opted for acting on the basis of existing crisis management legislation—for example, pandemic management laws—relied on a larger panel of policy instruments—including public health recommendations as well as various forms of incentives. Many of the countries concerned—such as Ireland, the Netherlands or the United Kingdom—also adapted their legislation throughout the pandemic waves, hence maintaining parliaments as watchdogs of the executive in crises—as documented by

Poyet's chapter. Second, strengthening crisis management legal frameworks minimize legal uncertainties during crises and allow for a better understanding of regulations by the public but also the implementing agencies. This benefit of legal preparedness is documented by the contribution of Churruca Muguruza, Cretu and Urrutia Asua on the protection of asylum rights during the pandemic as well as by Brzozowski, Hau and Rybczyńska. Last, legal preparedness also contributes to preserving high-quality democratic governance in crisis. This is particularly reflected in the Ehin's and Piret's contribution that show that countries that had special voting arrangements in place before the pandemic were more able to maintain electoral continuity.

BRING DECISIONS CLOSER TO CITIZENS

Emergency policies lead to a temporary restriction of individuals' rights to guarantee public safety. The chapters gathered in this volume largely document the various strategies used to restrict these rights in a proportionate manner. Focusing on the nature of the restrictions adopted matter but should not lead to neglect the quality of the procedures through which such restrictions are adopted. In other words, the stringency of restrictions is not necessarily a problem in itself as long as their adoption is perceived as legitimate by citizens. Our findings show that a way of increasing the legitimacy of emergency decision-making is to bring decision-making closer to citizens.

Contributions to this volume propose two ways of doing so. The first strategy is to decentralise emergency response. Magni-Berton documents that countries that opted for decentralized decision-making were no less efficient in managing the pandemic than those who preferred centralized forms of governance and this led most countries to decentralize their policies after the second wave. Brzozowski, Hau and Rybczyńska think along the same line and call for recognizing the effectiveness of subnational or regional approaches in managing restrictions, as seen in countries like Germany and Spain, is important, as it allows for tailored responses to local conditions. A second strategy consists in granting citizens formal ways of debating (and possibly contesting) the emergency legislation adopted. Kuebler reveals that in the case of Switzerland, direct democracy served as a safety valve that allowed citizen to voice their stances while preserving high levels of social cohesion, public trust and democratic quality.

ENSURING CROSS-NATIONAL COORDINATION

The study of pandemic containment strategies in Europe reveals a paradox. Compared to other continents, forms of policy coordination between states abound in Europe particularly in the field of public health. The EU mechanisms to coordinate crisis response, share information and monitor the spread of the virus were activated on time. Civil protection services also supported each other across national boundaries. Yet, governments initially reacted to the crisis in a very chaotic and uncoordinated manner and continued to do so as COVID-19 waves unfold. Explaining this paradox falls outside of the scope of this volume but our results call for strengthening policy coordination in crisis time. Some of our contributors call for a stronger role of the EU in that regards, particularly concerning the protection of fundamental rights. Conde Belmonte, Huesca González and Villacián Goncer argue that as the EU places freedom of movement at the core of its integration project, it should also ensure stronger coordination and consistency among EU member states in implementing travel restrictions. In doing so, the organization should ensure they align with the EU principles of proportionality and non-discrimination.

Beyond coordination functions, our contributors also see the possibility for the EU to set stronger standards for balancing the need to effectively respond to emergencies and the safeguard of democratic governance and fundamental rights. The EU appears as the right forum to develop a clear, EU-wide framework for assessing and responding to public health emergencies that respects free movement rights while effectively managing health risks. Given the EU's influence in setting global standards, there should be careful consideration of how EU-initiated data infrastructures and policies impact international travel and privacy rights beyond Europe.

Yet and given the size of the European Union and the varied levels of exposure to the pandemic, policy coordination can also take place in smaller fora, involving, for example, neighboring states characterized by a strong socio-economic interdependence.

Ensuring Transparency and Monitoring: Calling for the Principle of Evidence-Based Information Restriction

In addition to our findings, the EXCEPTIUS project revealed profound differences in access to data across countries. While in Northern Europe data were easily accessible, this is not the case for Southern and Eastern Europe. In particular, we were forced to abandon the collection of data on the enforcement of containment policies because they were particularly inaccessible. Moreover, in many countries the deliberations that led to important decisions were not open to the public, and even journalists did not have access to them.

This book is limited by this lack of data and, more generally, the understanding of crisis management suffers from this problem. The arguments for restricting access to some sensitive data are usually based on the risk of causing panic, loss of confidence, or compliance. We would like to argue that there is no evidence to support these expectations. In countries where data has been more accessible, trust has not decreased, mobility has not increased and more deaths have not been registered. While we can understand the fear that transparency might lead to debates and disagreements that are inappropriate at a time when coordination and solidarity are a priority, our comparative work does not document this pessimistic scenario.

On the other hand, transparency in itself is at the core of democratic and liberal values, and it is crucial to offer the scientific community the opportunity to effectively monitor the management of crises. As long as the scientific community has to assess to limited information, the improvement of the effectiveness of policies is slow, and this could increase, in time of crisis, deaths, poverty or disease.

This problem is the main obstacle for producing a rigorous comparative piece of research. We have experienced it in our data collection efforts and know how much it affects the quality of the evidence presented in this book. All we can do is call for the principle of evidence-based information restriction at the European level. According to this principle, no government should be allowed to restrict information unless it can provide evidence that this information has effects that the government explicitly wants to avoid in its policies. Among the best practices we have documented in this book, this principle is perhaps the first.

References

Bjørnskov, C., & Voigt, S. (2022). This time is different?—On the use of emergency measures during the corona pandemic. *European Journal of Law and Economics, 54*(1), 63–81.

Boin, A., Stern, E., & Sundelius, B. (2016). *The politics of crisis-management: Public leadership under pressure.* Cambridge University Press.

Győrffy, D. (2018). *Trust and crisis management in the European Union.* Springer Books.

Kelman, I. (2020). Pandemic by choice. *Chemistry & Industry, 84*(5), 40–40. https://doi.org/10.1002/cind.12_845.x

Lundgren, M., Klamberg, M., Sundström, K., & Dahlqvist, J. (2020). Emergency powers in response to COVID-19: Policy diffusion, democracy, and preparedness. *Nordic Journal of Human Rights, 38*(4), 305–318.

Voigt, S. (2022). Contracting for catastrophe: Legitimizing emergency constitutions by drawing on social contract theory. *Res Publica, 28*(1), 149–172.

Wenzelburger, G., & Wolf, F. (2015). Policy theories in the crisis? Comparing the explanatory power of policy theories in the context of crisis. In *Beitrag für die 2. International conference for public policy, Milan* (Vol. 24, p. 2017). www.icpublicpolicy.org/conference/file/reponse/1433840658.pdf. Zugegriffen.

Index[1]

---

[1] Note: Page numbers followed by 'n' refer to notes.